No Ordinary Disruption

No
Ordinary
Disruption

*The Four Global Forces
Breaking All the Trends*

RICHARD DOBBS
JAMES MANYIKA
JONATHAN WOETZEL

PUBLICAFFAIRS
New York

CONTENTS

Contents

—

AN INTUITION RESET

MANAGING A COMPLEX ORGANIZATION ISN'T EASY IN THE BEST OF times. It's especially difficult when the news continually reminds you that everything you thought you knew about how the world works seems to be . . . wrong. Or at least a little off. Dramatic changes come from nowhere, and then from everywhere. Major shifts can blindside even the most circumspect among us—first slowly, and then all at once. The fortunes of industries, companies, products, technologies, and even countries and cities rise and fall overnight and in completely unpredictable ways. Just consider some of the ways in which events on the ground have upended long-held assumptions, long-term projections, and basic beliefs about how things are supposed to work in the global economy:

- For years, the global retailing industry looked to American consumers, the most powerful and prolific in the world, as a proxy for the health of global shoppers. On Cyber Monday—the day after the Thanksgiving weekend—the media provided saturation coverage of the annual e-commerce binge. On December 1, 2014, Americans spent a record $2.65 billion online.[1] However, just weeks before, a much more significant online shopping bomb exploded. November 11 (11.11) is China's Singles Day—an unofficial holiday that has rapidly become a contrived occasion for consumption. Conceived in the 1990s by single college students as an anti–Valentine's Day, it is now an occasion for conspicuous online shopping in the world's second-largest economy. On November 11,

2014, Alibaba, China's biggest e-tailer, recorded sales of more than $9.3 billion, a record for a single day anywhere in the world.[2]

- In October 2013, the US Energy Information Administration made a stunning announcement. The United States, until recently an energy hog struggling with declining fossil fuel production, would surpass Russia as the world's largest producer of hydrocarbons in 2013. Yes, production of natural gas and oil had been rising sharply, thanks to the advent of fracking. But the pace of growth took the agency by surprise. Just a year before, it had projected that the United States wouldn't surpass Russia until 2020. In North Dakota alone, oil production increased twelvefold between 2004 and 2014, helping to reverse a decades-long decline in population.[3]

- On February 19, 2014, Facebook acquired WhatsApp, a five-year-old startup, for a stunning $19 billion. The instant-messaging app, started in mid-2009 by two former Yahoo employees, had enlisted 450 million users—more than Twitter and more than the entire population of the United States.[4] But many Wall Street bankers weren't familiar with the company. The free mobile-messaging application had its greatest appeal—and greatest number of users—in emerging markets. Facebook was able to easily afford the massive price thanks to its successful, swift pivot into mobile. From essentially zero in early 2012, Facebook grew its mobile advertising to 66 percent of total advertising revenue in the third quarter of 2014.[5]

- On September 24, 2014, the world took in a familiar scene of jubilant scientists at a mission control center celebrating a technical achievement. But this was different. The control center was in southern India, not southern Texas. And many of the scientists wore brightly colored saris. The team at the Indian Space Research Organization was celebrating its successful placement of a spacecraft into orbit around Mars. "We have gone beyond the boundaries of human enterprise and innovation," Prime Minister Narendra Modi proclaimed, taking his rhetorical cues from *Star Trek*. "We have dared to reach into the unknown." The most astonishing feature of the venture may have been its cost: a mere $74 million. Modi noted that the whole effort cost less than Hollywood spent making the science-fiction film *Gravity*. Aloft for nearly a year, the *Mangalyaan* was the embodiment of India's culture of frugal innovation. Using lightweight instruments, employing components adapted from other uses, and applying engineering prowess to bring down costs, India managed to become just the fourth country whose space organization successfully placed a spacecraft in Mars's orbit—and the first country to do so on its first attempt.[6]

These big, important stories incorporate common threads that are by turns bewildering and delightful. Speed, surprise, and sudden shifts in direction in huge global markets routinely impact the destinies of established companies and provide opportunities for new entrants.

In fact, ours is a world of near-constant discontinuity. Competitors can rise in almost complete stealth and burst upon the scene. Businesses that were protected by large and deep moats find that their defenses are easily breached. Vast new markets are conjured seemingly from nothing. Technology and globalization have accelerated and intensified the natural forces of market competition. Long-term trend lines, once reliably smooth, now more closely resemble sawtooth mountain ridges, hockey sticks (a plateau followed by a steep ascent), or the silhouette of Mount Fuji (rising steadily, then falling off). Five years is an eternity.

This new normal—a world in which China leads the globe in holiday consumption, the United States is the largest oil producer, a mobile messaging app is worth $19 billion, and India is a leader in space exploration—presents difficult, often existential challenges to leaders of companies, organizations, cities, and countries. The formative experiences of many senior leaders came during a period that was uniquely benign and placid for the global economy. With good reason, the twenty-five years leading up to the 2008 financial crisis came to be known, in the words of economists James Stock and Mark Watson, as the "Great Moderation."[7] Interest rates fell, helping to drive up the price of assets, whether stocks, bonds, or houses. Natural resources became ever more abundant and cheaper. Jobs were plentiful, and a seemingly endless supply of trained workers stood ready to fill them. When technology and trade disrupted and upended industries, most of those affected were able to find work in other sectors. As surely as night followed day, the value of our homes and investments rose each and every year. In developed economies, parents generally assumed that their children, upon becoming adults, would be more prosperous than they were. Whatever consumers and governments couldn't afford to buy with cash, they could pay for with borrowed funds. There were blips and bumps along the road, to be sure, but by and large, the tale of the Great Moderation was one of continuity and persistent trends.

That familiar world is no more. The financial crisis of 2008, the deepest economic contraction since the Great Depression, and a host of disruptive technologies, trends, and developments have conspired to ruffle the calm. Many of the long-standing trends that made life so pleasant for investors and managers during the Great Moderation have broken decisively. After nearly three decades of declining interest rates, the cost of capital cannot get cheaper, and it could rise over the next twenty years. After a prolonged period of falling and steady prices for natural resources, the cost of everything from grain to steel is becoming more volatile. The demographic surplus the world enjoyed as working-age populations grew and China joined the global trading system is likely to turn into a demographic deficit as population growth grinds to a halt and the world's labor force ages. Although inequality between countries continues to shrink, in many parts of the world, individuals—particularly those with low job skills—are at risk of growing up poorer than their parents.

That's just the beginning.

A radically different world is forming. The operating system of the world's economy is being rewritten as we speak. It doesn't come out in a splashy new release. It evolves, unfolds, and often explodes.

Four Great Disruptive Forces

We believe that the world is now roughly in the middle of a dramatic transition as a result of four fundamental disruptive trends. Any one of these disruptions, by itself, would probably rank among the largest economic forces the global economy has ever seen—including industrial revolutions in advanced economies. Although we all know that these disruptions are happening, most of us fail to comprehend their full magnitude and the second- and third-order effects that will result. Much as waves can amplify one another, these trends are gaining strength, magnitude, and influence as they interact with, coincide with, and feed upon one another. Together, they are producing monumental change.

The first is the shifting locus of economic activity and dynamism—to emerging markets like China and to cities within those markets. The emerging markets are going through the simultaneous industrial and urban revolutions that began in the nineteenth century in the developed world. The balance of power of the world economy is shifting east and south at a speed never before witnessed. As recently as 2000, 95 percent of the Fortune Global 500—the world's largest international companies, including Shell, Coca-Cola, IBM, Nestlé, and Airbus, to name a few— were headquartered in developed economies. By 2025, when China will be home to more large companies than either the United States or Europe, we expect nearly half of the world's large companies—defined as those with revenues of $1 billion or more—will come from emerging markets.[8] "Over the years, people in our headquarters, in Frankfurt, started complaining to me, 'We don't see you much around here anymore,'" said Josef Acker-mann, the former chief executive officer of Deutsche Bank. "Well, there was a reason why: growth has moved elsewhere—to Asia, Latin America, the Middle East."[9]

Perhaps equally important, the locus of economic activity is shifting *within* these markets. The global urban population has been rising by an average of sixty-five million people over the last three decades, equivalent to adding seven Chicagos a year, every year.[10] Nearly half of global GDP growth between 2010 and 2025 will come from 440 cities in emerging markets—95 percent of them small- and medium-sized cities that many Western executives may not even have heard of and couldn't point to on a map.[11] Mumbai, Dubai, and Shanghai, yes. But also Hsinchu, in northern Taiwan, which is already the fourth-largest advanced electronics and high-tech hub in the China region. And Brazil's Santa Catarina state, halfway between São Paulo and the Uruguayan border, which is now a regional hub for electronics and vehicle manufacturing and home to billion-dollar com-panies such as WEG Indústrias SA. And Tianjin, a city that lies around 120 kilometers southeast of Beijing. In 2010, we estimated that the GDP of Tianjin was around $130 billion, making it around the same size as Stockholm, the capital of Sweden. By 2025, we estimate that the GDP of Tianjin will have risen to around $625 billion—approximately that of all of Sweden.[12]

The second disruptive force is the acceleration in the scope, scale, and economic impact of technology. Technology—from the printing press to the steam engine and the Internet—has always been a great force in overturning the status quo. The difference today is the sheer ubiquity of technology in our lives and the speed of change. In their bestseller *The Second Machine Age,* Erik Brynjolfsson and Andrew McAfee of the Massachusetts Institute of Technology dubbed the current era the "second half of the chessboard." Brynjolfsson and McAfee give a modern twist to an old story about the power of exponential growth. Pleased with the invention of chess, a Chinese emperor offered the inventor his choice of prizes. At the outset, the inventor asked the emperor for a single grain of rice to be placed on the first square of the chessboard, two on the second square, four on the third, and eight on the fourth. The amounts doubled with each move. The first half of the chessboard was fairly uneventful. The inventor received spoons of rice, then bowls, then barrels. One version of the story has the emperor going bankrupt and being replaced by the inventor, as sixty-three doublings would have ultimately totaled eighteen million trillion grains of rice—enough to cover twice the surface area of the earth. "There have been slightly more than thirty-two doublings of performance since the first programmable computers were invented during World War II," the futurist and computer scientist Raymond Kurzweil has noted. As fast as innovation has multiplied and spread in recent years, it is poised to change and grow at an exponential speed beyond the power of human intuition to anticipate.

Processing power and connectivity are only part of the story. Their impact is multiplied by the concomitant data revolution, which places unprecedented amounts of information in the hands of consumers and businesses alike, and the proliferation of technology-enabled business models, from online retail platforms like Alibaba to car-hailing apps like Uber. Thanks to these mutually amplifying forces, more and more people will enjoy a golden age of gadgetry, of instant communication, and of apparently boundless information. Technology offers the promise of economic progress for billions in emerging economies at a speed that would have been unimaginable without the mobile Internet. Barely twenty years ago, less than 3 percent of the world's population had a mobile phone and less than 1 percent were on the Internet.[13] Today, two-thirds of the world's population has access to a mobile phone and one-third of all humans are able to communicate on the Internet.[14] Technology allows businesses to start and gain scale with stunning speed while using little capital, as WhatsApp did. Entrepreneurs and startups now frequently enjoy advantages over large, established businesses. The furious pace of technological adoption and innovation is shortening the lifecycle of companies and forcing executives to make decisions and commit resources much more quickly.

The third force changing the world is demographics. Simply put, the human population is getting older. Fertility is falling, and the world's population is graying dramatically. Aging has been evident in developed economies for some time. Japan and Russia have seen their populations decline over the past few years. The demographic deficit is now spreading to China and will then sweep across Latin America. For the first time in human history, aging could mean that the planet's population plateaus in most of the world. Thirty years ago, only a small share of the global population lived in the few countries with fertility rates substantially below those needed to replace each generation—2.1 children per woman. But by 2013, about 60 percent of the world's population lived in countries with fertility rates below the replacement rate.[15] This is a sea change. The European Commission expects that by 2060, Germany's population will shrink by one-fifth, and the number of people of working age will fall from fifty-four million in 2010 to thirty-six million in 2060, a level that is forecast to be less than France's.[16] China's labor force peaked in 2012, due to income-driven demographic trends. In Thailand, the fertility rate has fallen from 5 in the 1970s to 1.4 today.[17] A smaller workforce will place a greater onus on productivity for driving growth and may cause us to rethink the economy's potential. Caring for large numbers of elderly people will put severe pressure on government finances.

The final disruptive force is the degree to which the world is much more connected through trade and through movements in capital, people, and information—what we call "flows." Trade and finance have long been part of the globalization story. In recent decades, there's been a significant shift. Instead of a series of lines connecting major trading hubs in Europe and North America, the global trading system has expanded into a complex, intricate, sprawling web. Asia is becoming the world's largest trading region. "South-south" flows between emerging markets have doubled their share of global trade over the past decade.[18] The volume of trade between China and Africa rose from $9 billion in 2000 to $211 billion in 2012.[19] Global capital flows expanded twenty-five times between 1980 and 2007. People crossed borders more than one billion times in 2009, over five times the number in 1980.[20] These three types of connections all paused during the global recession of 2008 and have recovered only slowly since. But the links forged by technology have marched on uninterrupted and with increasing speed, ushering in a dynamic new phase of globalization, creating unmatched opportunities, and fomenting unexpected volatility.

RESETTING INTUITION

The four disruptions gathered pace, grew in scale, and started collectively to have a material impact on the world economy around the turn of the twenty-first century. Now they are disrupting long-established patterns in virtually every market and every sector of the world economy—indeed, in every aspect of our lives. Everywhere we look, they are causing trends to break down, to break up, or simply to break. The fact that all four are happening at the same time means that our world will change radically from the one in which many of us grew up, prospered, and formed the intuitions that are so vital to our decision making.

Discontinuities such as these could be seen as bringing only doom and gloom. But this would be wrong—by a long shot. Indeed, the same forces that lifted one billion people out of extreme poverty between 1990 and 2010 will help propel nearly two billion more people into the global consuming class in the next two decades.[21] This improvement in the economic status of so many people would save even more lives than the eradication of smallpox, one of the greatest medical achievements of the twentieth century. The rapid spread of technology will empower individuals and consumers in unprecedented numbers. Increasingly, companies will find that technology drives the marginal cost of delivering a new product, servicing a new customer, or completing a transaction toward zero. And as more people connect to the global communications and commercial systems, the force of network effects will make those systems more valuable—and create more value for those who can tap into them. As a result, the new world will be richer, more urbanized, more skilled, and healthier than the one it replaces. Its population will have access to powerful innovations that could address long-standing challenges, create new products and services for a growing consuming class, and present opportunities for a global entrepreneurial class. In many ways, we live in an age of recurring miracles.

These developments can play havoc with forecasts and pro forma plans that were made simply by extrapolating recent experience into the near and distant future. Many of the assumptions, tendencies, and habits that proved so successful have suddenly lost much of their resonance. We've never had more data and advice at our fingertips—literally. The iPhone or the Samsung Galaxy contains far more information and processing power than the original supercomputer. Yet we work in a world in which even, perhaps especially, professional forecasters are routinely caught unawares.

That's partly because intuition still underpins much of our decision making. It's human nature, and our intuition has been formed by a set of experiences and ideas about how things worked and are supposed to work. Changes were incremental and somewhat predictable. Globalization benefited the well established and well connected, opening up new markets with relative ease. Labor markets functioned quite reliably. Resource prices fell. But that's not how things are working now—and it's not how they are likely to work in the future. If we look at the world through a rearview mirror and make decisions on the basis of the intuition built on our experience, we could well be wrong. In the new world, executives, policy makers, and individuals all need to scrutinize their intuitions from first principles and boldly reset them if necessary. This is especially true for organizations that have enjoyed great success.

We have to rethink the assumptions that drive our decisions on such crucial issues as consumption, resources, labor, capital, and competition. We shouldn't discard experience and instinct, but rather augment them and adapt them to what we can see happening right ahead of us. We must think differently about strategy, constructing business plans, approaching markets, assessing competitors, and allocating resources.

The developed world used to drive consumption. As the huge, developed economies—Japan, the United States, Europe—went, so went growth in consumer spending. No longer. Now, the large new army of middle-class consumers in the emerging world propels global spending growth. China's e-tail market, which has grown at a compounded annual rate of 110 percent since 2003, is already the world's second largest, after that of the United States. By 2020, China's e-tail market, led by Alibaba and the legions of Singles Day shoppers, could be as big as today's markets in the United States, Japan, the United Kingdom, Germany, and France combined.

Commodity prices fell by almost half during the twentieth century in real terms, an astonishing development given that the global population quadrupled and global economic output expanded roughly twentyfold, massively boosting demand for different resources.[22] Why? Technological breakthroughs opened up access to resources and increased the efficiency of extraction. Companies enjoyed lower raw materials costs. More and more households had access to relatively inexpensive and abundant energy and food. But that trend began to break in 2000. In the first ten years of the new century, the price declines of the previous one hundred years were completely erased as soaring demand from emerging economies coincided with depleted reserves of many resources. The reversal of the past decade has brought higher volatility, which may persist regardless of future demand and supply trends.

Thanks to the actions of central banks, a host of disinflationary pressures, slack investment in the developed world, and a rise in savings, for thirty years the cost of capital has fallen progressively—for governments, for companies, and for consumers.[23] Between 1982 and 2013, the yield on the ten-year US government bond fell from 14.6 to just 1.9 percent.[24] This era of progressively easier money is very likely ending. The US Federal Reserve has already started the process of tightening monetary policy. Emerging economies are in the throes of a capital-intensive infrastructure boom exceeding that of the rebuilding of wrecked economies in the aftermath of World War II. The surging demand for capital comes when the world's savings are falling as people age and governments have to borrow more.

For decades the general trends were for the global labor force to rise and for more of the global labor force to be connected to the global system. What's more, thanks to a rapidly expanding economy in emerging markets, the new hands were able to find places to work. Across the globe, employers were generally able to find employees with appropriate skills. Between 1980 and 2010, 1.1 billion adults entered the twenty- to sixty-four-year-old age bracket and joined the world's labor force.[25] But due to a host of demographic factors, global labor force growth will *fall* by nearly one-third by 2030.[26] At the same time, technology is roiling labor markets as never before. Computers, which historically replaced manual and clerical workers, such as stenographers and bank tellers, are now beginning to replace knowledge and skilled workers, like journalists and stock analysts. By 2025, in fact, computers could do the work of 140 million knowledge workers, and robots could do the work of another 75 million people.[27] And yet there will still be high demand for skilled positions in engineering, software development, and health care. Four out of ten respondents in a McKinsey survey reported that they currently couldn't find the talent they need. This means that we're likely to see a strange dichotomy. By 2020, on our current trajectory, businesses could be short of 85 million workers with college degrees or vocational training; at the same time, 95 million lower-skilled workers could be unemployed.[28]

In the past, executives typically knew their main competitors at home and abroad, and they could often catch up to new competition that emerged. But competitive intensity has reached an entirely new level because of technology that gives the advantage to small, entrepreneurial companies over large, established businesses with high fixed costs. Today, new competition is coming from a wave of rapidly growing newcomers that are simply not on the strategic radar and that don't appear on the radar until they have gained critical mass. These newcomers play by a different set of rules. They have much lower cost bases, faster time to market, a ruthless understanding of their Western competitors, and a willingness to accept lower returns. The market position of Unilever's OMO laundry products in Kenya isn't being challenged by Procter & Gamble. Rather, OMO is under attack from Toss, made by Kapa Oil Refineries, Ltd., a Nairobi-based company that has shifted from industrial to consumer products.

While it is full of opportunities, this era is deeply unsettling. And there is a great deal of work to be done—in resetting our collective intuition, in developing new approaches to high-growth markets, and in becoming more agile as a way of dealing with breaking trends. The chapters that follow build on the efforts to understand trends by the McKinsey Global Institute (MGI), the economics and business research arm of the management consulting firm McKinsey & Co. Our thinking stems from McKinsey's work with companies and organizations around the world; meaningful conversations about the challenges and opportunities inherent in our world with corporate, government, and NGO leaders; deep, proprietary quantitative research by MGI over the last twenty-five years; and extensive and diverse personal experiences. One of us has lived in China for more than a quarter century, one of us has been based in Silicon Valley since 1993, and one of us has, since 1988, spent time in London, Mumbai, and Seoul. We have all been forced to continually reset our own intuition. The chapters that follow are divided into two broad sections. In the first four chapters, we describe the four great disruptive forces that are altering our world. In the final six chapters, we describe how you can—and should—respond to the challenges these forces present to key facets of modern leadership.

Analyzing the intelligence from these diverse sources and experiences has led us to the management imperative for the coming decade. Realize that much of what we thought we knew about how the world works is wrong. Get a handle on the disruptive forces transforming the global economy. Identify the long-standing trends that are breaking. Develop the courage and foresight to clear the intellectual decks and prepare to respond. These are lessons that apply as much to policy makers as to business executives. After all, urbanization, technology, and greater global connections are putting the same pressures on government that they are on business. In domains as diverse as labor, fiscal planning, trade, immigration, and resource and technology regulation, the emerging world will be exerting pressure on political, governmental, and NGO leaders and forcing them to reset their own intuitions.

We're not here simply to alert readers to perils or to flog the many wonderful opportunities that lie before us. Rather, we'll offer guidance on how you can reset your internal navigation system.

That process can't begin soon enough. In all the areas of the world economy that we discuss in this book, there is an urgent imperative to adjust to new realities. Yet, for all the ingenuity, inventiveness, and imagination of the human race, we tend to be slow to adapt to change. Behavioral economists throw around terms like *recency bias* and *anchoring*. Physicists point to the powerful force of inertia. Cynical analysts might refer to "pro forma disease"—because the last three years looked a certain way, the next five years will look much the same. However we identify it, there is a powerful human tendency to want the future to look much like the recent past. On these shoals, huge corporate vessels have repeatedly foundered. Revisiting our assumptions about the world we live in—and doing nothing—will leave many of us highly vulnerable. Gaining a clear-eyed perspective on how to negotiate the changing landscape will help us prepare to succeed.

PART I

The Four Disruptive Forces

1

—

BEYOND SHANGHAI

The Age of Urbanization

FEW PEOPLE FROM THE DEVELOPED COUNTRIES OF THE WEST HAVE
visited Kumasi, about 160 miles northwest of Ghana's capital, Accra, even
though getting there is much easier now than it was a few years ago. Kumasi Airport has thirteen flights daily to Accra, serviced by airlines such
as Antrak Air, Fly540 Ghana, Africa World Airlines, and Starbow, with
one-way fares starting as low as $20.[1] With a population of about two
million, Kumasi, hometown of former United Nations secretary general
Kofi Annan, is roughly the size of Houston, although its population density (21,000 per square mile) approaches New York's.[2] The capital of the
Ashanti region, the so-called Garden City, has long been a center of timber
and gold production.

The people of Kumasi are active consumers of basic, cheap goods. They
are not yet part of the massive global audience for midrange and premium
brands. Shopping activity centers on West Africa's largest open-air market,
Kejetia, a ramshackle collection of eleven thousand tin-roofed stalls. Multinational companies are scarce here. The leading hotel built to international
standards is a Golden Tulip, owned by the French company Groupe du
Louvre. Kumasi has a Standard Chartered Bank Ghana branch and eight
branches of Nigeria's Fidelity Bank. Only a few companies from developed economies have a presence in Kumasi. (Starbucks sells Kumasi-brand
coffee in the United States, but there is no Starbucks in town.) And why
should they? Kumasi is a poor backwater in a poor country. Ghana's per
capita income last year was about $3,880—163rd in the world.[3]

But Kumasi—and the thousands of emerging cities in emerging markets like it—is where the future of many companies will lie. Most of them just don't know it yet. As is the case with many developing world cities, it is on the verge of reaping the fruits of a radically condensed cycle of economic transformation.

The sweeping industrialization of emerging economies has shifted the center of gravity of the world economy east and south. Internal migration in those countries, from the farm and village to the city, is fueling astonishing growth. And it has happened at a speed never before seen in history. These developments are powering an explosive growth in demand, which compels us to reset our intuition. The megacities of these emerging economies— such as Shanghai, São Paulo, and Mumbai—are already on the radar of global companies. But the truly dramatic consumption growth will be in cities that most would find hard to locate on a map today, like Kumasi.

SHIFTING ECONOMIC CENTER OF GRAVITY

From the year 1 to 1500, the world's center of economic gravity*—a measure of economic power by geography—straddled the border between China and India, the countries with the globe's largest populations. But urbanization, and the industrial revolutions that accompanied it, started in Britain and then swept across continental Europe and the United States. As it did so, the center of gravity moved inexorably to the north and west— first to Europe and then toward North America. During World War I, the center of financial power hopped the Atlantic from London to New York. The shift was reinforced by two world wars, the effects of the Depression in Europe, and the spread of Communism in Russia and China. The East stagnated while the West, led by the United States, powered ahead. By 1945, the United States stood virtually alone as a vibrant global economic power.

The foundation for a trend break was laid in the decades following World War II. In the second half of the twentieth century, the economic pendulum gradually began to swing back to the East. Starting in the 1950s, Europe recovered, and Japan, embarking upon a remarkable recovery, rebuilt its industry. It grew to become the second-largest economy in the world

---

*Economic center of gravity is calculated by weighting locations by GDP in three dimensions and projecting the center to the nearest point of the earth's surface.

by the late 1980s. Japan was quickly joined by South Korea. The process accelerated when Asia's slumbering giants began to stir. Then, finally, economic reform took hold in the world's two most populous nations.

China began to liberalize its economy in 1978, and it has enjoyed a remarkable three-decade period of growth. India began to integrate into global markets and shift into higher gear in the 1990s, propelled by its rapidly rising information technology sector. Through the 1990s, developed nations still dominated the global industrial landscape. The United States was the world's largest manufacturer, and Japanese and Western European countries dominated the rankings of manufacturing giants. By 2000, the United States, with 4 percent of the world's population, accounted for about one-third of economic activity and about 50 percent of the world's global market capitalization. But these figures belied a shift that was gathering strength. Between 1990 and 2010, the world's center of economic gravity moved more quickly than at any other time in recorded history.[4] The shift in economic activity to emerging regions powered through the 2008 financial crisis and the resulting global recession. While Europe remained mired in recession, Japan struggled to exit its lost decade, and the United States muddled through a low-growth expansion, the developing world decisively picked up the mantle of economic leadership. Of the $1.8 trillion of new global economic activity in 2013, China alone accounted for $1 trillion, or 60 percent of it. That country is now the world's largest manufacturer.[5]

It's not just China. Emerging economies such as India, Indonesia, Russia, and Brazil are now major forces in global manufacturing. Manufacturing value added has doubled in real terms since 1990, from $5 trillion to $10 trillion today, and the share of that value added generated by large emerging economies has also nearly doubled, from 21 to 39 percent, over the past decade.[6] The share of global foreign direct investment going to emerging and transitioning economies rose from 34 percent in 2007 to 50 percent in 2010 and to over 60 percent in 2013.[7] The growth is just a foreshadowing. Between now and 2025, those regions together will grow 75 percent more rapidly than developed countries, and annual consumption in emerging economies will reach $30 trillion, accounting for almost half of the global total.[8] By 2025, the economic center of gravity is expected to be back in Central Asia, just north of where it was in the year 1.[9]

The pace and scale of forces at work are staggering. Britain took 154 years to double economic output per person, and it did so with a population (at the start) of nine million people.[10] The United States achieved the same feat in fifty-three years, with a population (at the start) of ten million people. China and India have done it in only twelve and sixteen years, respectively, each with about 100 times as many people.[11] In other words, this economic acceleration is roughly 10 times faster than the one triggered by Britain's Industrial Revolution and is 300 times the scale—an economic force that is 3,000 times as large.

THE URBAN CENTURY

Why now? An underlying trend is at work that supports and enables the developing world: urbanization. People have been moving to cities for centuries, attracted by the possibility of higher income, more opportunity, and a better life. But the scale and pace of today's urbanization is without precedent. We are in the midst of the largest mass migration from the countryside to the city in history.

The population of cities globally has been rising by an average of 65 million people a year over the last three decades—equivalent to the entire population of the United Kingdom—and the growth has been heavily driven by rapid urbanization in China and India.[12] While Europe and the United States urbanized in the eighteenth and nineteenth centuries and Latin America in the second half of the twentieth century, China and India, each with a population of more than a billion, are now in the middle of their urban shifts. "Urbanization is not about simply increasing the number of urban residents or expanding the area of cities," said Chinese premier Li Keqiang. "More importantly, it's about a complete change from rural to urban style in terms of industry structure, employment, living environment, and social security."[13]

For many in China, the change can't come soon enough. For example, Ta Ping village, in the Qinling Mountains, has a population of 103. About ninety minutes outside bustling Xi'an, it has about forty yards of paved road that are flanked by a couple of dozen buildings with terra-cotta roof tiles. It's common to see braids of drying corn nailed to the outside walls of the houses, which hold bare lightbulbs, wood-burning stoves, cement floors, and televisions. Here, twenty-eight families scratch out a meager existence. The able-bodied seek work in the cities, and the rest go into the mountains to gather herbs, grow some soybeans and corn, or subsist on extremely meager pensions of about 80 renminbi ($15) per month. "How

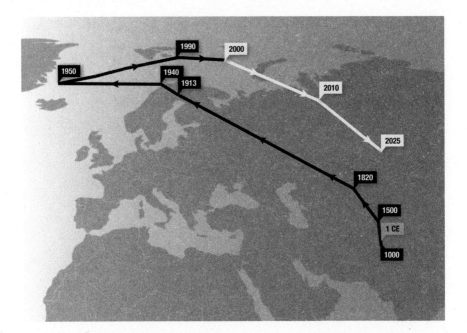

Evolution of the earth's economic center of gravity

---

1 CE¹

India and China account for two-thirds of global economic activity, and the world's center of gravity remains there for 1,500 years.

1950

Center of gravity shifts over three centuries to Europe—with the advent of the first Industrial Revolution in England—and then towards North America.

2025

In just twenty-five years starting in 2000, the rise of China, India, and other emerging economies could move the center back towards its origin.

1 The first century of the Current Era.
SOURCE: McKinsey Global Institute analysis using data from Angus Maddison; University of Groningen

should I be happy?" asks twenty-four-year-old Teng Ling Dang. "I'm poor, and my parents have illnesses." Teng, who didn't complete primary school, earns 70 renminbi (about $12) per day working at a brick factory in Luan, a nearby city. His marriage prospects are poor because he doesn't earn much money. And he can't leave for a higher-paying job on the coast because he must take care of his parents.[14]

Some 400 million people in China live in similar conditions, and the government is engineering their move to the city. "Urbanization," notes Stephen Roach, the longtime Morgan Stanley China expert who teaches at

Per capita GDP has risen in parallel with increases in the urbanization rate across regions

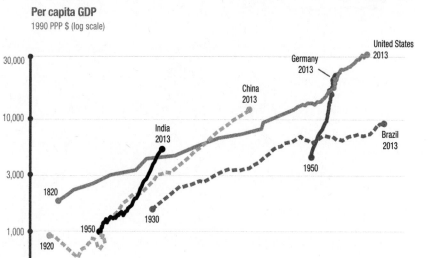

Per capita GDP
1990 PPP $ (log scale)

Urban population %

SOURCE: UN Population Data; The Conference Board; McKinsey Global Institute analysis

Yale, "is an essential ingredient of the 'next China.'"[15] On March 17, 2014, China released a new plan to respond to the flow of rural residents into cities. The central government foresees 100 million more people moving to China's cities by 2020. Current forecasts call for 60 percent of the country's population to live in cities by then.[16] In the near future, China has pledged to link every city with more than 200,000 people by rail and expressways, and to connect every city with more than 500,000 residents to its burgeoning high-speed rail network.[17] As goes China, so goes Asia and the rest of the developing world. By 2025, nearly 2.5 billion people will live in cities in Asia—that's one of every two urbanites in the entire world.[18] In little more than a decade, China could have more than triple, and India double, the number of urbanites the United States has today—about 250 million.

This matters because cities are where a country's population meets the modern world and the global economy. Cities turn poor peasants into more productive workers and into global citizens and consumers. The current

46 of the global top 200 cities will be in China by 2025

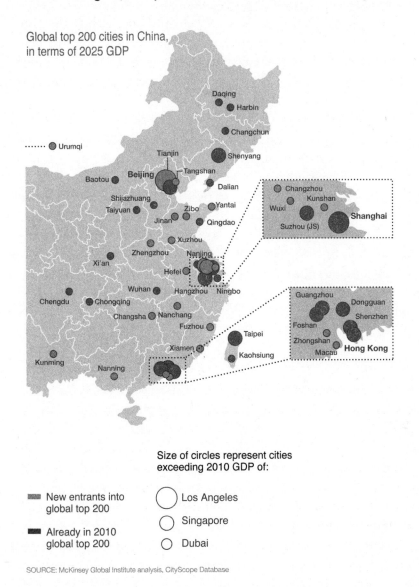

Global top 200 cities in China,
in terms of 2025 GDP

Size of circles represent cities
exceeding 2010 GDP of:

New entrants into
global top 200

Los Angeles

Singapore

Already in 2010
global top 200

Dubai

SOURCE: McKinsey Global Institute analysis, CityScope Database

wave of urbanization has played a key role in helping to lift 700 million
people out of poverty, most of them in China—thereby meeting the Millennium Development Goal of halving the number of people living in
extreme poverty five years ahead of schedule.[19]

Between 1990 and 2025, three billion people around the world are set
to become members of the consuming class, defined as having disposable

income greater than $10 per day. The vast majority of them will reside in the cities of emerging economies and enjoy opportunities that their parents could scarcely have imagined.[20] Never before has so much of the world's population been as fully engaged in the global economy. The first movie, the first taste of fast food, the first experience with the Internet, the first comprehensive medical checkup, the first bank account: these are all primarily urban experiences.

Tommy Xu grew up in a farming village outside Shanghai and remembers picking frogs out of rice paddies to sell. His village has long since been subsumed by Lujiazui, Shanghai's gleaming new financial district, which is studded with high-rise towers, parks, and malls. And Tommy, who held his marriage celebration at a KFC in the early 1990s, is now a senior official with a think tank in Beijing. His wife is a marketing executive with a publicly held firm. He drives an Acura. Tommy's is a singular story, but it is not atypical. In emerging markets alone, we project that this new army of urban consumers like Tommy will spend $30 trillion a year by 2030, up from $12 trillion in 2010.[21] They will account for half of the world's spending.

The Benefits of Cities

What's so great about cities? Throughout history, when people have moved out of farming to jobs in cities, their output has typically doubled. As subsequent generations come of age, their income also increases. To be sure, images of favelas, shantytowns, and slums are part of the landscape. Urban poverty is a real and potentially dangerous phenomenon. But economic historians tell us that for hundreds of years, people living in cities have enjoyed living standards one and a half to three times better than those of their country cousins.

There are many reasons that cities are such powerful engines of growth. Dense population centers generate productivity gains through economies of scale, specialization of labor, knowledge spillovers, and trade. These gains in productivity are reinforced through network effects. Recent research suggests that urban density drives superlinear productivity gains because it affords opportunities for greater social and economic interaction. People and skills attract businesses, which in turn lure migrants from rural areas looking for employment. Companies attract other companies that may want to do business or to share services such as roads, ports, and universities that offer a quick route into the talent pool. They invite ingenuity and the creation of new business models. Fan Milk International, now West Africa's largest maker of frozen dairy products, grew up in cities like Accra and Kumasi. It pioneered a sales model that worked for its environment. Bicycle vendors rode through the clogged streets with small containers (which could be consumed without being refrigerated). The company has added pushcarts and motorcycles to the mix, and it erects kiosks powered by solar panels (the electricity grid in many of its markets is unreliable) to keep its yogurt and milk cool. Having expanded to seven countries in Africa, Fan counts sales of about $160 million and enjoys high profit margins. Danone in 2013 bought a 49 percent interest in the company at a valuation of $360 million.[22]

The scale of the city means that urban populations benefit in other ways as well. Cities tend to have more extensive education systems than rural areas, and urban businesses and workers both benefit from the fact that building infrastructure and delivering public services is more efficient and cost effective. Evidence from India shows that it can be 30 to 50 percent less expensive for large cities to deliver basic services, including water, housing, and education, than it is for more sparsely populated rural areas to do so.[23] A virtuous cycle ensures that successful cities are able to further boost productivity by attracting better infrastructure, innovation, talent, and economic diversity.

Higher education is a crucial component of economic development. In the United Kingdom and the United States, it is not uncommon to find colleges and universities in rural settings. But in the developing world, they are almost exclusively an urban phenomenon. Kumasi is home to the Kwame Nkrumah University of Science and Technology, one of the leading science and technology universities in West Africa. Founded in 1950 as a technical school, it's a full-fledged university set on an eight-square-mile campus, with six colleges, including schools of business, law, and medicine. (Kofi Annan studied there in the late 1950s before leaving for the United States.) It attracts bright, ambitious students from other West African countries as well as Ghana.

ADAPTING TO URBANIZATION

Cities have been around for millennia. A person traveling to Europe, the Middle East, Africa, Latin America, or Asia would encounter common,

familiar features—the central square, walls, administrative and government buildings, a large religious complex, the market. Today's rapid urbanization, however, is altering the very definition and concept of cities. And
cities are developing in unpredictable ways. In 1950, New York City and
Tokyo were the only two urban areas with more than ten million people.
Today, more than twenty geographic agglomerations have populations of
more than ten million.[24] China has two cities—Shanghai with twenty
million people and Beijing with sixteen million—whose populations are
roughly the size of the entire country of the Netherlands.[25]

The movement of the economic future to the cities of emerging economies impels a fundamental shift in the way business leaders need to think
about managing growth. The rising urban tide opens up unprecedented
access to new consumers, an array of new economic opportunities, and a
unique chance to innovate. Infrastructure, smart city technologies, and
urban services are in high demand. Huge armies of urban talent are joining the global labor pool. And these densely packed markets function as
laboratories in which companies can experiment with different business
models, technologies, products, and strategies. Capitalizing on these new
growth markets is far from simple; it requires masterful city-level market
intelligence, ruthless prioritization, and navigation of risks. However, business leaders need to start seeing these new urban markets as opportunities
rather than risks. This is not just a matter of semantics. There's a big difference between the way resources and talent are mobilized to take advantage
of an opportunity and protecting against risk. It's the difference between
playing offense and defense.

Get to Know the Newcomers

In the past, many large companies have done well by focusing on developed
economies combined with the megacities of emerging economies. Today,
that combination will gain them exposure to markets with 70 percent of
the world's GDP. But by 2025, this combination will generate only about
one-third of global growth, which will not be sufficient for large companies
trying to position themselves for growth.[26] In contrast, between 2010 and
2025, 440 cities in developing nations will generate nearly half of global
GDP growth.[27]

But only about 20 or so of these emerging-market dynamos are likely
to be familiar names, such as Shanghai, Mumbai, Jakarta, São Paulo, or
Lagos. The other 420 are names that don't roll off the tips of our tongues.

How many people have spotted Surat, Foshan, or Porto Alegre on their strategic radars? Probably not many, despite the fact that all three have populations of more than four million and are considerable economic forces in fast-growing economies. Surat, in western India, accounts for about two-fifths of the nation's textile production. Foshan is China's seventh-largest city in terms of GDP. And Porto Alegre is the capital of Rio Grande do Sul, the fourth-largest state in Brazil. Each is growing rapidly and has a vibrant and expanding base of consumers. Each will contribute more to global growth between now and 2025 than Madrid, Milan, or Zurich.

Navigating this new landscape will be far from straightforward. Many of these emerging-market cities aren't widely known outside their own nations. Operating costs in some of the cities will far exceed those in home markets. Income and demographic trends will vary from country to country and city to city, and even within cities, as the consumption of different products and services starts to rise at different income levels. To make the best decisions, companies will need extensive city-level market intelligence to determine which cities—or clusters of cities with similar characteristics—to focus on.

Create New Services

Consumer ownership models are changing, and cities are at the heart of the shift. Urban populations tend to have higher disposable incomes. In many cities, residents—especially younger ones—are increasingly comfortable renting services rather than buying assets, opening up opportunities for businesses that are smart about spotting consumers' new needs.

Fueled by technology and assisted by dense urban networks, home-based services and transportation have been perhaps the most prominent examples of innovative services. In 2011, Homeplus, a Korean retail chain owned by British retailer Tesco, opened the world's first virtual supermarket in a subway station in Seoul. Using an app, commuters can scan the barcodes of life-size pictures of grocery items on the walls and screen doors of the railway platform and have the groceries delivered to their homes the same day. The service was so popular that in one year, Homeplus expanded its virtual stores to more than twenty bus stops. US start-up Instacart now offers customers in ten cities the ability to order goods from multiple stores through one website and get them delivered in one hour. Car-sharing services such as Zipcar and Lyft and transport services such as

Uber are becoming increasingly popular among urban residents who have chosen not to purchase their own cars.

The growing ubiquity of such shared services may be hard to replicate outside dense urban environments, but they are not unique to developed economies. In many emerging-market cities, similar services are already routinely offered though informal arrangements with mom-and-pop stores and service providers in local communities and neighborhoods. As incomes rise, consumers in those cities will be increasingly willing to pay for higher-quality services. One example of this trend comes from India, where house calls by doctors were common a generation ago but grew less prevalent as cities became more congested. Today, Portea Medical offers home health care in eighteen Indian cities, using geospatial information to efficiently send the nearest clinician to a patient's home, capturing health data and uploading it to an electronic platform, and deploying predictive analytics to analyze health trends and recommend interventions.

Tap Urban Talent and Innovation Pools

Cities are increasingly attracting talented, highly educated young people, with larger cities able to attract and retain talent better than smaller cities can. McKinsey research indicates that three-quarters of Europe's GDP gap with the United States can be explained by the fact that more Americans live in big cities—even American middle-sized cities tend to be larger than large European ones. This matters because larger cities tend to have greater network effects and higher wage premiums compared to rural areas. More densely populated cities are more attractive to innovators and entrepreneurs, who tend to congregate in places where they have greater access to networks of peers, mentors, financial institutions, partners, and potential customers. Cities exhibit superlinear scaling characteristics; with every doubling of a city's population, each inhabitant becomes, on average, 15 percent wealthier, more productive, and more innovative.[28]

Companies that seek to tap large cities for talent often worry about the cost of doing business in urban locations. The cost challenge has been made more complex by recent trends that have seen a reversal of the traditional urban ecosystem of businesses locating downtown (or in midtown) and high-skilled residents living in suburbs. Today, many cities are seeing the development of downtown and midtown residential and mixed-use space as workers—increasingly white-collar professionals—seek to live in the urban core.

Firms that locate outside the core—to benefit from lower costs or to locate large assets such as factories and warehouses—can find it harder to attract technical talent that increasingly wants to live near the center of large cities. Companies that can get inside the core can enjoy access to a rich and growing talent base. Universities located in urban settings are benefiting from the influx of talent—making it even more of an imperative for businesses to locate nearby. In June 2014, Pfizer opened a new one-thousand-person R&D facility in Cambridge, Massachusetts, close to MIT. In Pittsburgh, Carnegie Mellon's Collaborative Innovation Center has attracted companies such as Google, Apple, and Intel, which have set up R&D facilities on campus. Many large cities in the developed world are seeing the growth of innovation districts that attract tech start-ups and small, design-oriented manufacturers. TechCity in London, 1871 in Chicago, 1776 in Washington, DC, and 22@ in Barcelona are all examples of such urban collaborative spaces. In San Francisco, SFMade, a nonprofit set up in 2010, seeks to promote local manufacturing in the city. In New York, Made in NYC has a similar aim, looking to support nearly seven thousand small local manufacturers. And in Europe, organizations such as Design for Manufacturing Forum connect industrial designers, engineers, and manufacturers with the fast-growing "maker" movement to create a decentralized, lean manufacturing ecosystem around urban clusters in cities like Rotterdam.

Think of Cities as Laboratories

Cities are demographic and political microcosms well suited for both private- and public-sector experimentation. Compared with their rural counterparts, city leaders often have greater license to experiment, be it in school reform or regulation of self-driving cars. Private- and public-sector leaders are increasingly collaborating on R&D to find innovative solutions to evolving city needs. As a result, cities are becoming increasingly important partners in innovation—particularly for companies that need to pilot new products and services in self-contained markets before rolling them out nationally.

Some of these "experiments" in urban innovation are driven by new technologies that repurpose legacy installations. Telekom Austria has converted hundreds of disused phone booths in Vienna into electric-car-charging stations where drivers can pay for fuel with a text message. In New York City, a partnership between Cisco and 24/7 has repurposed

250 of the city's unused phone boxes into interactive information touch screens.[29] From technology demonstrations to marketing campaigns, cities can be attractive targets to test new ideas and business models in a rich and diverse environment that is still of manageable scale.

Urban administrators benefit from these innovative pilot programs as well. Take infrastructure as an example. On the outskirts of Lima, Peru, engineers at the local University of Engineering and Technology have found an innovative way to tackle the lack of access to clean drinking water by harnessing one of the city's most abundant resources: humid coastal air. Essentially, they installed a humidity collector, which turns water vapor in the air into liquid when air gets in contact with the cooler surface of water condensers, and a water purifier on top of a large advertising billboard. The system produces nearly one hundred liters of clean drinking water a day, which flows through a pipe to a tap at the base of the installation.[30] In Umea, Sweden, long, dark winters and a chronic lack of sunlight have spurred a local company, Umea Energi, to install therapeutic UV light in thirty bus stops. Commuter traffic has since risen by 50 percent.[31] MIT's Senseable City Lab illustrates the potential of smart city technologies. The lab focuses on studying cities and urban life through new kinds of sensors and hand-held electronics. On its new campus in Singapore, the Senseable City Lab has worked closely with Singapore's Land Transport Authority and developed three interactive applications that provide insight into the city's transportation infrastructure.[32]

Manage Operational Complexity

For businesses looking to locate or expand in cities, operating costs are high and rapidly growing. Emerging-market megacities such as Shanghai and Mumbai are already home to some of the priciest commercial real estate in the world. In built-up areas, infrastructure can get congested easily, further raising the cost and unpredictability of doing business. Some Latin American and Asian cities are beginning to lose their power as engines of prosperity because they are clogged with traffic, scarred by urban sprawl, polluted, and crime ridden. Any visitor to Jakarta is familiar with the traffic gridlock that results from 1.5 million vehicles using roads designed for 1 million. Traffic congestion alone costs Indonesia's capital city an estimated $1 billion a year in lost productivity.[33] In Mercer's Annual Cost of Living survey, the most expensive city for business isn't San Francisco or Tokyo. Rather, it's Luanda, Angola, where a dearth of quality office space and living

quarters, poor public services and supply chains, and underdeveloped business and physical infrastructure impose huge costs on corporations.[34]

On top of land costs, businesses face other challenges, such as stringent
zoning rules, land-use regulations, and environmental rules—in emerging
and developed cities alike. These regulations may still be manageable for
service companies, but businesses that require heavy machinery, land, or
warehouses face prohibitive costs of operation. While many large emerging-
market cities remain significant industrial hubs in their own right, growing
demand for commercial and residential space is squeezing out industrial
users. Mumbai's Parel neighborhood housed textile mills for more than one
hundred years; over the past thirty years, the mills have given way to up-
scale restaurants, premium office space, and luxury hotels and apartments,
including World One, slated to be among the world's tallest residential
buildings when it is completed in 2015.

Companies are trying a range of solutions to such pressures—and are
finding new opportunities. In March 2014, Panasonic decided to pay bo-
nuses to expatriate workers in China to compensate for their exposure to
high pollution.[35] In July 2014, Google expanded its office space in downtown San Francisco, buying an eight-story building and leasing 250,000
square feet nearby. The company now has a cluster of offices near the San
Francisco waterfront. In Bangalore, the hub of India's IT industry, companies run their own buses and power generators to ensure that unreliable
public transport and electricity supply don't affect commercial activity. And
to provide better reliability of urban delivery, logistics providers are investing in two-tier urban distribution centers and smart trucks with real-time
telematics, hoping to minimize delivery delays and reduce unpredictability.

Companies are also trying to partner with city administrations to offer
solutions to these challenges. Infrastructure financing and delivery is one
area; public-private partnerships were successfully used to build New Del-
hi's Metro Rail, modernize Singapore's water system, develop a public
cable-car system in Medellín, Colombia, and invest $3.5 billion in various
transportation projects in Vancouver. In March 2014, Kumasi's government announced the construction of a sky train, an elevated transit system,
to relieve chronic traffic. Standard Bank of South Africa is financing the
$170 million project.[36] Technology and smart apps are other areas where
large companies and start-ups have collaborated with cities. Transport for
London shared its data to encourage new apps such as BusIT London,
which suggests the best bus route for any journey, given the user's current

location; NextBus provides real-time bus information in several cities in the United States and Canada. The San Francisco Municipal Transportation Agency partnered with tech companies and parking meter providers to develop SFPark, a parking solution that combines new meters with sensors, mobile apps, and dynamic pricing to reduce congestion and parking delays.

It is easy for the leader of a business to take a quick look at Kumasi, and at the thousands of up-and-coming cities in the developing world, and conclude that his or her company is not missing out on all that much by not being there today. But at a time of rapid, surprising change, snapshots that capture a moment in economic time can be deeply misleading. In this age of Instagram, we must apply new filters to the mental and financial pictures we take. Our intuition—the nerve center that turns images into narratives—has to reset so that it processes the incoming data intelligently. The portraits we take of cities must capture the dynamism underneath the surface and highlight the brightness of opportunities, while toning down the alarming flares of risk. Most of all, they must be able to project forward motion.

2

—

THE TIP OF THE ICEBERG
Accelerating Technological Change

LONDON IS A CITY CHOCKABLOCK WITH ICONS RECOGNIZED BY PEO-
ple around the world—Big Ben, Westminster Abbey, Buckingham Palace,
and the thousands of black cabs that ply the crowded, twisting roads and
lanes. For tourists and locals alike, the black cabs are a quintessential part
of the London experience. London cabbies are justly proud of their trade,
heritage, and skill. They must pass a notoriously tough multiyear training course, known simply as "the Knowledge," which requires drivers to
memorize over sixty thousand streets.[1] On average, drivers take the final
exam twelve times before passing. Yet on June 11, 2014, London cabbies
decided that they had had enough.[2] That afternoon, more than ten thousand black cabs blocked off London's iconic areas in a wide-ranging strike.
They brought Trafalgar Square, Parliament Square, and Whitehall to a
standstill. The reason? In a word, Uber.[3] To be more precise, they were
protesting London's handling of transport start-ups like Uber, whose business model depends on a GPS-enabled smart-phone app that cheaply and
efficiently connects riders to drivers and that acts like a taxi meter. Cabbies
argue that the city's Private Vehicles Act bars privately hired vehicles from
having taxi meters.[4]

Advances in digital technology are fueling the rise of new, nimble competitors that have their sights set on a slice of London's lucrative taxi market.[5] Protection from competition and high barriers to entry have allowed
London's cabbies to thrive, even though they've been reluctant to embrace
new technology: the knowledge obviates the need for GPS, and most taxis
only take cash—and keep prices high. The average journey is estimated to

cost about £27.[6] Hailo, a smart-phone app that allows customers to hail a black cab virtually, did not launch until the end of 2011.[7]

Drivers of London's black cabs—along with those in several other European cities that day—were channeling their anger at San Francisco–based Uber. Since launching in 2009, Uber has been an enormous success, rapidly expanding into more than 230 cities in fifty countries.[8] Backed by Google Ventures and private equity firm TPG, among other high-profile investors, Uber in June 2014 closed a round of financing that valued the company at $18 billion.[9] Since Uber entered London in 2012, the city has been one of its fastest-growing markets, with over seven thousand drivers active in late 2013.[10]

As car-hailing apps proliferate—Uber's competitors include Hailo, Addison Lee, and Kabbee—black cabs have been caught in the slow lane. Hailo, originally designed to work exclusively with black cabs, has responded to Uber's success by opening up its services to private-hire vehicles, a move seen by many cabbies as a significant betrayal. In response, Hailo's offices were vandalized.[11] Meanwhile, on the day of the June protest, Uber announced that it would welcome black cabs into its service.[12]

London's cabbies aren't alone in finding their once-venerable and impregnable business models rapidly upended with apparent ease. Advances in technology have always disrupted the status quo. But they have never done so across so many markets and at the speed and scale that is being seen today. As digital platforms reduce to near zero the marginal costs of scaling up business activity, such platforms are enabling new business models, new entrants, and even new market models such as peer-to-peer transactions and the "sharing" economy. With lowered barriers to entry, it is now common to see small companies take on incumbents and gain critical mass in a matter of months. The boundaries separating sectors have become blurred, and digital capabilities are often driving the shift of economic values between players and sectors. While companies struggle with technological churn, consumers are big beneficiaries—far beyond the extent captured in official data releases. Take, for instance, the ability to search the Internet, a service provided by Google, Microsoft's Bing, and Apple's Siri, among others. Consumers would have happily paid a great deal for this service. As recently as the 1980s, customers paid each time they dialed 411 to get a phone number. But from the outset, web search has generally been free. As a result, it is not captured in official statistics such as GDP. The acceleration of the "metabolic rate" of the global economy has profound implications for all consumers, businesses, and governments. Accelerating technological changes shortens the lifespan of ideas, business models, and market positions. It forces leaders to rethink the way they approach and manage information, the way they define, monitor and respond to competition, and the way they navigate and respond to technological churn. And it also creates significant opportunities for reinvention, growth and differentiation.

ACCELERATING INNOVATION

From the first stabs at mechanization during the Industrial Revolution to the computer-driven revolution we are living through now, technological innovation has always underpinned dynamic economic change. But today is different because, as noted in the introduction, we are in the second half of the chessboard.

In a process that is both gratifying and terrifying, the period between historic breakthroughs has been decreasing by orders of magnitude. More than five hundred years passed between Gutenberg's printing press and the first computer printer. It then took only another thirty years for the 3-D printer to be invented. Two hundred years separated the spinning jenny, the yarn-producing machine invented in 1764, from GM's Unimate, the world's first industrial robot.[13] It took only a quarter of that time for Shaft, the world's most advanced humanoid robot, to be invented. As W. Brian Arthur, a former Stanford economist, who pioneered the study of positive feedback and wrote *The Nature of Technology,* noted, "With the coming of the Industrial Revolution—roughly from the 1760s, when Watt's steam engine appeared, through around 1850 and beyond—the economy developed a muscular system in the form of machine power. Now it is developing a neural system."[14]

Moore's law, which holds that the processing power of computer technology doubles every eighteen months, has long underpinned our expectations of technological change.[15] Faster, more powerful computers, combined with access to exponentially increasing amounts of data, have altered our vision of what is possible. In the 1990s, sequencing the human genome was a project equivalent to constructing the Panama Canal—a multiyear endeavor that required armies of workers and battalions of steam-powered shovels. A team of scientists spent thirteen years and $3 billion to unlock the mysteries of the human blueprint.[16] Today, a $1,000 machine could soon be available that will be able to sequence a human genome in a few hours.[17]

THE DISRUPTIVE DOZEN

More technological change is coming—faster. The list of possible "next big things" grows longer every day. A lot of noise and confusion surround transformative technologies, with claims and counterclaims that range from the utopian to the catastrophic. We cut through the clutter and highlight the twelve technologies that could truly challenge the status quo in the years ahead.[18] They range from the familiar to the more surprising. We estimate that select applications of each of these technologies could generate a potential economic value of between $14 trillion and $33 trillion a year by 2025.[19] (Our measure of economic value is a broad one that encompasses measurements such as revenues, money saved through efficiency, and consumer surplus.) The disruptive dozen fall into four broad categories.

1. *Changing the building blocks of things.* To successfully sequence the first human genome in 2003, it took thirteen years, $3 billion, and teams of scientists from all over the world. Rapid advances in technology mean that the speed of gene sequencing has exceeded Moore's law. Barely a decade later, in January 2014, Illumina, the world's leading seller of gene sequencing machines, unveiled the HiSeq X, a supercomputer that can sequence twenty thousand genomes a year at a cost of $1,000 each.[20] The rapidly declining cost of gene sequencing is spurring studies in how genes determine traits or mutate to cause disease. Increasingly affordable genetic sequencing combined with big data analytics will allow rapid diagnosis of medical conditions, pinpointing of targeted cures, and potentially even the creation of customized organisms through synthetic biological methods, with applications in agriculture, food, and medicine.

    Advances in materials science are another disruptive innovation. The process of manipulating materials at the molecular level has made nanomaterials possible. Such breakthroughs have already transformed ordinary materials such as carbon and clay to take on surprising new properties—greater reactivity, unusual electrical

The period between historic breakthroughs has been decreasing dramatically

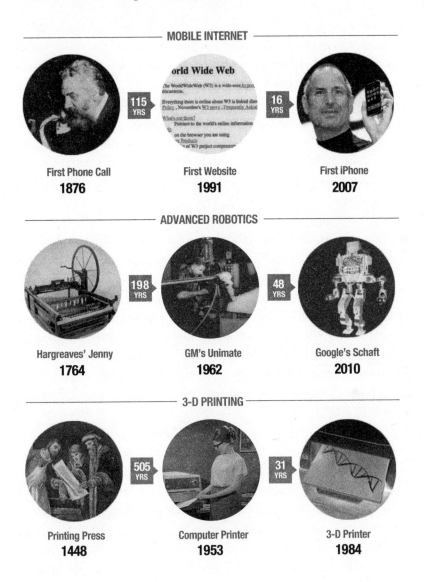

MOBILE INTERNET

115 YRS — 16 YRS

First Phone Call
1876

First Website
1991

First iPhone
2007

ADVANCED ROBOTICS

198 YRS — 48 YRS

Hargreaves' Jenny
1764

GM's Unimate
1962

Google's Schaft
2010

3-D PRINTING

505 YRS — 31 YRS

Printing Press
1448

Computer Printer
1953

3-D Printer
1984

properties, and greater strength. Nanomaterials have already been used in products ranging from pharmaceuticals to sunscreens to bicycle frames. Now, new materials are being created that have attributes such as enormous strength and elasticity and remarkable capabilities such as self-healing and self-cleaning. Smart materials and memory metals (which can revert to their original shapes) are finding applications in a range of industries such as aerospace, pharmaceuticals, and electronics.

2. *Rethinking energy comes of age.* In North America, fracking—a combination of horizontal drilling and hydraulic fracturing—has unleashed a shale energy boom that few saw coming. In less than a decade, the price of natural gas has fallen from more than $12 per unit (million British thermal units) to around $4 to $5 per unit in the United States. And as gas supply outstrips demand and prices remain low, producers are turning to fracking for oil in formations like North Dakota's Bakken Shale. Other unconventional sources are also being explored, including coal-bed methane and methane clathrates.

Meanwhile, even as the unconventional fossil fuel revolution takes off, the cost of renewable electricity generation continues to fall rapidly. Since 1990, the cost of solar cells has dropped from nearly $8 per watt of capacity to one-tenth that amount. Countries around the world—including large emerging economies such as China and India—are working on aggressive plans to accelerate adoption of wind and solar installations and increase the amount of energy they produce. By 2025, solar and wind power could become a source of 15 to 16 percent of global electricity generation, up from 2 percent today, and reduce emissions by up to 1.2 billion tons of CO^2 annually.[21]

Finally, energy storage technologies are also seeing disruption. Technologies such as lithium-ion batteries and fuel cells are already powering vehicles and portable consumer electronics. Prices for lithium-ion battery packs for cars could fall from over $500 per MWh to $160 per MWh by 2025, even as their life cycle increases. Such advances in energy storage have the potential to make battery-powered vehicles cost competitive. When used in the electric grid to improve reliability, reduce outages, and enable distributed generation, energy storage can dramatically improve the efficiency of our utility grids and bring electricity to remote and underserved areas around the world.[22]

3. *Machines working for us.* Industrial automation has been around for several decades, and the robots on the factory floor are now changing fast. Past generations of robots were isolated from humans,

sometimes bolted to the floor or even caged. They cost hundreds of thousands of dollars and needed engineers to program instructions into them, a process that could take several days. Today, a new generation of increasingly capable robots with enhanced perception, dexterity, and intelligence is being developed thanks to advances in machine vision and communication, sensors, and artificial intelligence. One example is Baxter, a $22,000 general-purpose robot that can work safely alongside humans. It can learn a new routine simply by having a human guide its arms through the motions needed for the task. Baxter even has a "head," which it nods to indicate that it has understood instructions, and a "face" with a pair of eyes, which take on different expressions. As their capabilities grow, robots are performing tasks once considered too expensive or delicate to automate. Their application extends beyond industry to services, robotic surgery, and even human augmentation.

Autonomous vehicles are another disruptive technology that has made dramatic advances in a single decade. In 2004, DARPA (Defense Advanced Research Projects Agency) funded the Grand Challenge, a competition that offered $1 million to the first driverless car that could drive 150 miles across the Mojave Desert. Nobody won the prize money; the best-performing car (from Carnegie Mellon) managed a little over 7 miles. Ten years later, Google's fleet of self-driving cars has already logged 700,000 miles in city streets—with the only accident occurring when a human was operating one of the Toyota Prius cars. Today, new car models offer the latest advances in driver-assist systems, such as braking, parking, and collision avoidance. By 2025, the driverless revolution in ground and airborne vehicles could be well underway, especially if the regulatory framework keeps pace with the changes.

Finally, additive manufacturing technologies could become another disruptive force in production. While they are not new, 3-D printers are becoming more prevalent because of better technology and performance, new materials, and falling prices. Their use in simple consumer goods and prototypes is widely known. Today, they are also used in medical and dental products, such as hearing aids, dental braces, and prosthetic limbs, and are starting to be used in other high-complexity, low-volume applications, such as aerospace components and turbines. New applications are proliferating. The world's first 3-D printed car, the Strati (made by start-up Local Motors), was assembled and driven in Chicago in September 2014. Artificial human organs have already been 3-D printed, using a sugar-based hydrogel to create a scaffolding of a kidney or other body part and an inkjet-like printer to spray onto it stem cells from the patient's own tissue. Over the coming decade, such uses could expand further. The manufacturing process will "democratize" as consumers and entrepreneurs start to print their own products.

4. *IT and how we use it.* We may think of the mobile Internet as a familiar technology, but with over one billion people already using smart phones or tablets, it is dramatically changing the way we perceive and interact with the world around us. Consider the rapid growth of the Internet of Things—embedded sensors and actuators in machines and other physical objects that are being adopted for data collection, remote monitoring, decision making, and process optimization in everything from manufacturing to infrastructure to health care. Sensors in limekilns can tell operators how to optimize temperature settings; in consumer goods, they can inform manufacturers about how products are being used; and in bridges, they can warn city administrators about maintenance needs. Today, over 99 percent of physical objects remain unconnected, highlighting a vast opportunity.[23]

Increasingly affordable, capable, and connected mobile computing devices are spurring innovation in services and worker productivity and are creating vast consumer surplus in the process. This trend is only likely to grow in strength as smart mobile technology brings another two billion to three billion people, predominantly from developing economies, into the connected world over the coming decade.[24] Cloud technologies are supporting these information trends. Cloud technologies are already making the digital world simpler, faster, more powerful, and more efficient and are changing how companies manage their IT. In the years ahead, cloud technology will continue to spur growth of new business models that are asset light, flexible, highly mobile, and scalable. The technologies will continue to expand, increasingly accompanied by advances in machine learning, artificial intelligence, and human-machine interaction. These changes make it possible for computers to do jobs that it was assumed only humans could perform. From IBM's Watson supercomputer—which beat human champions on the TV quiz show *Jeopardy!*—to automated discovery processes in the legal world and even software that can automatically write sports coverage, knowledge work is being automated on a scale we couldn't imagine just a few years ago.

A Digital, Data-rich Thread Runs Through It All

Digitization is the common thread running through many of these technology disruptions. At its most basic, digitization is a simple proposition: converting information into 1s and 0s so that it can be processed, communicated, and stored in machines. That simple notion has transformed our lives in the past thirty years in the form of personal computers, consumer electronics, and the global Internet. Now it underlies these new disruptions. Digitization slashes to nearly zero the cost of discovering, transacting, and sharing information. In the process, it creates a deluge of information—big data. Information used to be precious and scarce; think of a book having to be borrowed from a library for only a few weeks. Now it is ubiquitous; according to Eron Kelly, a senior director for product management at Microsoft, "in the next five years, we'll generate more data as humankind than we generated in the previous 5,000 years."[25] One exabyte of data is the equivalent of more than four thousand times the information stored in the US Library of Congress.[26] By 2020, the volume of data could reach more than forty thousand exabytes—an increase of nearly three-hundredfold since 2005. [27]

Digitization is changing the world around us in three ways. First, it converts physical goods into virtual ones. E-books, news websites, MP3 files, and other forms of digital media have largely disrupted sales of LP records, cassette tapes, CDs, DVDs, and printed media. In the future, 3-D printing could redefine the sale and distribution of physical goods. Items such as shoes, jewelry, and tools may in the future be sold with the transfer of an electronic file, allowing the buyer to print the object on demand or at the point of consumption.

Second, digitization enhances the information content of many of our routine transactions, enriching them and making them more valuable and productive. Examples include the digital tracking of physical shipments with the use of RFID tags and the use of 2-D barcodes to convey information to consumers.

Third, digitization is creating online platforms that facilitate production and transaction and allow minnows to compete head-to-head with

12 The Disruptive Dozen

Twelve technologies have massive potential for disruption in the coming decade

CHANGING THE BUILDING BLOCKS OF EVERYTHING

1. Next-generation genomics

Fast, low-cost gene sequencing, advanced big data analytics, and synthetic biology ("writing" DNA)

2. Advanced materials

Materials designed to have superior characteristics (e.g., strength, weight, conductivity) or functionality

RETHINKING ENERGY COMES OF AGE

3. Energy storage

Devices or systems that store energy for later use, including batteries

4. Advanced oil and gas exploration and recovery

Exploration and recovery techniques that make extraction of unconventional oil and gas economical

5. Renewable energy

Generation of electricity from renewable sources with reduced harmful climate impact

MACHINES WORKING FOR US

6. Advanced robotics

Increasingly capable robots with enhanced senses, dexterity, and intelligence used to automate tasks or augment humans

7. Autonomous and near-autonomous vehicles

Vehicles that can navigate and operate with reduced or no human intervention

8. 3-D printing

Additive manufacturing techniques to create objects by printing layers of material based on digital models

IT AND HOW WE USE IT

9. Mobile Internet

Increasingly inexpensive and capable mobile computing devices and Internet connectivity

10. Internet of things

Networks of low-cost sensors and actuators for data collection, monitoring, decision making, and process optimization

11. Cloud technology

Use of computer hardware and software resources delivered over a network or the Internet, often as a service

12. Automation of knowledge work

Intelligent software systems that can perform knowledge work tasks involving unstructured commands and subtle judgments sharks. Online exchanges and platforms like eBay and Alibaba, two of the linchpins of global e-commerce, allow even the smallest companies and individuals to become micro-multinationals. More than 90 percent of eBay commercial sellers export to other countries, compared with an average of less than 25 percent of traditional small businesses.[28]

The data avalanche is set to become more powerful only because of a movement toward "open data," in which data are freely shared beyond their originating organizations—including governments and businesses—in a machine-readable format at low cost. More than forty nations, including Canada, India, and Singapore, have committed to opening up their electronic data, everything from weather records and crime statistics to transport data. The excitement about open data has largely revolved around the potential to empower citizens and improve the delivery of public services, ranging from urban transportation to personalized health care. We estimate that select applications of open data could help unlock more than $3 trillion in economic value every year—an amount equal to 4 percent of global GDP.[29]

Kenya became the first sub-Saharan African nation to launch an open data initiative in 2011, with the hope that making government procurement data more transparent would enable the country to save up to $1 billion a year. "We are moving to e-procurement, so now . . . our pen will cost 20 shillings, not 200, and times to process payments will be faster," said Bitange Ndemo, permanent secretary of Kenya's Information and Communications Ministry. "But it isn't just about removing the manual aspects. The much more powerful thing, open data, is making the public aware."[30] Pune, India, uses data analytics to identify accident-prone locations and isolate common factors in accidents (such as the lack of crosswalks or too-short traffic-light cycles) in order to improve the city's traffic infrastructure.[31] The OpenStreetMap project, set up after the 2010 earthquake in Haiti, combined data from different sources and became a critical source of reliable information for government and private aid agencies in delivering supplies to hospitals, triage centers, and refugee camps.[32]

ACCELERATING ADOPTION

It's not simply that computers run more quickly today. So do consumers. One of the most striking aspects of the new age of accelerated technological change is the sharply increased pace of adoption. Historically, new technologies encountered a certain amount of friction on their way to world domination. It took a while for people to become comfortable with using new gadgets, for manufacturing to scale up, for distribution channels to develop, and for other businesses to create more compelling reasons for people to purchase the devices.

After Alexander Graham Bell invented the telephone, more than fifty years elapsed before half of American homes had one. It took radio thirty-eight years to attract fifty million listeners. Adoption curves are much steeper in the twenty-first century.[33] Half of all Americans acquired a smart phone within five years of the devices' introduction. After reaching six million users in its first year, Facebook multiplied that number by one hundred times in its next five years of existence.[34] In less than two years, WeChat, the mobile text and voice messaging communication service developed by China's Tencent, has reached three hundred million users—more than the entire adult population of the United States.[35] Accelerated adoption invites accelerated innovation. In 2009, two years after the iPhone's launch, developers had created around 150,000 applications.[36] By 2014, that number hit 1.2 million, and users had downloaded more than 75 billion total apps, over 10 for every person on the planet.[37] As a distribution system for digital goods, the Internet is friction free. The only obstacles to scale are consumer interest and curiosity.

The types of rapid adoption curves seen in the digital sector also characterize physical goods and their manufacturing process. A new generation of industrial robots with enhanced perception, dexterity, and intelligence is being developed thanks to advances in machine vision and communication, sensors, and artificial intelligence. Sales of industrial robots grew by 170 percent in just two years between 2009 and 2011, and the industry's annual revenues are expected to exceed $40 billion by 2020.[38]

The pace of this change will continue to accelerate. The more people online, the more people connected, the more rapidly innovations can spread. About 2.5 billion people were online around the world in 2013, and nearly 4 billion people are expected to be online by 2018.[39] If current trends in innovation and adoption continue—and there is every reason to think that they will, as technology becomes ever more affordable and products can easily go global—it will not be uncommon for new offerings to be used by hundreds of millions of people in less than a year. This is a true disruption to the status quo.

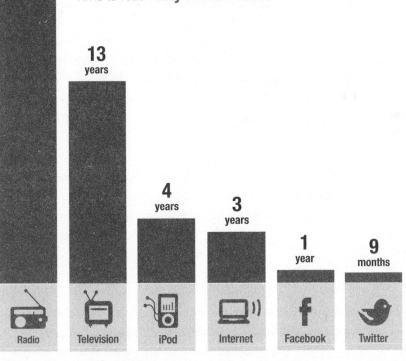

38
years

Technologies being adopted at record speed

Time to reach **fifty million users**

13
years

4
years

3
years

1
year

9
months

Radio

Television

iPod

Internet

Facebook

Twitter

SOURCE: The Social Economic Report, McKinsey Global Institute

WHY IT MATTERS

The benefits from the application of data, digitization, and disruptive technologies discussed in this chapter are tremendous—think of the ease and speed with which you can experiment with new business models and the value you can extract from the data you already collect. Or the drastically reduced marginal costs of scaling up the production and distribution of goods and services. Or of how quickly you can now reach customers around the world, thanks to a proliferation in the number of platforms, distribution channels, and payment systems that abet them. Or even of the insights you can glean from your data to improve design, pricing, and marketing of your products—as well as all aspects of your operations.

But monetizing the value of these technologies isn't always easy. MGI research indicates that the consumer is king in our technological age. As much as two-thirds of the value created by new Internet offerings is captured as consumer surplus—in the form of lower prices, improvements in productivity, or greater choices and convenience.[40] The disruptive technologies discussed earlier will likely deliver the lion's share of their value to consumers, even while providing companies with sufficient profit to encourage adoption and production. To illustrate the scale of the opportunity, consider this change: on July 31, 2013, the US Bureau of Economic Analysis released GDP figures that for the first time categorized research and development and software into a new category of "intellectual property products." We estimate that digital capital is now the source of roughly one-third of total global GDP growth, with intangible assets (think of the value of Google's search algorithm or Amazon's recommendation engine) being the main driver.[41]

For businesses and governments alike, failing to navigate today's technological tide will mean losing out on a huge economic opportunity as well as increasing vulnerability to potential disruptions. Digitization and technological advances can transform industries in the blink of an eye, as BlackBerry has learned. History is littered with such corporate casualties. The breathless wait for an updated smart phone may be a delicious pleasure for consumers. For businesses, however, anticipating and preparing for the next wave of the technological tsunami can be the difference between success and failure. Early birds will be challenged to place technology bets amid the extraordinary diversity of new technologies. For instance, within the realm of additive manufacturing—just one of the dozen disruptions we identify—a wide range of technologies and materials exists. They include laser sintering with powdered metal, fused deposition molding with melted plastic, and 3-D printers, which range in size and cost from $1,000 hobby printers to industrial-scale printers costing hundreds of thousands of dollars. Even if you are not an early bird in their application, you will need to determine *when, how,* and *whether* to take advantage of them—and be prepared to follow fast.

Lastly, understanding technology is now a core skill required of every business leader. You don't need to know how to use the programming language SQL or be able to run a 3-D printer, though. Far more important is the ability to zero in on what your most tech-savvy customers are doing. Leaders must build and manage systematic ways of keeping the skills of employees up-to-date and must ensure that executive teams and boards remain well informed about the latest technological developments. Long-established strategic planning processes will also need to be reimagined— to include reliable monitoring of trends, to plan for a range of scenarios, and to jettison old assumptions about potential sources of competition and risk.

Adapting to Technological Disruption

On the first day of classes at Ivy League colleges, it was common for the dean to warn students: "Look to the left, look to the right. One of you won't be here next year."[42] A similar dynamic is unfolding in the top echelons of the corporate world. In 1950, the average S&P 500 company could expect to stay on the index for more than sixty years.[43] In 2011, that average was down to eighteen years, and the trend shows no sign of easing. At the current rate of churn, thanks to mergers and acquisitions, the rapid rise of upstart companies, and frequent falls of incumbent firms, 75 percent of the S&P 500 will be replaced by 2027.[44] Companies are increasingly finding that their era of dominance is more like the career of a professional athlete than the tenure of a distinguished college professor—it lasts a few years rather than a few decades.[45]

While there is no technology silver bullet that is effective across different sectors, functions, and markets, we find that business leaders who adhere to five principles stand the best chance of staying on top and reinventing themselves to keep up with the "new normal."

How digitization transforms industries

The position of companies on this curve depends on the degree to which their companies and customers have embraced digitization.

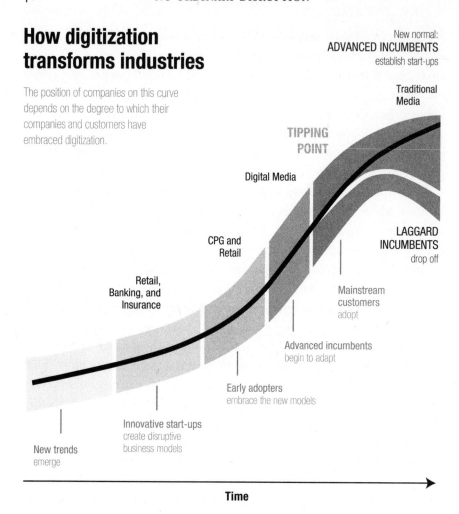

New normal:
ADVANCED INCUMBENTS
establish start-ups

Traditional Media

TIPPING POINT

Digital Media

CPG and Retail

Retail, Banking, and Insurance

LAGGARD INCUMBENTS
drop off

Mainstream customers
adopt

Advanced incumbents
begin to adapt

Early adopters
embrace the new models

Innovative start-ups
create disruptive
business models

New trends
emerge

Time

Make the Most of Your Digital Capital

Many companies are starting to awaken to the important role their currently unstructured data can play in sharpening existing processes and future business strategies. Everywhere we look, companies are putting data to use—driving market share, reducing costs, raising productivity, and improving products and services. Retailers are using big data to optimize prices dynamically, forecast demand, generate recommendations, and improve stock management. Manufacturers are using big data to create bespoke products that better serve customer needs and to optimize their supply chains. At Alibaba, China's largest online merchant, the live data room resembles NASA mission control. Data-as-service start-ups are booming, and giants such as IBM, Microsoft, Oracle, and SAP have spent billions of dollars in the past several years snapping up companies that develop software for advanced data analytics.

In fact, intangible digital assets—such as behavioral data on consumers and tracking data from logistics—can be the seeds of entirely new products and services. The disruption in taxi services is one example. Uber uses algorithms to determine "surge" prices in times of peak demand.[46] Lyft, another on-demand ride-sharing start-up, employs a "happy hour" pricing model to lower rates in times of soft demand.[47] Health care is another example of a sector where the marriage of data, analytical models, and decision-support tools—all key components of digital capital—can create immense economic value, improve customer experience, and create difficult-to-replicate capabilities. Some five million Americans suffer from congestive heart failure, which is treatable with drug therapy or implantable devices.[48] Medtronic has built an industry first, CareLink Express Service, a remote heart-monitoring network that connects implanted cardiac monitoring devices to sites where physicians can remotely view and interpret data, improving the quality and efficiency of patient care in the process. During the pilot phase of the program, patient wait times fell sharply, to less than fifteen minutes.[49] "This kind of data is the currency of the future," notes Ken Riff, vice president of strategy and patient data management at Medtronic.[50]

Look to Exploit Lower Marginal Costs of Digital

Digitization significantly reduces the costs associated with the access, discovery, and distribution of goods and services. More efficient distribution and lower barriers to entry have spurred more individuals, entrepreneurs, and businesses to participate in the digital marketplace and experiment with new business models. Digitization has drastically lowered geographic barriers as well, fueling the growth of micro-multinationals, microwork, and micro supply-chain companies.

Kiva, the world's largest online platform for peer-to-peer microlending, has facilitated loans worth more than $630 million, mostly in the emerging world.[51] Kickstarter, a crowd-funding platform that connects entrepreneurs to individuals interested in funding creative projects, has facilitated pledges of more than $1.4 billion to fund 70,000 creative projects since 2009.[52] Small or individual registered investment advisors are the fastest-growing segment of the investment advisory business in the United States; they purchase turnkey back-end systems from companies like Fidelity and Charles

Schwab to get all the capabilities they need in order to provide direct advice to consumers.[53]

In markets such as search, e-commerce, social media, and the sharing economy, the low marginal costs of digital infrastructure allow upstarts to build business models with near-limitless scale. WhatsApp, the mobile messaging platform that Facebook recently snapped up for $19 billion, reached 500 million monthly active users within five years of its launch.[54] Snapchat surpassed the photo-sharing activity on both Facebook and Instagram with 400 million users only two years after its foundation.[55] Sharing economy start-ups are growing at breathtaking speed. In 2013, some 450,000 active users were launching the Uber app every week, and more than a million Lyft users had requested a ride with the tap of a button.[56]

Traditional players have also benefited from changes in marginal cost economics to enter new markets, grow rapidly, or optimize processes and cost structures. French telecom operator Free Mobile reinvented the "mobile attacker model" by exploiting a large and active digital community of brand fans and advocates as its core asset. Free Mobile signed up more than 2.6 million new subscribers in less than three months in 2012 and captured 13 percent market share in one year with no above-the-line budget.[57] Luxury retailer Burberry is synonymous with best-in-class multichannel customer experience; its flagship store at 121 Regent Street in London boasts the world's tallest retail screen, real-life digital feeds, and RFID chips that are sewn into Burberry products. These tiny chips trigger bespoke content in front of RFID-enabled mirrors.[58] Nordstrom, the luxury department store, first exploited the marginal cost advantages of digital for internal purposes, to develop shipping and inventory-management facilities. The company then turned its digital investments outward, building a strong e-commerce site, mobile-shopping apps, kiosks, and capabilities for managing customer relationships across channels.

Find New Ways to Monetize Consumer Surplus

There's an interesting and perhaps counterintuitive implication to the rise of big data and increasingly cheap digital business tools. In theory, both trends should be immense boons to the companies that can afford to gather, maintain, and use data to their advantage. Consumers, however, remain king and queen in our age of accelerating technological change. Consumers capture as much as two-thirds of the value created by new Internet offerings in what is known as consumer surplus—lower costs, better products, and improved quality of life.[59] The challenge for companies is how to get consumers to pay for all of the great new stuff—video, content, games, storage, messaging, convenience—being made available to them.

So far, only a few monetization models have proven effective at shifting value back to companies. One is advertising revenue, which has fueled the highly profitable growth of tech giants such as Facebook and Google. The advertising revenue model will remain viable, but users' expectations surrounding the ability to target, measure, and analyze ads effectively will continue to rise.

Direct payments and subscriptions reflect an increasing ability to charge for online content. Under this model, the use of "freemium" pricing strategies—offering no-fee basic services and charging for enhanced features such as the ability to avoid advertising, virtual goods in games, or a higher level of service and access to valuable features—is increasingly common. Examples range from Zynga and Spotify to LinkedIn and Apple. Joining LinkedIn is free, for example. Upgrading to premium membership—monthly prices start at $59.99 per month for the Business Plus account—affords the user greater insight into who has been looking at his or her profile, the ability to send more messages to potential leads, and the use of more advanced search filters.[60]

A third model is monetization of big data, either through innovative business-to-business offerings (for example, crowd-sourcing business intelligence or outsourced data science services) or through developing more relevant products, services, or content for which consumers are willing to pay. LinkedIn, for example, makes 20 percent of its revenue from subscriptions, 30 percent from marketing, and 50 percent from talent solutions, a core part of which is selling targeted talent intelligence and tools to recruiters.[61]

You will have to keep experimenting in order to capture more consumer surplus for your business. Turning traditional transaction-based e-commerce into subscription models is one increasingly popular way. In an effort to lock in consumer loyalty and repeat business, a host of companies have created offerings that put the relationship on autopilot. In retail, for instance, Glossybox, based in Berlin, Germany, has already shipped over four million boxes of new beauty products to Internet subscribers, many of whom pay a $21 monthly fee for five surprise luxury items.[62] Companies like Dollar Shaving Club and Harry's, which ship razor blades and cartridges to customers each month for a fixed price, are challenging long-standing incumbents like Gillette. Graze, a UK-based subscription service for weekly personalized healthy snack boxes, nearly doubled its revenues in 2013, to £40.2 million ($64.1 million).[63] In media, experimentation with digital content monetization models is commonplace. Creating digital paid subscriptions as well as bundling digital and print subscriptions has helped the *New York Times* mitigate declines in advertising and print circulation. CEO Mark Thompson has dubbed the adoption of an aggressive paywall "the most important and successful business decision in years." The *Times* boasts more than 875,000 digital subscribers, and circulation revenues now surpass advertising revenues.[64] Piano Media, a start-up in Slovakia, created a paywall system that encompassed most leading media in that country. In its original revenue model, the company split subscription revenue with the original site through which the user joined (30 percent) and other media sites based on the time users spent on each site. Piano drove subscriptions and proved the concept in a five-million-strong, linguistically closed market, before moving onto other Central European markets in 2012.[65] In August 2014, Piano extended its reach by acquiring Press+, a US-based pioneer of micropayments and paywalls that is nearly nine times Piano's size in revenues.[66]

Don't Wait for the Dust to Settle

The instinct, in the face of rapid technological churn, can be to wait for the dust to settle before placing your bets on a new technology. But time is the enemy. Today's technology could be outdated tomorrow, and a seemingly irrelevant acquisition or strategic move may wind up shaking up the industry. Figuring out which of the dozen types of 3-D printing technologies will become standard is a time-consuming effort with a low likelihood of success. Most companies struggle to make such efforts an integral part of their business-as-usual processes.

For many established companies, placing big bets on early technologies is simply not an option due to strictly defined risk appetite, high hurdles for new investments, and legacy IT systems. In the auto insurance industry, for instance, many established players continue to limit investments in telematics and behavioral data to small-scale pilot programs, while they nervously watch new nimble attackers enter the space. Embracing innovation could potentially redefine the way companies monitor customers' actions—and hence set prices and assess risk. Companies in the beauty business have also been caught off guard by technology. Mink, a 3-D printer that allows customers to "print" customized makeup from the comfort of home, threatens to challenge the healthy margin of incumbents once it launches at its target retail price of $200 in 2015.[67]

Tech giants have stood out as an unsurprising exception to the rule, using their deep pockets and eagle eyes for the latest innovations to place large bets on the next transformative technologies. Google acquired Android in 2005 when the mobile Internet was in its infancy.[68] The following year, when online video advertising was in its infancy, it paid $1.6 billion for YouTube.[69] Both proved to be masterstrokes, defying the prevailing conventional wisdom. Google cofounder Larry Page gives a sense of the nervousness that thinking in advance of the crowd can engender. Talking about the decision to buy Android, he said, "I felt sort of bad and sort of guilty. Why am I spending time on this? Why aren't I spending time on, you know, search or advertising or something that was more core to our business? But it turned out to be a pretty important thing to do."[70]

Large companies in other sectors have realized that establishing symbiotic relationships with vibrant tech start-ups can be an increasingly effective way to place technology bets. Doing so minimizes risk and disruption to the core business, while potentially providing companies with the option to take ownership of or deploy promising new products and services. Companies do so by embedding accelerators and innovation labs, which provide supportive environments, mentoring, equipment, and funding to promising entrepreneurs, in their existing structures.[71] In 2012, General Electric launched GE Garages, a lab incubator concept focused on reinspiring innovation in advanced manufacturing. GE Garages sets up workshops in the United States to provide start-ups with access to equipment, such as 3-D printers, computerized numerical control machines, and laser cutters, and to give them access to expert advice and potential partners. In 2014, GE took the concept global; the most recent GE Garage established is in Lagos, Nigeria.[72] In 2013, Allianz launched its first Digital Accelerator, cosponsored by Google, which focuses on how big data can help drive the development of new insurance and finance business models, in Munich.[73]

Think Technology for Your Talent, Organization, and Investments

Some companies have successfully institutionalized the technology mindset by appointing a chief digital officer and elevating the role throughout the organization. In 2008, Sona Chawla joined Walgreens, the large US pharmacy and retail chain, from Dell as senior vice president of e-commerce. A couple years later, she was promoted to president of e-commerce, and in 2013 she became the president of digital and chief marketing officer, reporting directly to the CEO.[74] Under Chawla, Walgreens acquired drugstore.com in 2011 and developed one of the most popular US mobile health apps, which allows customers to refill prescriptions by scanning bar codes and set personal medication reminders.[75] Today, more than 40 percent of the chain's online refill requests come from the app, and multichannel customers spend 3.5 times more than brick-and-mortar customers.[76]

Other companies have used the "acqui-hire" approach—buying a startup in order to acquire the team that runs it—or established partnerships to catch up on promising trends and accelerate access to intellectual property, talent, and technology. Yahoo laid out $1 billion for Tumblr in part to bring wunderkind founder David Karp into the fold.[77] In May 2014, Walmart acquired Silicon Valley–based ad software company Adchemy for $300 million and incorporated Adchemy's sixty-person team into @Walmart Labs, the company's in-house tech shop.[78] In 2013, Sephora, the cosmetics retailer with 1,300 stores in twenty-seven countries, acquired Scentsa, a specialist in digital technologies, to improve the in-store shopping experience and keep Scentsa's technology out of the reach of competitors. [79]

German media conglomerate Axel Springer has embraced technology and digitization in its investment approach. In 2014, it sold off its regional newspapers along with its women's and TV magazines, then invested heavily in three digital pillars: paid content, digital advertising, and online classifieds.[80] It also launched the Berlin-based Axel Springer Plug and Play Accelerator. In 2013, the company started a joint venture with private equity firm General Atlantic, dedicated to digital classifieds.[81] An in-house VC outfit, Axel Springer Ventures, has investments in start-ups, such as price comparison sites and loyalty shopping apps, and in a leading early stage investment fund.[82]

There's no guarantee that any of these efforts will enable companies to thrive in an age of rapid technological advance. But in a world in which business models and strategies grow old quickly, leaders must constantly think about ways to rejuvenate their enterprises.

3

—

GETTING OLD ISN'T
WHAT IT USED TO BE
Responding to the Challenges
of an Aging World

IT'S NOT UNCOMMON FOR A ROBOT TO VACUUM THE FLOOR. IN Japan, robots are quickly evolving to perform the functions of butlers, home health-care aides, and companions. Combining robotic hardware known as WAM (whole arm manipulator), arms with computer intelligence, researchers at Japan's Nara Institute of Science and Technology and Barrett Technology have invented robotic arms that can help people in and out of their jackets, shirts, and pajamas. Robovie-R3, a humanoid bot designed by ART and Vstone, based in Osaka, is like the *Star Wars* character R2-D2 come to life. Robovie-R3 shuffles alongside mall shoppers at speeds up to 1.5 miles per hour, takes the hand of elderly users as they navigate through crowds, and totes shopping baskets—all without demanding to stop for coffee.[1]

It's not uncommon for first-time visitors to Tokyo to remark that the metropolis looks like the future. In Japanese factories, like the highly efficient plant in Toyota City that produces the Prius, robotic equipment has long substituted for human labor. But Robovie-R3 and other recent robotic products are designed to meet needs other than production for industry—specifically the real and current human need in what is now, with a median age of forty-six and 24 percent of the population over sixty-five, the oldest country in the world.[2] Add low levels of immigration and anemic fertility rates (1.4 births per woman over the course of a lifetime), and there simply aren't enough people to care for Japan's growing elderly population.[3] At a meeting with journalists, officials at Toyota City were asked how their country would cope with its demographic problem. The response—"Maybe the robots will take care of us"—was not encouraging.[4]

Global analysts are fond of painting a picture of a young world on the move, just waiting to grow up. In large chunks of the globe, that is indeed the reality. In Pakistan, where the median age is 22.6 years, nearly 55 percent of the population is under 25.[5] In sub-Saharan Africa, more than 40 percent of the population is under the age of 15.[6] Every major consumer and services company is figuring out how to tap into the rising number of young consumers.

But there's a flip side to this coin, and it is one of the most overlooked trend breaks evident in the world today. In the years after World War II, the world seemed to get younger, and the population grew in virtually every country, rich and poor. Improvements in vaccinations, declining infant mortality, and the absence of massively destructive world wars created a virtuous circle. As the world's population kept growing, the working-age cohort grew apace, fueling economic growth. This demographic surplus has paid enormous dividends. More people meant more demand for goods and services, more houses, and more schools, which in turn created more jobs and more tax revenues. With technology acting as an amplifier, these people all worked more productively.

Now, simply put, the world is getting older. We have been aware of this development for some time, but long-term forecasts are becoming reality. In many large and highly developed economies—and in the world's largest developing economy, China—people are living longer and having fewer children. The baby-boom generation is getting older and easing into retirement, while fertility is falling sharply. These trends are reaching a tipping point. Sometime in the next few decades, they will very likely cause the population of most of the world—with the exception of Africa—to plateau for the first time in modern history.[7] Large swaths of the world will have dramatically older populations, aging workforces, and ballooning government social programs. In this regard, Japan, whose population has already started to decline, really does look like the future.

These developments require a reset of our intuition to change the way we think about the elderly—as consumers, customers, employees, and stakeholders.

Fertility rates have declined globally

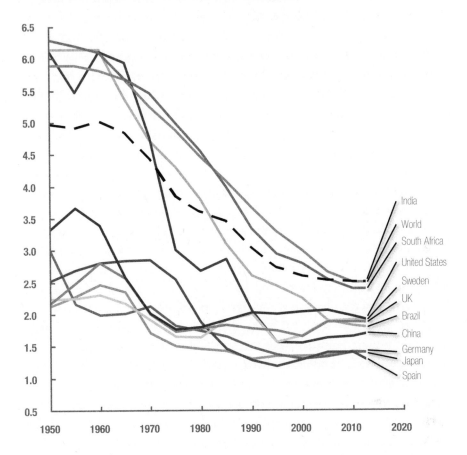

NOTE: Fertility rate is the average number of children a hypothetical cohort of women would have at the end of their reproductive period if they were subject during their whole lives to the fertility rates of a given period and if they were not subject to mortality. It is expressed as children per woman.
SOURCE: UN population data; McKinsey Global Institute analysis

FALLING FERTILITY

Global experience suggests that as nations grow wealthier, their populations become less fertile. As economies develop, residents are more likely to use birth control, women have more choices, parents are less likely to regard large families as an economic necessity, and families are less likely to view having a large number of children as a hedge against high infant mortality rates. Typically, the richer the country, the lower the number of children born over a woman's lifetime. The total fertility rate (the average number of children that would be born per woman if all women lived to the end of their childbearing years) is 1.4 children per woman in Germany, for instance, while it is over 6 in countries like Niger, Somalia, and Mali.[8] While recent research indicates that the fertility trend can reverse in a limited way in high-income countries, particularly those with high immigration—for example, the United Kingdom, which has a fertility rate of 1.96—and countries that implement policies to help families manage children and careers, the long-term trend toward lower fertility rates is unlikely to be disrupted.[9]

Thirty years ago, only a small share of the global population in just a few countries had fertility rates that were substantially below those needed to replace each generation—about 2.1 births per woman in developed countries and about 2.5 births per woman in developing countries.[10] Fertility drove most population growth in developing countries, with 1970 rates as high as seven children per woman in Mexico and Saudi Arabia and five per woman in India, Brazil, and Indonesia.[11] In many advanced economies with low fertility rates, immigration propelled population growth. Between the 1960s and 2012, the share of immigrant-born children in the total population quadrupled in the United Kingdom (from 3 to 12 percent), more than doubled in the United States (from 6 to 14 percent), and increased by half in Canada and France.[12] By 2014, however, thanks to broadly rising prosperity, about 60 percent of the world's population lived in countries with fertility rates below replacement rates.[13] This includes most of the developed world as well as some large developing countries such as China (1.5), Brazil (1.8), Russia (1.6), and Vietnam (1.8).[14] Net migration is also anticipated to decline in eighteen of the world's nineteen largest economies (the exception is Mexico).[15]

The 2006 Alfonso Cuarón film *Children of Men* painted a vision of a dystopic future in which the birth of a child was a rarity, even a miracle. Things haven't quite come to that, but in nearly every European country, the fertility rate is below the replacement rate. Across the European Union (EU), the population is expected to increase by 5 percent until 2040 and then start to shrink.[16] In Germany (2014 fertility rate: 1.4), which has long stood out for its weak population growth, the European Commission believes the population could shrink by 19 percent by 2060.[17] The country's working-age population is expected to fall from fifty-four million in 2010 to thirty-six million in 2060.[18]

Proportion of elderly in global population is increasing rapidly

Global population by age group (1950 – 2050), %

■ 65+
▨ 15–64
▨ 0–14
● Dependency ratio (per 100 people)

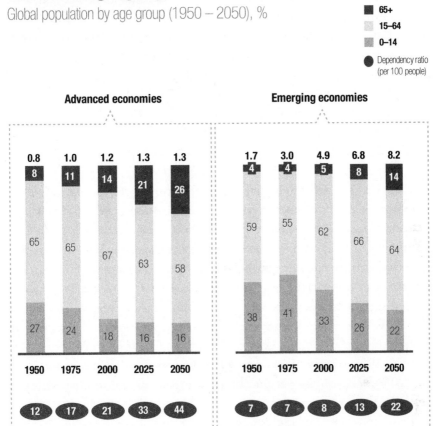

NOTE: Old age dependency ratio = Population aged 65+ over population 15-64
SOURCE: McKinsey Global Institute analysis, UN population data

Germany has been able to mask its decline by attracting immigrants from Russia, Turkey, Africa, and elsewhere. But not all countries possess the economic strength or cultural attributes necessary to attract new residents. Many European countries with low fertility rates are already suffering from massive brain drain, as young people leave to seek their fortunes elsewhere. Regions of Europe surrounding the Baltic and Black seas are already depopulating and could turn into ghost towns in the coming decades. The population of Bulgaria is expected to fall by 27 percent by 2060, and the populations of Latvia, Lithuania, and Romania could fall by similar amounts.[19] The exception to this trend is the United Kingdom, which may overtake Germany as the EU's most populous country by 2060—thanks to the high birth rate among families whose forebears were immigrants and to relatively high immigration today. This is not only a European phenomenon. The peak days of global population growth are potentially behind every continent except Africa. Annual population growth could drop from its rate of 1.43 percent between 1964 and 2012 to as low as 0.25 percent over the coming fifty years, a trend that will have profound impacts on the global economy and politics.[20]

AGING POPULATIONS

The outstanding and often unappreciated feature of the trend break era is the way in which forces act in concert to amplify and produce change at a more rapid scale. We've already seen this with urbanization and technological change. The same dynamic is apparent in demographics. At the same time that fertility rates are broadly declining, life expectancy is rising. Put another way, comparatively few new people are being created, while those created several decades ago are sticking around a lot longer. The rise of global life expectancy is one of the great feel-good stories of the postwar era. Around the world, life expectancy at birth rose from forty-seven years in 1950–1955 to sixty-nine today. A few decades from now, between 2045 and 2050, the average person alive can expect to live to an impressive seventy-six years.[21]

The demographic tables, simply put, have turned upside down. In 1950, developed countries had twice as many children (aged fifteen years and under) as older persons (aged sixty years and over). By 2013, older persons outnumbered children by a margin of 21 percent to 16 percent of the populations in such countries. Given current trends, by 2050 developed economies will have twice as many older persons as children.[22] Moody's, the credit-rating agency, in 2014 projected that the number of "superaged" countries—where more than one-fifth of the population is sixty-five or older—would rise from 3 today (Germany, Italy, and Japan) to 13 in 2020 and to 34 in 2030.[23]

This cycle won't play out only in the developed world. China is currently the most populous nation in the world and a rising economic power. On a steaming spring day, throngs of newly minted graduates pose for photos in caps and gowns in scenic spots in Wuhan, an interior city that is home

Without migration and policy changes, many countries will see their labor force shrink dramatically

Countries with large forecasted absolute workforce decline

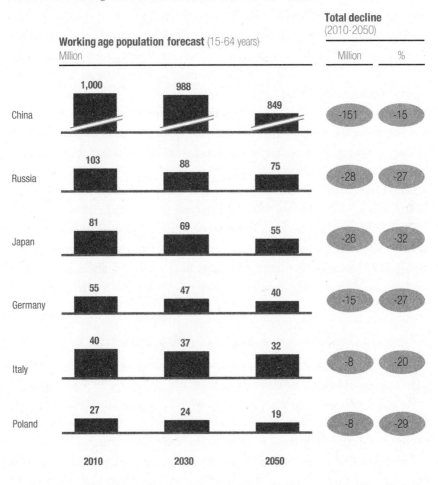

Working age population forecast (15-64 years)
Million

Total decline
(2010-2050)
Million   %

	2010	2030	2050	Million	%
China	1,000	988	849	-151	-15
Russia	103	88	75	-28	-27
Japan	81	69	55	-26	-32
Germany	55	47	40	-15	-27
Italy	40	37	32	-8	-20
Poland	27	24	19	-8	-29

SOURCE: UN Population Data; McKinsey Global Institute analysis

to dozens of higher educational institutions and boasts some 1.2 million students.[24] But for quite different reasons, Wuhan and the rest of China are experiencing a demographic pinch similar to Europe's. The median age in China is about thirty-seven, roughly the same as in the United States.[25] The number of Chinese aged fifty-five or older is likely to rise to more than 43 percent of the population in 2030, from 26 percent today.[26] The Chinese refer to their impending aging challenge as the "4:2:1 problem."

Every adult child today must care for two parents and four grandparents. By 2040, China could have more dementia patients than the rest of the developed world combined.[27] The world's workshop, peopled by armies of workers performing labor-intensive tasks, will in time become the world's nursing home.

Beyond sheer demographics, technology is adding to the trend of aging. We expect to see significant increases in life expectancy over the next decade as new technologies help people live healthier and longer. For instance, next-generation genomics—the combination of sequencing technologies, big data analytics, and technologies that are able to modify organisms—has the potential to give humans far greater power over biology, helping to cure diseases such as cancer and cardiovascular disease that currently kill around twenty-six million people a year.[28] Based on the assessment of cancer experts, we estimate that genomic-based diagnoses and treatments will extend patients' lives by between six months and two years in 2025.[29] Additionally, desktop machines could make gene sequencing part of every doctor's diagnostic routine, and 3-D printing could soon let doctors "print" biological structures and organs. Finally, advances in materials science could lead to the development of nanomaterials for drug delivery.

Graying—and Shrinking—Labor Force

Falling fertility, slowing population growth, and aging populations will all have a profound impact on the labor force of the future. New workers will enter at a slower rate. Older people may work for much longer than they do today. And the definition of the labor force itself may change from today's twenty- to sixty-four-year-olds to include older age groups.

"May your heart always be joyful. And may your song always be sung. May you stay forever young." So goes the lyric from Bob Dylan's "Forever Young." Difficult as it may be to believe, the raspy-voiced troubadour is seventy-three. He still tours. Mick Jagger, a great-grandfather who turned seventy in July 2014, struts around arena stages in leather pants. Baseball player Jamie Moyer pitched—and pitched well—until the age of forty-nine. US Supreme Court justices routinely stay on the job until their eighties; the median age of today's court is sixty-four.[30] In coming years, such phenomena are likely to be more common in lower-profile jobs.

Why? Based on current trends and definitions, the annual growth rate of the global labor force is set to weaken from around 1.4 percent annually between 1990 and 2010 to about 1 percent to 2030.[31] In 1964, the working-age group (fifteen to sixty-four) accounted for 58 percent of the total population, reaching a peak of 68 percent in 2012.[32] In the next fifty years, however, the working-age population is expected to drop to 61 percent, while the share of elderly (sixty-five and up) in the total population could increase to 23 percent, from 9 percent in 2012.[33] In China, some 70 percent of the population works today, one of the highest such shares in the world. But in January 2013, China's National Bureau of Statistics announced that the country's working-age population actually fell in 2012. And as the country's population ages, the proportion of Chinese who are working should fall to 67 percent by 2030. We estimate that developed economies will add about thirty million workers by 2030, only a 6 percent increase from 2010.[34] Moody's predicts that between 2015 and 2030, the world's working-age demographic will grow at only half the rate it did between 2001 and 2015.[35] Most of the growth will be in a handful of countries such as the United States, the United Kingdom, and Canada.

Longer life expectancy and lower investment returns will mean that the elderly will be less able to afford to retire. And because unfavorable demographics—fewer people working, more people receiving benefits—can increase budget deficits, governments will come under increased pressure to boost retirement ages. So, worldwide, the share of older workers (above fifty-five years) in the workforce is expected to increase from 14 percent in 2010 to 22 percent by 2030. The graying of the workforce will be felt most acutely in advanced economies and in China, where the share of older workers will increase to 27 and 31 percent of the workforce, respectively.[36]

A STRUCTURAL CHANGE

While these demographic changes have long been predicted, countries are struggling to cope with them. Despite spending $265 billion a year on family subsidies, Germany still encounters difficulties changing cultural attitudes toward increased fertility.[37] Research suggests that China's fertility rate is unlikely to recover quickly, if at all.[38] And for many countries, including the Nordic nations, Japan, and Russia, immigration—often an effective means of changing a nation's demographic profile—is culturally and socially problematic. The aging and shrinking of the workforce is unprecedented in modern history, and the disruption will affect us all. The number of likely retirees will grow more than twice as fast as the labor pool, leaving fewer workers to pay for the elderly.[39] Over the next two decades, the total population of retirees is expected to reach 360 million.[40] Roughly 40 percent of expected retirees will be in advanced economies and China. And of those retirees, roughly 38 million will be college-educated workers with valuable skills.[41]

In addition to creating pressure on global pension funds, these trends will pressure the world's pool of savings and create a host of new fiscal stresses.[42] A 2013 Standard & Poor's report found that without policy changes, age-related spending will accelerate the growth of median net general government debt in advanced economies from less than 40 percent today to 190 percent in 2050.[43] The conflicts in US states and cities over underfunded pensions, such as the scenario currently playing out in Illinois, are simply the opening skirmishes of a much larger battle.

Governments in economies with established social security and pensions systems are clearly becoming increasingly alarmed about the cost. OECD (Organisation for Economic Co-operation and Development) research shows that the average pension age in thirty advanced economies fell from 64.3 years in the early 1950s to a low of 62.5 years in the early 1990s for men, a drop of nearly two years.[44] For women, the average age fell from 62.9 to 61.0 in the same time period. That trend has broken. Since the mid-1990s, fourteen countries have increased or plan to increase pension ages for men, and eighteen have done so or plan to do so for women. Over the next forty years, almost half of OECD countries are set to increase the pension age. But, as the OECD noted, this is just "running to stand still," because life expectancy is rising. The United Kingdom's Turner commission on pension reform has suggested that the state pension age should be increased to seventy years.[45]

Faced with the lengthening retirement periods of their former employees, the private sector is increasingly moving away from defined-benefit pension plans. Starting in the 1980s and accelerating in the 2000s, advanced economies have seen a shift toward defined-contribution plans.* Between 1980 and 2008, the proportion of US private-sector payroll

---

*With defined-benefit (DB) plans, an employer pays its retired employees a fraction of their salary at retirement for the rest of their lives. In contrast, defined-contribution (DC) plans require the employer to match a portion of employees' annual contribution to their retirement accounts. While DB and DC plans come in a wide range of flavors, fundamentally, DB plans place the risk of financial solvency and longevity of payments on the employer or other plan sponsor; DC plans shift these risks to employees.

Between 1950 – 2050, the ratio of retirees to children will have increased

Number of retirees per (ten) children

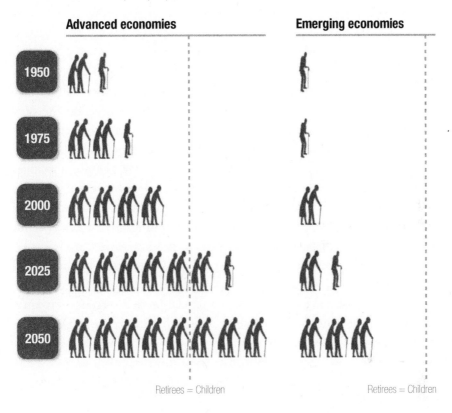

NOTE: Retirees to children ratio = Population aged 65+ over population <15
SOURCE: UN population data; McKinsey Global Institute analysis

workers enrolled in defined-benefit pension plans fell from 32 percent to 20 percent; the proportion plummeted to 16 percent in 2013. Meanwhile, the proportion of workers in contribution-only plans grew from 8 percent in 1980 to 42 percent in 2013.[46] Many employers have frozen their defined-benefit pension plans, and most others are expected to freeze and terminate theirs altogether in coming years.[47]

Attitudes about retirement are also beginning to shift in reaction to the financial pressures that many older people anticipate. In the United States, a poll of Americans aged fifty or older showed that nearly one-third thought it was highly likely that they would do some paid work during retirement, and another 28 percent thought it somewhat likely. Yet one in five reported that they had already faced age discrimination in the workplace—before retirement age—and many of those who had looked for work after retirement had found it difficult.[48]

Adapting to the Aging Trend

As a leader in your business, you can't afford to stand still and watch as employees and customers age. Adapting to the new reality will require some fundamental changes in the way most businesses operate and how they manage customers, employees, and stakeholders over their life spans. The health-care industry is at the forefront of these demographic changes. For companies like Hospital Corporation of America, aging is a double-edged sword. Rising numbers of people covered by Medicare and of Americans suffering from health issues common to old age will drive demand for services at its 165 hospitals and 113 freestanding surgery centers. But the same trend will push rising numbers of its experienced professionals out of the workplace, at least as it is currently structured. When a nurse practitioner retires, she may take thirty-five years of accumulated experience with her—knowledge that can be crucial in an emergency. Hospital Corporation of America has come to realize that it can use flexible work arrangements as an important means of keeping older workers engaged for longer periods. So a nurse might shift from full-time work to take a few shifts when needed, continuing to earn income while avoiding the stress and long hours that accompany full-time posts.[49]

Coping with a Graying Employee Pool

Employers have long focused on youth. In Silicon Valley, executives in their late twenties are often made to feel past their prime. Older workers can be more expensive, so they are often the first to be bought out or let go during restructurings. But in a graying world, employers have to reset their intuition. Rather than seeing older employees as legacy costs, they must view them as assets and resources. Employers want to be fishing in the deepest and most populated parts of the talent pool. As demographics shift, there will be more skilled, educated, talented, and experienced people congregating in the deeper waters.

Historically, the mentality of both employers and the employed has been black and white. Workers are on staff, full-time, and in the office every day until they no longer work for the company. Employers have grown accustomed to dictating the terms and conditions of employment, while unions have become accustomed to negotiating on behalf of full-time employees. However, technology, virtual ways of working, and shifting demographics may change this paradigm. In order to engage workers who are older, and for whom the attraction of a full-time job may be decreasing over time, companies have to become more comfortable dealing with shades of gray. A range of arrangements can help keep employees and companies tethered to one another, but on terms that may be more appealing to older employees.

In Japan, companies like Toyota, which used to maintain strict age-based retirement programs, have implemented reemployment programs that enable retiring workers to apply for positions at Toyota or its affiliated companies. Toyota rehires about half of its retiring employees through the program, allowing the company to retain their skills and experience as it maintains flexibility of production. In return, the retiring employees gain a stream of income, social interaction, and the opportunity to continue plying their trade on a part-time basis.[50]

Such policies are becoming increasingly important in designing career paths that fit senior skills and constraints. In France, Axa launched its Cap Métiers program, aiming to promote internal job mobility for its staff and particularly targeting older workers. Axa offered non-front-line staffers a job guarantee and vocational training if they decide to change their roles; 30 percent of its staff, including a large proportion of senior workers, switched jobs during the initial years of the program. The electronic systems group Thales, determined to raise the number of employees over fifty-five by 5 percent annually, implemented an integrated policy to anticipate career evolution—for example, through a systematic career review for those aged over forty-five—developing vocational training and mentorship and managing the transition between work and retirement.[51]

Another crucial initiative is to offer specific training to help retain older workers, redefine their roles, and keep their skills updated. British Gas, a leading UK energy supplier, removed age limits on its training and apprenticeships programs. The average age of apprentices and trainees has risen, with some trainees as old as fifty-seven. The company also actively encourages senior employees to act as mentors to younger workers and deploys flexible practices to support older workers and caregivers.[52]

Fearing labor shortages as baby boomers age, some companies in the United States have adjusted human resources needs to the well-established migratory patterns of older Americans, from the Northeast, Midwest, and Plains to Florida and the Southwest in the winter. CVS, the drugstore giant, realized that if it "doesn't learn how to recruit and retain older people," it wouldn't "have a business," Steve Wing, the company's director of workforce initiatives, said. So CVS rolled out its Snowbird Program, under which pharmacists, photo supervisors, and cosmetics salespeople in New England can work at stores in Florida during the winter. The program has greatly improved satisfaction for the more than a thousand employees who have been participating each year. It shouldn't come as a surprise that retention rates of the mature workers were 30 percent higher than the industry average.[53]

Marketing to an Aging Demographic

Consumer-facing companies today are obsessed with their performance in "the demo"—the twenty-five-to-fifty-four demographic. Strategists construct elaborate plans to grab customers when they are young and forming preferences, hold on to them as they mature and pass through their peak earnings and consumption years, and then let them go as soon as they hit their fifties. But in the evolving world, older consumers will make up a larger portion of the market and will be active consumers for a longer time. If more older people are likely to be working longer, they are more likely to have more disposable income. As these customers' preferences and needs change over time, companies have to reset their intuition so that they can meet older consumers on their own terms.

For example, people facing a difficult transition to retirement tend to become more cost conscious. In France, for example, the gap between the annual purchasing power of households aged 50 to 54 and those aged 70 to 74 is on average €18,000. By 2030, this gap is expected to increase to €22,000.[54] Elderly consumers face trade-offs that force a change in purchasing tactics. While nonretirees are more inclined to "shop smarter," looking for bargains on brand-name products online, retirees prefer to seek value, by, for example, buying supermarkets' private-label goods.[55]

There is a second important trend in consuming patterns. Seniors typically reduce their spending on housing, food away from home, and apparel as they move to retirement, while they increase spending on food at home, medical services, and, surprisingly, electronics. Of particular importance is their focus on health and wellness, addressing the need to remain mobile and independent. Products and services that address these needs will have a fast-growing market to capture. Danone, for example, recently launched Densia—which strengthens bone density—in Spain, and it plans to expand to other European markets, such as France.[56]

As new generations enter this fast-growing segment, it will be important to keep attuned to their needs and not blindly rely on the approaches used in earlier eras. This is especially true for rapidly growing countries like China. Given current demographic trends, China will add 125 million elderly consumers between today and 2020. Their spending patterns will likely differ from those of the current retired generation, which lived through the Cultural Revolution and allocates little to discretionary categories—only 7 percent toward apparel, for example. In fact, our latest Chinese consumer survey shows the spending patterns of today's 45- to 54-year-olds—who will be the older generation in 2020—are more similar to those of 34- to 45-year-olds, with a greater emphasis on discretionary spending, for example. Companies will need to rethink what older Chinese consumers want.[57]

The breakdown of traditional family structures will strongly impact the elderly, who will pursue community and digital connectivity. Online platforms and other business innovations could address isolation, a factor particularly relevant to elderly people who live alone. Tapping the desire for a sense of community, ElderTreks offers holiday travel to seniors.[58] Thomas Cook (India) launched Silver Breaks tourism packages targeting affluent Indian travelers over sixty years of age with features such as easy-access transportation, relaxed itineraries, and special diets.[59] And as older consumers become more used to technologies such as laptops and smart phones, business leaders should expect them to become a major growth driver in these categories. Singapore's telecommunications operator Sing-Tel, for example, anticipated this trend by developing Project Silverline, which encourages donations of old iPhones, refurbishes them with apps developed specifically for senior users and commits to one-year sponsorship of talk and data plans for the beneficiaries.[60]

Advertising tactics to build product awareness will need to be adapted as well. Low-concept advertising campaigns pitched at seniors have been a staple of late-night television jokes—the Clapper sound-activated light switch, adult diapers, and reverse mortgages pitched by aging stars like Henry Winkler, who played the Fonz on the 1970s sitcom *Happy Days*. But companies that have latched onto these trends are becoming more sophisticated and nuanced in their marketing. In 2007, Unilever's Dove launched

Pro-Age, a line of deodorants, hair-care products, and skin-care products targeted at female consumers between the ages of fifty-four and sixty-three. The launch was accompanied by provocative ads showing unclothed models in its target demographic, complete with age spots, wrinkles, and gray hair. One of the spots in the campaign racked up more than 2.5 million views on YouTube.[61] In anticipation of aging baby boomers' needs and issues with the older brand image, Kimberly-Clark embarked on a series of clever repositioning campaigns from 2011 to 2013 for its Depend brand of incontinence products. The campaign involved younger, unexpected celebrities—including actress Lisa Rinna and pro football players—who were willing to break through the stigma associated with incontinence and demonstrate how well the product fits into an active lifestyle.[62]

Products and Services for Seniors

Smart marketers have always segmented their core markets by consumer demographics and other important characteristics. Around the world, companies, nonprofits, and public institutions are developing new products and services that cater to older people and are thinking in innovative ways about the lifelong value of their customers. Youth must be served, the saying goes. But so, increasingly, must the elderly.

The design of cities and social care will also need to be rethought with new consumer needs in mind. Housing developments with community spaces and tailored activities, retrofitted apartments, easy medical access, and infrastructure centered on shorter trips in electric golf carts may soon become mainstream. In Singapore, where the issue of an aging population has been on the national agenda since the 1980s, mass transit and housing policies, combined with projects such as City for All Ages, are gradually transforming communities to become more accommodating to the elderly.[63] Even in India, a country better known for its youth bulge, the topic is very much alive. There are already over one hundred million people over the age of sixty; the elderly segment is expected to grow to over three hundred million by 2050, according to United Nations estimates.[64] The first national Association of Senior Living in India was formed in 2011 as a trade association of companies serving the small, fragmented, but rapidly growing market for senior living communities.[65] Real estate developers like Tata Housing and Max India Group have announced plans to create residential communities specifically for seniors.

In the private sector, retail, health-care, tech, financial, and leisure companies are among the early birds in developing tailored services and products for the graying market. Here, too, Japan leads the way. Malls are often designed as havens for teenagers and young shoppers. But in 2012 Aeon, a retail-focused conglomerate, opened a senior-focused mall in Funabashi in Chiba prefecture, the first effort in a larger push to reorient many of its 157 malls to tap into the ¥101 trillion ($1.18 trillion) consumption opportunity that Japan's silver spenders represent.[66] At the mall, people can use escalators that move at a slower-than-usual speed, get a medical checkup, and buy groceries that have price tags in large type. And for those who just want to meet new people, the mall offers a senior dating service—the Begins Partner program—which was perhaps one of the reasons about five thousand people waited to enter on opening day.[67]

Age-friendly customization of products and services in retail banking is increasingly common. Telephone, online, ATM, and physical touch points are getting a makeover to cater to customers' differing visual, hearing, and access needs. In Canada, TD Canada Trust developed a toolbar, designed with a TV remote in mind, to help customers easily navigate the web, adjust font size and volume, and instantly access help. Brazil's Banco Bradesco provides a phone for people with hearing difficulties. In Germany, Deutsche Bank has designed its ATMs to be as barrier-free as possible and equipped them with Braille and voice guidance.[68] Aging-themed investing and tailored fraud protection services for customers with dementia and Alzheimer's are examples of propositions that are likely to become more mainstream over the coming decade.

Beyond tailoring marketing, products, and services, companies and organizations have to innovate and conceive of new products as well. Steve Jobs famously noted that consumers didn't know what they wanted until he showed it to them. Responding to—and anticipating—urgent consumer needs often drives significant innovation in product development. Deploying human and financial capital to fundamentally reimagine products for older people will likely pay significant "silver" dividends.

In 2013, Amazon launched a new retail initiative, the 50+ Active and Healthy Living Store, with nutrition, wellness, exercise and fitness, medical, personal care, and other targeted products. The company said it launched the initiative to "offer customers in the 50+ age range a place to easily discover hundreds of thousands of items that promote active and healthy living."[69] In the United Kingdom, Saga creates products and services exclusively for customers aged fifty and up, covering a range of needs from insurance and travel to health and dating. The company has roughly 2.7 million customers and a market capitalization of £1.7 billion in late 2014.[70] Israel's CogniFit developed a brain-training application that lets the elderly assess their cognitive skills and gives personalized brain training, which is rapidly spreading worldwide through its mobile app.[71]

In tech, Fujitsu has innovated extensively with a focus on the silver segment. In 2013, the company introduced the second generation of senior smart phones called the Raku-Raku ("easy, easy" or "comfortable, comfortable"). Modeled on an Android device, it is designed to be easier on older eyes and bodies; the touch-screen controls are more like buttons, scrolling only goes up and down, and text and icons are large enough to see clearly without bifocals. The phone can even slow down the speech of the person at the other end of the line. After reaching more than twenty million handset sales in 2011, Fujitsu made the product available in other countries, like France, through local partnerships.[72] Fujitsu in 2014 also issued a prototype of a cane with a built-in navigation system that helps people get where they're going and allows them to be tracked. Future iterations will have the capability to monitor heart rate and temperature and to call for help if necessary.[73]

The cane is still in the works, but it stands as a powerful metaphor. Here's a passive object, a tool that most consumers spend their lives trying to avoid, that is synonymous with debilitation. But technology paired with an understanding of an evolving market has quickly shifted and reset the way we think about it. It's proactive, highly useful, less stigmatizing, and empowering.

This cane, in other words, is able.

4

—

TRADE, PEOPLE, FINANCE, AND DATA

Greater Global Connections

SHANGHAI'S SPRAWLING DOWNTOWN OFFERS A SNAPSHOT OF GLO-
balization past, present, and future. The Huangpu River carves an arc past
the Bund, home to the Beaux-Arts corporate headquarters buildings the
colonial powers erected in the nineteenth century. On the eastern shore,
Pudong, which was a collection of rice paddies and villages thirty years ago,
has sprouted into a modern financial center. The gleaming skyscrapers—
ICBC Tower, HSBC Tower, Citigroup Tower, Deutsche Bank Tower—
belong to the giant financial institutions that act as portals for the vast
amounts of capital flowing around, in and out of the country. From here, a
maglev (magnetic levitation) train shuttles tourists and businesspeople eighteen miles in seven minutes to Pudong International Airport, which saw
47.2 million passengers come through its massive terminal in 2013.[1] While
barges still ply the waters and dock at the city's wharves, the real action
takes place at the giant Yangshan Port. The world's busiest port, connected
to the mainland by the 20.2-mile Donghai Bridge, handled about thirty-
two million containers in 2013, more than double the volume in 2004.[2]

The story of trade in Shanghai—and in China—is no longer simply a
matter of dollars and euros arriving in exchange for manufactured goods
shipped to the United States and Europe. Goods, services, and people flow
in and out of all of Shanghai's ports of entry at a pace that is noteworthy
for its size and growth. Oil arrives from Congo, motorcycles leave for Vietnam, tourists fly to Paris, investments flow through the banks to factories
in China's interior, and funds flow out to buy bonds in New York. The
often-frenetic activity embodies the rising pace, intensity, and complexity

of global connections, the higher flows of people, goods, services, money, and information.

These tides have been rising for decades. Connections have always risen along with growth. But the long-term trend is accelerating. In the twentieth century, things moved, often at slow speed, from one point to another along reliable routes. In the twenty-first century, things, people, and information move much more quickly, often at the speed of sound, sometimes at the speed of light. And in this second great wave of globalization, cross-border flows of goods, services, finance, and people are growing and dispersing rapidly. Driven and amplified by the disruptive forces of growing prosperity in the emerging world and by the spread of the Internet and digital technologies, these flows—and the greater connections they spawn—are changing the nature of the game. With each passing year, more goods, services, people, information, and capital move around from place to place. These flows add between 15 and 25 percent to global GDP growth each year. If the impact of these disruptive forces continues, flows could triple in volume by 2025.[3]

Few countries and companies are sitting this out. As Ann Pickard, executive vice president of Arctic at Royal Dutch Shell, notes, "I think the world is far more interconnected. We've got Alaska thinking about Norway thinking about Greenland. The interconnectedness becomes absolutely important."[4] The web of the world economy is ever more intricate and complex. These flows present both opportunities and the potential for crisis. Companies have never been more able to reach more new customers, tap into new sources of financing, and find new sources of both supply and demand. But greater global interconnections have also produced a proliferation of channels that can transmit shocks across sectors and borders. A disruption in a seemingly remote area—an earthquake in Japan, a political crisis in Ukraine, a fiscal meltdown in Greece—can have instantaneous effects around the world. In order to tap into this flow of energy without getting shocked, it is imperative to understand how these interconnections affect your business, and then to reset your intuition accordingly.

A New Wave of Globalization:
Trade in Goods and Services

The growth of trade is a centuries-long trend that has accelerated with containerization and higher productivity of transportation networks. Today, a host of new technologies and networks are amplifying the trend. The rise of consumers and businesses in emerging economies is remaking, intensifying, and deepening the process of globalization. The network of supply chains is growing more complex and has greater geographic reach, and the volume of goods and services moving around the world is on a scale and at speeds that are unprecedented. With the notable blip of 2009—the first year since 1944 in which the global economy shrank—the connections, and the volume of stuff flowing through them, have been growing much more rapidly than the economy as a whole.[5]

- Between 1980 and 2012, the value of total goods trade grew at a 7 percent compounded annual growth rate, while the value of services traded rose at an 8 percent annual rate.[6]
- In the same period, thanks to rapidly expanding supply chains, goods flows increased nearly tenfold in value, from $1.8 trillion to $17.8 trillion, and amounted to 24 percent of global GDP.[7]
- Fueled by dramatic declines in the cost of international communications and a sharp increase in travel, global services flows nearly tripled between 2001 and 2012, from $1.5 trillion to $4.4 trillion, or 6 percent of global GDP.[8]
- By 2011, the volume of global trade in goods and services had surpassed 2008 levels. Today, the world is more trade intensive than ever. The cross-border movements of goods, services, and finance in 2012 reached $26 trillion, or 36 percent of global GDP—1.5 times the share of GDP in 1990.[9]

International trade hasn't simply grown in volume. It has broadened and branched out, like a river moving through its delta. In 1990, more than half of all goods flows were between developed countries. The typical transaction might have been a Toyota Celica shipped from Japan to the United States. But in 2012, such transactions accounted for only 28 percent of all goods flows.[10]

Since 1990, trade routes have evolved from hubs in the United States and Western Europe into a global web of trade, with Asia as the largest trading region. Emerging economies now account for 40 percent of all goods flows, and 60 percent of those go to other emerging economies—known as south-south trade. In 1990, this trade accounted for 6 percent of global goods flows; it rose to nearly 24 percent by 2012.[11] It might, for example, involve a barrel of oil going from Congo to China, or soybeans farmed deep in Brazil shipped to Malaysia, or an Indian pharmaceutical shipped to Algeria. China's bilateral trade with Africa has exploded, from about $10 billion in 2000 to nearly $200 billion in 2012.[12] Trade between emerging economies is likely to continue to grow as a share of global trade as incomes in these countries increase, boosting the number of consumers with a voracious appetite for goods of all kinds, and as business activity grows.

In an important trend break, technology is shifting trade from the formerly exclusive province of large companies to an activity that all sorts of companies—even individuals—can participate in. Online platforms such as eBay and Alibaba facilitate production and cross-border exchanges. More than 90 percent of eBay commercial sellers export to other countries, compared with less than 25 percent of traditional small businesses.[13] The types of goods being traded are changing as well. In the past, labor-intensive products shipped from low-cost manufacturing locations and commodities originating in resource-rich nations dominated global flows. Today, trade in knowledge-intensive goods like pharmaceuticals, semiconductors, and aircraft make up nearly 50 percent of the total value. Trade in knowledge-intensive goods is growing 30 percent faster than trade in labor-intensive goods such as apparel and toys.[14] Twenty years ago, the prototypical traded object may have been a $3 T-shirt. Now it could be a 30-cent pill, a $3 e-book, or a $300 iPhone.

FINANCE

For decades, oil was the main liquid asset moving around the world. Today, the flows of black gold are abetted—and eclipsed—by the rapid movement of a different commodity: money. Finance enables trade, and the flow of capital has become a phenomenon in its own right. It is easier to ship large sums of money and credit than it is to send oil or shoes—you don't have to put electronic money on a tanker or a container ship. So it is not surprising that financial globalization has proceeded at an even faster pace than trade globalization since 1990. Between 1980 and 2007, annual cross-border capital flows increased from $0.5 trillion to a peak of $12 trillion, a twenty-three-fold increase that was in large measure driven by Europe's monetary and trade integration.[15] Such flows fell sharply in the aftermath of the 2008 financial crisis and then bounced back. In 2012, estimated financial flows stood at $4.6 trillion, nearly five times the level in 1990.[16]

Trade routes have expanded and trade patterns have become increasingly more complex

Total trade flows between regions [1]

········· USD 50–100 billion

▬▬▬ USD 100–500 billion

▨▨▨ USD 500 billion or more

● Participation in world trade, %

1990 United States and Western Europe were the main hubs for trade flows

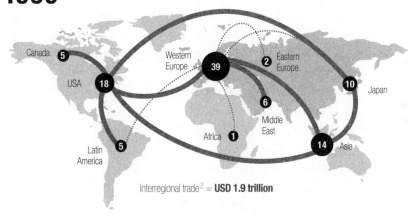

Interregional trade [2] = **USD 1.9 trillion**

2013 Trade flows became an elaborate web as Asia and Middle East became large players

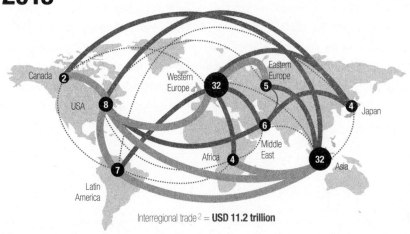

Interregional trade [2] = **USD 11.2 trillion**

1 Includes only merchandise.
2 This value does not include the trade flows between countries in a region. If intraregional trade flows are included, the total trade for 2009 is $18.3 trillion. Overall value estimate for 2013, breakdowns calculated on data until August 2010. Updated February 2011/ May 2014.
SOURCE: Global Insight – World Trade Service; McKinsey Global Institute analysis

As with the trade in physical goods, the flow of capital is becoming more varied and complex. Developing countries, long the recipients of private capital flows, are now emerging as *sources* of global foreign direct investment, and the web of cross-border investment assets has grown in depth and breadth. For example, Angola, a former Portuguese colony, has reportedly invested between 10 and 15 billion Euros into high-profile Portuguese assets in sectors such as media, banking, telecommunications, and energy.[17] The investment office of S. D. Shibulal, one of the founders of Indian outsourcing giant Infosys, has purchased more than seven hundred apartments in the Seattle area.[18] In May 2014, Chinese dairy firm Bright Foods paid about $1 billion for a majority stake in Tnuva, an Israeli dairy cooperative.[19] Financial outflows from emerging economies rose from 7 percent of the global total in 1990 to 38 percent in 2012.[20]

Capital markets are the main international arenas in which money flashes around the world in seconds. But today, the big players are not just clustered in the traditional power centers of New York, London, and Tokyo. They're also in Abu Dhabi, Mumbai, and Rio de Janeiro. While the assets of households in the United States and Western Europe grew on average 3 to 4 percent annually between 2000 and 2010, those of households in emerging markets rose much more quickly: by 23 percent annually in the Middle East and North Africa and by 16 percent in China, for instance. Total assets are still much smaller in emerging regions than they are in developed economies, but they are catching up.[21]

The forces of financial globalization were severely weakened in the 2008 recession and its aftermath. By 2012, cross-border capital flows had fallen 60 percent from their 2007 peak.[22] But the long-term trend remains intact. As the global financial and banking system reconstitutes itself and becomes better capitalized, and regulation becomes more effective and coordinated, the financial system could effectively reset and enable the rapid growth of financial globalization to resume.

PEOPLE

People, too, are increasingly interconnected globally. While the number of people traveling, working, and studying globally has increased steadily for centuries, the past few decades have seen an explosion in the volume of those movements. Once people move to cities and earn higher incomes, it becomes much easier to move or travel to other countries. The number of international migrants—people living outside their country of birth—grew from 75 million in 1960 to 232 million in 2013, according to the United Nations Department of Economic and Social Affairs.[23] In the first ten years of the new millennium, the rate of immigration doubled compared with the 1990s. One of the new characteristics of immigration is that movement between developing regions has grown faster than immigration from developing to developed countries. The labor market, too, is becoming truly global for the first time. And the phenomenon manifests up and down the income and skills ladder.

Between 1994 and 2006, the ratio of foreign-born to US-born scientists and engineers working in the United States doubled. In Silicon Valley, more than half of business start-ups over that period involved a foreign-born scientist or engineer; one-fourth included an Indian or Chinese immigrant.[24] Since 2012, 30 percent of Romanian resident doctors have left the country and moved to wealthier European Union countries, such as the United Kingdom, Germany, and France, in search of higher pay.[25] More than 130,000 Bangladeshi migrant workers are working in Qatar, one of the richest Gulf states, with many of them engaged in building venues for the 2022 World Cup.[26] In his book *China's Second Continent,* the veteran foreign correspondent Howard French cites a common estimate that some one million Chinese citizens have moved to Africa in the past two decades. In Latin America, comparatively more prosperous southern countries like Chile, Argentina, and Brazil are exerting the type of magnetic force that the United States does to the north. In Buenos Aires, many of the taxi drivers and virtually all the people staffing corner fruit and vegetable stands are Bolivian. The International Organization for Migration reports that the Bolivian population in Argentina has increased by 48 percent since 2001 (to 345,000) and that the country's Paraguayan and Peruvian populations have grown even faster.[27]

People are not just traveling more frequently for work. World tourism has also expanded exponentially. In 1950, only about 25 million people traveled beyond their own countries. In 2013, there were more than 1 billion international tourists. Their impact is massive, not just due to the money they spend but for the rich exchange of culture and knowledge they bring. Estimates put the GDP of the global tourism industry at $2 trillion and its payroll at more than 100 million people.[28] More than 110 million US citizens—more than double the number in 2000— had valid passports in 2013.[29] More than 100 million additional Chinese tourists are expected to travel abroad by 2020.[30] Galeries Lafayette, the Parisian department store, now has an Asian department to accommodate the rising number of shoppers coming from China. At the top of Vail Mountain, the ski resort in Colorado, it is common to see Australian instructors teaching Mexican skiers how to negotiate black diamond slopes.

Students, too, are crossing borders in large numbers. More than 750,000 international college students study in the United States, 200,000 more than in 2006. A quarter of these students are Chinese.[31] At Lake Forest College, a small liberal arts institution outside Chicago, of the 410 entering members of the class of 2015, 63, or 15 percent, hailed from thirty-three different countries. President Steven Schutt spends a portion of his year recruiting students—not just in New York and Boston, but in Shanghai and Beijing. "US education is a brand that travels well," he notes.[32]

DATA AND COMMUNICATION

Perhaps the most dramatic change in recent years has been the speed at which information is flashing around the world. More than two-thirds of humans have a mobile phone, and the proportion is rising rapidly. "Today, there are more phones than people. . . . And we can call almost any part of the world at almost no cost through Internet services such as Skype," notes Kishore Mahbubani, dean of the Lee Kuan Yew School of Public Policy at the National University of Singapore. "This level of teledensity means that people have become interconnected at a level never seen before in history."[33] One-third of the planet is online. At more than 1.35 billion, the community of Facebook users is equivalent to the population of the world's largest nation. Global online traffic rose from eighty-four petabytes a month in 2000 to more than forty thousand petabytes a month in 2012—a five-hundred-fold increase. Cross-border voice traffic has more than doubled over the past decade, and Skype call minutes have increased more than 500 percent since 2008.[34]

These connections have already had an enormous impact and are poised to have an even greater one, especially in developing countries. Internet-related consumption and expenditure is now bigger than either global agriculture or the worldwide energy sector.[35] In 2005, mobile subscriptions in aspiring countries—defined as the thirty countries with the economic size and dynamism to become significant global players—accounted for 53 percent of worldwide subscriptions; just five years later, that share had risen to 73 percent. By 2015, 1.6 billion of the estimated total 2.7 billion Internet users globally are likely to be from aspiring countries.[36]

Many areas with large populations still have a great deal to gain from going online. Mobile subscriptions in Africa have rapidly increased, from fewer than 25 million in 2001 to around 720 million in 2012.[37] This has significantly expanded Africans' access to markets and services; the impact of mobile telephony on GDP has been three times as large as in developed economies. However, Internet penetration in Africa lags behind, and the Internet's contribution to GDP in Africa averages just 1.1 percent, half that of its contribution in other emerging economies.[38] Although Internet penetration is only around 16 percent on the continent, some 25 percent of Africa's urban population goes online daily, with Kenyans (47 percent) and Senegalese (34 percent) leading the way.[39] The economic opportunity this online gap represents is vast. By 2025, the number of Internet users in Africa could quadruple, to six hundred million, while the number of smart phones could rise more than fivefold to 360 million, bringing a $300 billion annual Internet contribution to GDP.[40] Rocket Internet, the Germany-based global digital incubator, in 2013 struck a $400 million investment deal with South African mobile network operator MTN to develop a host of e-commerce start-ups in the Middle East and Africa.[41] The joint venture will provide Rocket Internet with access to a huge number of new customers and allow it to further accelerate its practice of launching and scaling business models that been proven to work elsewhere. Examples of Rocket's success in Africa include the Jumia e-commerce platform (modeled on Amazon.com), the Easy Taxi taxi-ordering app (modeled on Hailo), Carmudi auto classifieds, and the Jovago hotel-booking system.[42]

WHY IT MATTERS

The rise, diversification, and power of global flows are not just fascinating; they are of significant importance to businesses all over the world for several reasons.

First, the more connected you are, the better off you are. Although some companies and workers have been and will continue to be displaced by increased connectivity, research further reinforces long-held economic theories suggesting that countries, cities, and companies receive a net benefit by participating in flows. In advanced economies, multinational firms— with their global networks of customers, suppliers, and talent—tend to make outsize contributions to growth and productivity. Prior to the 2008 recession, multinationals made up less than 1 percent of all US companies, but they generated 25 percent of gross profits, 41 percent of productivity gains, and nearly 75 percent of the nation's private-sector R&D spending.[43]

Connectedness matters for countries, too. Global flows add between $250 billion and $450 billion—or 15 to 25 percent—to global GDP growth each year and contribute to faster growth for countries that participate. In fact, the most connected countries can expect to increase GDP growth from flows by up to 40 percent more than the least connected countries.[44] Germany ranked as the most connected country in the world in 2012.[45] Developed economies by and large dominated the rankings, though some large emerging economies have made significant gains in the past two decades. India and Brazil, for instance, jumped fifteen and sixteen ranks, respectively, thanks to their participation in global flows of services (India) and commodities and finance (Brazil). China rose five spots due its participation in goods and financial flows. The fastest riser of all, Morocco, leaped twenty-six spots in the connectedness ranking.[46]

Second, global interconnections are rewriting the rules of the game and are one of the major factors changing the basis of competition, as we will see in Chapter 9. The new landscape of global flows offers more entry points to a far broader range of players. Large companies from emerging markets are increasingly formidable competitors. Traditional sector boundaries are blurring. Small businesses and start-ups can be instantly global. Whereas in the past, developed-economy multinationals competed against each other, today's competitors can be individuals and companies in all shapes and sizes, from anywhere in the world and from unexpected sectors. Put differently, if a business today has data and a platform that engage millions of people, few attractive business opportunities in just about any sector are "unthinkable" for it.

Third, global flows provide companies with new ways to put their assets to productive use. Large firms can mobilize cash assets on their balance sheets to provide financing to companies and projects that can unlock new markets, as General Electric has done in Africa. For GE, Africa is one of the most promising growth regions, having produced revenues of $5.2 billion in 2013. GE in 2014 partnered with the Millennium Challenge Corporation to provide $500 million in financing for the Ghana1000 project, a huge, 1-gigawatt power plant the company is helping to build in Western Ghana.[47] Beyond tapping tangible assets, companies are able

Trade routes have expanded and trade patterns have become increasingly more complex

Connectedness index, 2012[1]

Percentile of participation (selected countries)

■ 1–10   ▦ 11–25   ▨ 26–50   ☐ >50

Rank	Flows of					Change in rank 1995–2012[2]
	Goods	Services	Finance	People	Data and communication	
1 Germany						+1
2 Hong Kong					N/A	-
3 United States						-1
4 Singapore						+1
5 United Kingdom						-1
9 Russia						-
16 Saudi Arabia						+19
20 South Korea						-
21 Japan						-1
25 China						+5
30 India						+16
43 Brazil						+15
47 Argentina						-6
49 South Africa						+4
53 Morocco						+26

1 Migrants data from 2010 used for people flows; 2013 cross-border Internet traffic used for data and communication flows. For data on complete country set, download the full report, *Global flows in a digital age: How trade, finance, people, and data connect the world economy.*
2 Calculations exclude data and communication flows, for which data are not available for 1995.
SOURCE: IHS Economics and Country Risk; TeleGeography; United Nations Comtrade database; World Development indicators, World Bank; Word Trade Organization; McKinsey Global Institute analysis

to mine intangible assets—knowledge, competencies, data—that can help them participate in global flows. Some do so for philanthropic purposes. Coca-Cola used its market distribution expertise in sub-Saharan Africa to manage the storage and delivery of AIDS drugs in countries such as Tanzania. "We're not lending our trucks or our fleet, or our motorcycles," as Coca-Cola CEO Muhtar Kent put it. "We're lending our expertise."[48]

Finally, a more interconnected world leads to some surprising new outcomes. Several decades ago, the sovereign default of a small economy like Greece would barely register on the world's financial radar. (Indeed, Greece has been in default on its debt around half the time since gaining independence in the nineteenth century.)[49] But with Europe on a single currency and a high level of integration in the financial sector, Greece's fiscal woes threatened banks in Germany, France, and the United Kingdom. Similarly, natural disasters or seemingly isolated geopolitical conflicts can disrupt supply chains or access to markets for players around the globe. Commodity prices are also showing an interesting new pattern. The correlation between commodity prices and the price of oil is now greater than at any time since the oil-shocked 1970s. In the 1980s and 1990s, prices of commodities such as corn, wheat, beef, and timber were largely uncorrelated with the price of oil (or even negatively correlated, in the case of timber); they now move in lockstep. This phenomenon can be explained by several factors: the growth in demand for resources from developing giants such as China; the fact that some resources (oil) are substantial input costs for other resources (grains); and the rise of technology that allows substitution between resources (like corn-based ethanol for oil). The combination of increasing correlation, surging demand, and supply constraints points to more volatility in commodity prices in the years to come.

When it comes to dealing with such disruptions—and the opportunities and risks they present—the most agile companies will have a significant advantage. In fact, the companies that perform well on measures of agility, such as shifting capital reallocation from year to year, post significantly higher performance with lower risk. Based on data from more than 1,600 companies, we found that total return to shareholders of the top one-third most agile companies—those with the highest capital reallocation year after year—was 30 percent higher than that of the least agile companies, whose capital allocation remain fixed year after year.[50]

The auto sector provides an excellent illustration of the increasing focus on agility. In recent years, Volkswagen has moved toward a modular architecture that provides greater flexibility for manufacturing several products on the same assembly lines.[51] BMW maximizes asset agility through the use of its Mobi-Cell, a robot that can be moved from plant to plant. Toyota standardizes line design and a host of processes across models to ensure greater flexibility. But other sectors have been striving to become more agile as well, often by sharing information and working more closely with suppliers. Helix, a maker of high-performance vacuum pumps, breaks its manufacturing processes into so-called subprocesses and shares each subprocess with suppliers. In case of a disruption in Helix plants, suppliers can easily take over parts of the manufacturing processes. A leading retailer in the United States shares its data with suppliers at the point of sale through an integrated IT system, so that the suppliers can also be aware of real-time delivery flows.[52]

Adapting to an Interconnected World

Most executives have thought in global terms for years. Yet established multinationals, mostly from advanced economies, remain significantly underweight in emerging markets, even as newcomers from these countries are expanding aggressively. The accelerations in global interconnectivity require an intuition reset on the part of companies. They must plan early to scale up globally, tailor business models to new markets, get to know new competitors, develop global talent, and prepare for shocks and volatility in an increasingly interconnected world economy. Businesses that focused mainly on cost effectiveness in global supply chains now need to consider how "value" chains may evolve—who the participants may be, which regions could play a role, and how value could shift along the value chain.

Just as the introduction of electricity was an important factor in pushing the world's industrialized economies into higher gear a century ago, the current of economic energy from global economic flows coursing through the system offers similar potential today. Incumbent firms will need to brace for a new wave of competition propelled by the lower cost of starting and scaling up a business in the new era. Capturing the opportunities emerging from these flows requires business leaders to rethink the positioning of their companies' physical locations, the way they use digital platforms, the nature of the competition they face, and the prospect of potential shocks.

Prepare for Entrants from Anywhere

It is important that companies position themselves smartly to take advantage of flows. Here, too, the technology revolution is providing unrivaled opportunity for companies of any size and age to be instantly international. Start-ups can immediately tap into global networks for talent (oDesk), funding (Kickstarter and Kiva), and suppliers (eBay and Amazon) through a host of online platforms. We have dubbed this rapidly growing class of companies that are born global "micro-multinationals." Virtually all technology start-ups have some cross-border links from the outset. Among many examples of new micro-multinationals is Solar Brush, a Berlin-based start-up that has developed lightweight robots that clean solar panels. The company has an office in Chile, has presented at a business plan competition in Washington, DC, and is targeting customers throughout the United States and the Middle East.[53] Shapeways, a company founded by Dutch entrepreneurs and based in New York, provides 3-D printing services and a platform to sell 3-D printed designs to customers around the world.[54]

The instantly plugged-in phenomenon isn't confined to the technology and digital sectors. Even traditional industries such as manufacturing are increasingly seeing small businesses with multiple-country production sites and global operations, practices once reserved for established multinationals. In the United Kingdom, many small and midsized engineering companies serve customers around the world and operate multiple plants in a mixture of low-cost and advanced-economy locations. Bowers & Wilkins, a UK-based firm that makes high-end speakers and has consolidated turnover above £100 million, has invested in a purpose-built factory in China, which now makes much cheaper models of its original product.[55] Colbree, an electrical and military equipment parts manufacturer, operates plants in the United Kingdom and Thailand. "Having the Thailand plant has been a big help to gaining new customers which are keen to benefit from the lower costs that are possible with the factory in Asia," explains Robert Clark, Colbree's general manager. "But at the same time they like to see us maintain our most advanced production technology in Britain."[56]

These instantly global new entrants are not confined to developed economies. In fast-growing developing economies, more than 143,000 Internet-related businesses launch every year.[57] Jumia, a Nigerian e-commerce company that now operates in Ivory Coast, Kenya, Egypt, and Morocco, in 2013 became the first African winner of the World Retail Award for

"Best Retail Launch of the Year."[58] M-pesa, a mobile-money service started in Kenya, is now disrupting traditional banking, payments, and money-transfer service providers across Africa.

Build New Global—and Digital—Ecosystems

Digital platforms enable companies to expand rapidly and profitably to customers further away from their home markets than was possible in the past. Building cross-border ecosystems ranging from global supply chains to innovation networks could help companies take advantage of this opportunity.

Many companies are exploiting global interconnections and digital platforms to weave together networks of suppliers, distributors, and after-sales service providers—not just for procurement but also for preemptive maintenance that reduces production downtime, and for more efficient parts supply. The Boeing Edge, a new service division of Boeing, is seeking to transform the company from a traditional supplier of aviation equipment into something that more closely resembles a "digital airline." The company aims to use the vast amounts of data that the airline business generates to build an integrated information platform. By connecting real-time data from aircraft, passenger engineers, maintenance groups, operations staff, and suppliers, Boeing believes it can help its customers—airlines—maximize efficiency, profitability, and environmental performance.[59] And as firms like Boeing and Airbus push toward increased digital tracking of individual parts and components, companies such as Fujitsu and IBM are becoming part of the aerospace ecosystem through their RFID and other automated intelligence tracking products and services.

Companies are also relying on digital platforms to reach potential partners, to connect customers, suppliers, and financiers and to crowd-source ideas. Etsy, an online global marketplace in which independent artisans sell a wide range of products, connects thirty-million buyers and sellers and exemplifies the twenty-first-century digital ecosystem. The company recently partnered with Kiva to help crowd-source funding for its artisans. In addition to providing a digital portal that links buyers to sellers, Etsy provides entrepreneurial education and connects designers to suppliers. In 2013, the Etsy community generated more than $1.35 billion in total sales, a 50 percent increase from 2012.[60]

Pharmaceutical company AstraZeneca launched a digital open innovation platform in 2014 and aims to connect with researchers and academics at the UK Medical Research Council, the US National Institutes of Health, and similar organizations in Sweden, Germany, Taiwan, and Canada, among others.[61] Consumer packaged goods companies, including Unilever and Procter & Gamble (P&G), often engage customers in new product development. Unilever's "Challenges and Wants" digital portal is a tool for developing partnerships with innovators on topics from sustainable laundry products to improved packaging.[62] And German equipment-maker Bosch uses its innovation portal to connect with individual and institutional researchers in power tools, new materials and surfaces, and the automotive aftermarket.[63]

Exploit Your Position in Global Flows

Countries and cities that have developed as hubs for certain types of flows have created a competitive advantage. Companies tapping into these hubs will likewise be able to benefit.

Take the United States, which is ranked number one in people flows, as an illustration.[64] Broadly speaking, US-based firms are unrivaled in their ability to attract global talent. Those positioned in hubs that are already global capitals—New York for finance, Houston for energy, Los Angeles for entertainment—are particularly well situated to do so. The impact of foreign entrepreneurs in Silicon Valley, for instance, has been significant. One-third to one-half of Silicon Valley high-tech start-ups have foreign-born founders. Foreign-born residents represent 36 percent of Silicon Valley's population, almost triple the national average of 13 percent. Among all adults in Silicon Valley, 46 percent have at least a bachelor's degree, compared with the national average of 29 percent. Foreign talent has provided critical engineering skills, often developed at US universities, the lack of which might otherwise have hampered Silicon Valley's growth.[65]

Take Frankfurt as another illustration. It is the highest-ranked city in terms of participation in data and information flows globally and is home to the German Commercial Internet Exchange, which handles over one-third of Europe's Internet traffic.[66] The city houses over five thousand software firms, such as SAP and Symantec, and is Germany's hub for industries that benefit from proximity to high bandwidth and connectivity, such as financial services and games development. Ironically, even in an area of instant communications, companies are realizing the benefits of locating people-intensive operations in close physical proximity to other firms. In the late twentieth century, many businesses tried to carve out their own environments in vast campuses and office parks in the suburbs of North America. But the efforts to isolate corporate headquarters have often proven to be unproductive and are falling away in favor of sites that are more integrated into cities.

If your business is not yet taking advantage of being located in a major hub, considering whether to move to one should be on your agenda. Western multinationals have moved portions of their operations to Singapore precisely because it is a major conduit for Asian flows of goods, services, and finance. Singapore has the highest density of regional head offices relative to its GDP in the world. Nearly half of all large foreign subsidiaries in emerging Asia outside China are located in the city.[67] Examples of companies that have located in Singapore include P&G, which moved its beauty and baby-care divisions from Cincinnati in 2012 to position itself in the growing Asian market.[68] Unilever opened a new state-of-the art leadership development center in Singapore in 2013—its first training center outside the United Kingdom.[69] In 2009, Rolls-Royce relocated its marine business from London to Singapore, reflecting Asia's emergence as the world's center for shipping.[70]

Be Agile in an Interconnected World

Fostering global interconnections also means reevaluating the way you think about opportunity, risk, and volatility—and how to respond nimbly. On the one hand, an interconnected world should bring opportunities to diversify risk and improve stability. In a highly connected world, it is much easier to offer round-the-clock customer service by English-speaking call agents in locations such as the Philippines and Costa Rica. However, disruptions can now travel around the world much faster and through the same channels that enable diversification and redundancy. Shocks can be transmitted—more quickly than ever—through financial and physical markets, the same way pain travels throughout the nervous system. Now that supply chains are longer than ever, and trade relationships of all types span the globe, they are in many ways more fragile. Product quality issues, supply-chain problems, and natural or man-made disasters can quickly and massively affect businesses in unexpected and uncontrollable ways. "These days, there are things that just come shooting across the bow—economic volatility and the impact of natural events like the Japanese earthquake and tsunami—at much greater frequency than we've ever seen," said Ellen Kullman, chief executive officer of DuPont. "And the world is so connected that the feedback loops are more intense."[71]

The external environment is volatile, with capital markets increasingly characterized by more extreme events

Number of "3-sigma" days, where S&P 500 price changes are beyond three standard deviations from mean

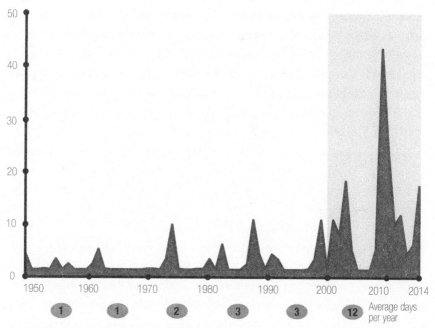

SOURCE: Standard & Poor's; McKinsey Global Institute analysis

In the old paradigm, companies sought to insulate themselves from disruptions by bulking up, relying on proven strengths, and sticking to their core competencies. Today, however, agility is increasingly becoming a focus. Agility, the ability to act quickly and nimbly in response to problems that arise, is a vital attribute for thriving in the age of accelerating global flows. Companies that invest in preparing for, detecting, and being able to respond quickly to sudden crises will have a vital competitive advantage. After seven of its factories were hit by the Tohoku earthquake in March 2011, the semiconductor manufacturer Fujitsu recovered its production levels in less than a month. The speedy recovery was possible because Fujitsu had changed its production processes after a 2008 earthquake in Iwate. The new emergency response strategy included devising ways to rapidly restore electricity, water, and other utilities in case of disaster. It also built redundancy in manufacturing across plants so that unaffected factories could cover for damaged facilities.[72]

It's easier for a business to develop these kinds of agile responses to the opportunities and risks presented by global linkages than it is for a nation to do likewise. But it is no less vital that countries do so. As we've noted, the more nations are connected to global trade, the faster they tend to grow. In order to reduce their exposure to global shocks, some countries have started implementing systematic mitigation measures that reduce their vulnerability.

Tanzania is one country that recently diversified its trade exposure, mitigating further risks from dependency on advanced economies. Tanzania once relied heavily on the export of agricultural commodities to developed economies. In recent years, it has enacted reforms aimed at liberalizing financial markets, diversifying production, building a manufacturing base, and focusing more on exports to emerging nations like China and India. As a result, the proportion of Tanzania's exports sent to Asian and African countries has risen from 30 percent in the early 2000s to more than 60 percent today. In 2009, when the developed world remained mired in a deep recession, Tanzania's economy grew 6 percent.[73]

———————

Like information technology, the rising flows of global connections are both a tool to be exploited and an unavoidable force to be reckoned with. The keys are understanding them on their own terms and making concerted efforts to ride the waves without drowning in them. Smart planning, a willingness to change, and an openness to new ways of conducting and managing business will all be vital attributes in harnessing the power of global flows.

PART II

Intuition Resets

5

———

THE NEXT THREE BILLION

Tapping the Power of the New Consuming Class

VERY FEW PEOPLE HAVE HEARD OF CLARKS VILLAGE SHOPPING CEN-
ter in the small town of Street, in southwest England. Even fewer count
it among the globe's "must-visit" shopping destinations. And virtually nobody would associate it with the boom in emerging-market consumerism.
Yet as a closer look at the history of and recent visitor patterns to Street
reveals, emerging markets—specifically China—have had a surprising influence on this small town in rural Somerset.

In the nineteenth century, Street's most prominent Quaker family, the
Clarks, and their shoe factories were the town's lifeline. As Clarks brand
grew in strength and international presence, Street flourished, surviving
the Industrial Revolution and two world wars largely unscathed. But it
couldn't weather the rise of low-cost manufacturing in Asia in the late
twentieth century.[1] As the quality of Chinese- and Vietnamese-produced
shoes rose, Clarks needed to move production offshore to remain competitive. By 2005, every one of Clarks' UK factories had shut down.[2]
In Street, redundant factory buildings were converted to form Clarks
Village, a designer outlet shopping complex that opened to the public in
1993.[3]

Fast-forward twenty years, and the shopping complex—with more than
ninety-five stores, over a thousand employees, and four million visitors each
year—has become a new lifeline for the town. In an era when many dere-
lict high-street stores are sad reminders of the recent recession, Clarks Village is booming.[4] The unlikely ingredient in Clarks Village's secret recipe?
Emerging-market consumers. Chinese tourists have become an increasingly

important source of retail, leisure, and hospitality-industry income across the United Kingdom, contributing over £550 million ($878.5 million) to Britain's economy in 2013.[5] Building on its unique tourist-route location, on the way to Cornwall and Devon, Clarks Village has added organized tourist bus visits and VAT advice to its offerings. So, in addition to attracting price-conscious British shoppers, Clarks Village now draws thousands of Chinese tourists who are aware of the premium certain brands command in their home country. The shopping center's vision is now, as the manager put it, "for Clarks Village to be a 'must do' destination for international visitors to the West Country."[6] In an interesting twist, Chinese tourists are now flocking to Clarks Shoe Museum and are an increasingly powerful force behind the prosperity of Street.[7] "Clarks shoes are a phenomenon in China; their quality and design are famous," says Stephanie Cheng, managing director of London-based China Holidays Ltd.[8]

TREND BREAK

Two decades ago, the notion of shoppers from China, or any emerging market, driving economic activity in Street—or anywhere else—would have seemed preposterous. For centuries, less than 1 percent of the world's population enjoyed sufficient income to spend it on anything beyond basic daily needs. As recently as 1990, 43 percent of the population in the developing world lived in extreme poverty, earning less than $1.25 per day, and only one in five people on the planet earned more than $10 a day—the level of income at which households reach the "consuming class" threshold and can afford to buy discretionary items.[9] The vast majority of those consumers were in advanced economies in North America, Western Europe, and Japan.

Over the past two decades, the amplifying forces of industrialization, technology, and the urbanization of emerging economies have driven incomes higher for billions of people, lifting 700 million out of poverty and adding 1.2 billion new members to the consuming class.[10] From a societal perspective, this level of poverty eradication prevents more deaths from poverty-related diseases and hunger than the lives saved per year through eradication of smallpox, often hailed as the greatest health-care achievement of the twentieth century.[11] From a market perspective, it means the center of the global consuming class, with huge spending power, is shifting east and south. By 2025, we expect the consumer class to add another 1.8

Three billion people joining the consuming class between 1990–2025

For the first time in world history, the majority of the global population is set to become consumers

Share of population in consuming class

Consuming class

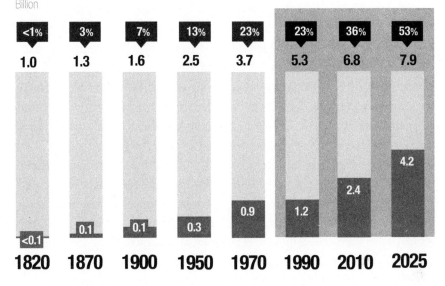

World population[1]
Billion

1820	1870	1900	1950	1970	1990	2010	2025
<1%	3%	7%	13%	23%	23%	36%	53%
1.0	1.3	1.6	2.5	3.7	5.3	6.8	7.9
<0.1	0.1	0.1	0.3	0.9	1.2	2.4	4.2

1. Historical values for 1820 through 1990 estimated by Homi Kharas; 2010 and 2025 estimates by McKinsey Global Institute.
2. Defined as people with daily disposable income above $10 at purchasing power parity (PPP). Population below consuming class defined as individuals with disposable income below $10 at PPP.
SOURCE: Homi Kharas; Angus Maddison; McKinsey Global Institute Cityscope database

billion people and total 4.2 billion. Much has been made about the world's population crossing the 7 billion threshold in 2012. But the 3 billion additional members of the world's consuming class added in just thirty-five years is a far more significant milestone.[12] That's as many new consumers added as there were people on the planet in the mid-1960s.[13] As Sanjeev Sanyal, Deutsche Bank's global strategist, notes, "The real story for the next two decades will be emerging economies' shift to middle-class status. Although other emerging regions will undergo a similar shift, Asia will dominate this transformation."[14]

Tipping Point

Incomes have been rising, and the consumer class has been expanding, for some years. But we have reached a tipping point where the spending of a new generation of consumers in emerging economies has become an overwhelming force.

By 2030, almost six hundred million people with annual income greater than $20,000 a year will live in emerging markets—roughly 60 percent of the global total. They will account for an even higher proportion of spending in categories such as electronics and automobiles. Seven emerging markets—China, India, Brazil, Mexico, Russia, Turkey, and Indonesia—will be fueling almost half of all global GDP growth over the coming decade.[15]

The billion-plus populations of China and India are at the heart of the phenomenon. Technological progress, in which millions of people in emerging economies now have access to the Internet and mobile communications, is fueling consumption. In India, discretionary spending jumped from 35 percent of average household consumption in 1985 to 52 percent in 2005, and it looks set to hit 70 percent by 2025.[16] In China, a new generation of consumers born after the mid-1980s—Generation 2 or G2—will be crucial for the economy. While their parents lived through many years of shortages and were primarily concerned with building economic security, G2 consumers have been raised in relative material abundance. They are confident, willing to pay a premium for the best products, eager to experience new technology, and heavily reliant on the Internet for price information.

To illustrate the strength of the consumption wave, China should overtake the United States in terms of spending on consumer electronics and smart phones by 2022. The speed of change is extraordinary. In 2007, ten million flat-screen televisions were sold in China. Five years later, sales were fifty million units—more than were sold that year in the United States and Canada combined.[17] And it's not just basic products: the Chinese are moving upmarket. China has already overtaken the United States as the world's largest market for all car sales, and in 2016, China will outstrip the United States in sales of premium cars.[18] Tesla Motors is already shipping its expensive electric sports cars to China.[19] Trading up is becoming an ever more important part of China's consumer story. In some luxury goods categories, emerging-market consumers are the fastest-growing segment of the market. That explains why L'Occitane, the privately held French beauty products company, floated its 2010 IPO in Hong Kong and not on the Euronext in Paris.[20]

Many of these new consumers will come from relatively unknown "Middleweight" cities in emerging markets

- ■ Advanced Economies
- ■ Emerging Economies - Megacities
- ■ Emerging Economies - Middleweight cities
- ▦ Emerging Economies - Small cities and rural areas

Example cities in China

6 megacities: Shanghai, Beijing, Chongqing, Tianjin, Guangzhou, Shenzhen
236 middle-weight cities: Haerbin, Lanzhou, Qinhuangdao

Contribution to GDP and GDP growth by type of city, %

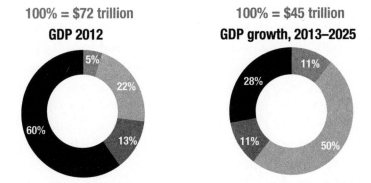

100% = $72 trillion
GDP 2012

5%
22%
60%
13%

100% = $45 trillion
GDP growth, 2013–2025

11%
28%
11%
50%

1 Megacities are defined as metropolitan areas with ten million or more inhabitants. Middleweights are cities with populations of between 150,000 and ten million inhabitants.
2 Real exchange rate (RER) for 2007 is the market exchange rate. RER for 2025 was predicted from differences in the per capita GDP growth rates of countries relative to the United States.
SOURCE: McKinsey Global Institute Cityscope database

Although there will be turbulence and periods during which the rate of economic growth of emerging markets may slow, we expect these trends to continue at least through 2025. In fact, even under pessimistic scenarios, we believe the emerging economies will likely continue outperforming developed economies. The annual consumption in emerging markets will reach $30 trillion by 2025.[21] Some 440 emerging-market cities, including 20 megacities (population over ten million), will account for nearly 50 percent of the additional GDP growth between now and 2025.[22]

TECHNOLOGY WILL BENEFIT CONSUMERS

The spreading reach of the Internet also means that these new consumers will be plugged in and online. China already has more than six hundred million Internet users, equivalent to 20 percent of the global Internet population.[23] More than a quarter of Brazilians using the Internet have opened Twitter accounts, making Brazil the world's second-most enthusiastic tweeting nation.[24] In India, consumers are leapfrogging the traditional technology trajectory. Landlines may be slow to reach remote villages, but more than nine hundred million Indians are mobile users.[25] A desire to cater to the nearly 300 million Indians who are illiterate is spurring the development of voice-activated websites and services.[26] Of Facebook's 100 million users in India, more than 80 percent access their accounts through mobile devices.[27]

In 2013, we witnessed two firsts for the Chinese e-commerce market. First, China's e-tail market, which has been growing at a stunning compound annual rate of more than 100 percent since 2003, overtook the United States to become the world's largest, with an estimated $300 billion in sales.[28] By 2020, China's e-commerce market could be as big as today's markets in the United States, Japan, the United Kingdom, Germany, and France combined. Second, as we noted in the introduction, on November 11, 2014—Singles Day in China—Alibaba recorded sales of more than $9.3 billion, a record for a single day anywhere in the world, and more than triple the combined online purchase of US consumers during Black Friday and Cyber Monday in 2013.

In a phenomenon that is often underplayed and challenging to quantify, the consuming classes will also receive most of the value created by most of the new disruptive technologies. Free information, apps, and online services, lower-cost goods, greater access to information, and lowered barriers to communications will enrich the lives of billions. Unfortunately, this is not picked up in the way we measure GDP. Established companies, on the other hand, may find themselves temporarily shortchanged and unable to monetize the newly created consumer surplus. Technology disruption has historically represented as a negative-sum game for the disruptor and the disrupted. Think of Apple's iTunes and the rise of digital music sales: following the introduction of iTunes in 2003, physical music sales in the United States fell from $11.8 billion to $7.1 billion in 2012, adjusted for inflation; industry revenues have fallen by more than half. The consumer receives the benefit.[29]

How to Adapt

We are dealing with very large numbers. And it is easy to be overwhelmed by the single overriding growth story. But the $30 trillion consumption opportunity is as granular as it is vast. New-growth markets come in a range of sizes and development stages, and new customers span a multitude of ethnic and cultural backgrounds. Their tastes and preferences are

Technology is opening up new routes to these consumers

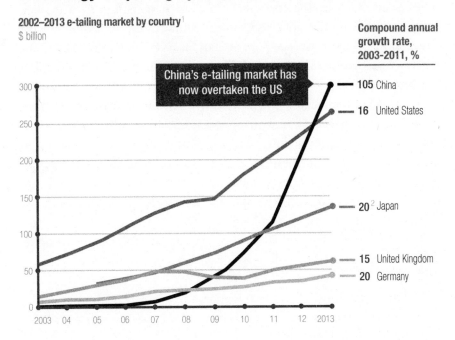

2002–2013 e-tailing market by country [1]
$ billion

Compound annual growth rate, 2003-2011, %

China's e-tailing market has now overtaken the US

- 105 China
- 16 United States
- 20 [2] Japan
- 15 United Kingdom
- 20 Germany

300
250
200
150
100
50
0

2003   04   05   06   07   08   09   10   11   12   2013

1 Excluding online travel.
2 Japan's compound annual growth rate covers 2005–2013.
SOURCE: Euromonitor; Forrester; US Census Bureau; Japanese Ministry of Economy, Trade, and Industry; iResearch; McKinsey Global Institute analysis

constantly evolving, in many cases accelerated by the mutually amplifying forces of interconnectivity and technology. As these new markets grow, they are also fragmenting into many segments with a proliferation of product varieties, price points, and marketing and distribution channels.

Even for the most seasoned executives, the sheer speed and scale of change can be daunting, and many continue to be held hostage to their existing strategy bias. The success stories are plentiful: we've been hearing for years about emerging-market "insiders" like Unilever, which has made great inroads in the Indian consumer market, and SAB Miller, a South African firm that grew into one of the largest beer companies. But we've seen a great number of failures as well. Yahoo and Amazon have both stubbed their toes badly in China. India has proved a formidable challenge for many otherwise successful multinationals.

To succeed in this emerging climate, business leaders have to reset their intuition. Under the old model of global expansion, big firms that had conquered their home markets could thrive by methodically planting their flags in fertile foreign soil, all directed from a headquarters thousands of miles away. But winning consumers in these new high-growth markets requires a radical reallocation of resources, a smart shift in capabilities, and a rethinking of multiple aspects of operations. New emerging markets are not vast homogenous entities that will readily accept products and services transplanted whole from developed markets. Nor are these new consumers simply looking for watered-down, low-price versions of existing products. As executives navigate these new opportunities, they also don't have the luxury of waiting and watching. Growth is often explosive in these emerging markets, with sudden bursts of 70 to 100 percent expansion possible in certain product categories. Leaders must learn to reallocate resources to these new-growth markets with speed and at scale, while managing risk and diversity at an entirely new level.

The companies that will succeed in the race for these extraordinarily diverse emerging markets will most likely share four traits.

- They will think of the next opportunity in terms of cities and urban clusters, not regions or countries, and reallocate their capital and talent accordingly.
- They will customize and price products to meet local tastes and needs and will build faster, lower-cost supply chains and innovative business models in order to be cost competitive and deliver price points across a broad spectrum.
- They will design and control multichannel routes to market and rethink their brand and marketing and sales strategies.
- They will overhaul organizational structures, talent strategy, and operating practices to reflect the new shift.

Focus on Cities and Urban Clusters, Not Regions or Countries

Global consumption is experiencing an unprecedented shift in power toward emerging-market cities. The continued rise of megacities—familiar entities with populations of ten million or more, such as Shanghai, São Paulo, and Moscow—is driving this trend. But the truly dramatic consumption growth will come from middleweight cities such as Luanda, Harbin, Puebla, and Kumasi, four hundred or so of which will generate the GDP equivalent to the entire US economy by 2025.[30] In China, the shift in the weight of consuming households from the megacities on the east coast to interior middleweight cities (populations of between two hundred thousand and ten million people) is already visible. In 2002, only 13 percent of China's urban middle class lived inland, with the remaining 87 percent living in coastal areas; that figure is set to rise to nearly 40 percent by 2022.[31]

The consumer landscape in these new-growth cities remains incredibly diverse. India embraces about twenty official languages, hundreds of dialects, and four major religious traditions. The residents of Africa's fifty-three countries speak an estimated 2,000 languages and dialects. Even cities close to each other in the same country can be very different.[32]

Many global companies, for example, make the mistake of conducting Brazilian consumer research in São Paulo, not realizing that the cosmopolitan city has more in common culturally with New York, 4,771 miles away, than with Curitiba, the capital of Parana state (population 1.7 million), which is just 210 miles away.

Take the southern Chinese cities of Guangzhou and Shenzhen, which are roughly the same size and only one hundred kilometers apart. The majority of people living in Guangzhou speak Cantonese. In Shenzhen, Mandarin-speaking migrants make up more than 80 percent of the population. These differences have deep business implications.

Chinese premium auto buyers from coastal cities like Hangzhou and Wenzhou, who have long been exposed to international brands, are looking for cars that reflect their social status. They react favorably to advertising that appeals to this impulse. But in interior cities like Taiyuan and Xi'an, drivers rely heavily on word-of-mouth and in-store experience to reassure themselves that cars provide what brands advertise.[33]

Given the granularity of the $30-trillion opportunity and the rapid urbanization of these economies, the answer to "where next?" will be found in urban clusters and cities. In consumer goods, companies that target older generations will consider Shanghai and Beijing among the most attractive markets. By contrast, companies that sell baby food will find more than half of the top cities that are experiencing a baby boom and whose households have sufficient income to buy their products are in Africa. In midmarket apparel, nine out of the top ten growth cities, including Chongqing, Guangzhou, Shenzhen, will be in emerging markets. But in luxury apparel, developed-market cities will continue to fuel growth, with only four emerging-market cities—Saint Petersburg, Moscow, Seoul, and Singapore—among the top ten.[34]

Rather than competing in the cutthroat retail markets in emerging-market megacities, many executives will find better growth opportunities in the rapidly growing middleweight cities. In Brazil, the GDP of São Paulo state is larger than that of the entire country of Argentina. Competitive intensity is high and retail margins thin as a result. For new entrants to Brazil, the populous but historically poor northeast of the country, where boomtowns like Salvador are expected to grow 2.4-fold by 2015, may offer better prospects, even if setting up operations is more difficult.[35] This is not exactly a new idea. Walmart grew into America's largest retailer from the inside of the country out, finding underserved towns and avoiding highly competitive metropolitan markets.

Anticipating when to take action will matter as much as choosing where to compete. Growth in emerging markets is rarely linear. The demand for a particular product or category of products typically follows an S-curve trajectory. Consumption takes off and enters an explosive growth "hot zone" once consumers have enough money to buy a product. At higher GDP-per-capita income levels, markets tend to become more saturated and then enter a slower-growth "chill out" zone. Take Nigeria's beverage market as an example. While cities such as Warri, Benin City, and Port Harcourt have already entered the beverage hot zone, larger cities like Lagos, Ibadan, and Abuja are still walking toward the takeoff point. By understanding the dynamics of the product category and the local marketplace, companies can time market entry—ideally right before a category enters the hot zone—and benefit from the fastest growth stage in each city.[36]

Understanding and coping with the trade-offs between growth and costs is a complex business. One way to start is by segmenting and clustering the new-growth-market cities similarly to the way you segment consumers. Multiple smaller cities with common demographic, socioeconomic, and cultural characteristics, as well as infrastructure and retail landscape, could form an urban cluster and provide scale efficiencies across all aspects of operations. You can then orchestrate your expansion cluster by cluster, focusing on "going deep" before "going wide."

Think Locally, Act Globally

On its own, understanding where and when to focus isn't sufficient. To ensure relevance and achieve scale in the new market, you must decide how and how much you need to tailor your products or services.

As these new consumers emerge over the next decade, their needs, preferences, and consumption behavior will vary vastly across product categories, geographies, and segments. Although some trends travel the globe, there is no such thing as a "global consumer." LG refrigerators have larger vegetable compartments in India than in Brazil, where freezer compartments are larger. Nestlé instant coffee is sweeter in China than in most other markets.[37]

A deep understanding of consumer needs and preferences and of smart segmentation will continue to differentiate leaders from the pack. And companies will increasingly need to craft more nuanced product strategies that balance scale and local relevance. In recent years, many companies have assimilated a polarized caricature of emerging-market customers— the free-spending, luxury-loving nouveaux riches at the high end, arrayed against the bottom of the pyramid. But given the increasing proliferation of customer needs and rising sophistication of data and analytics, these are neither the only strategic alternatives nor necessarily the most apt.

Seek, rather, to understand markets on their own terms. A careful understanding of local tastes and flavor preferences propelled consumer goods companies such as Frito-Lay in India and Tingyi and Wrigley in China to meteoric growth.

- Frito-Lay has captured more than 40 percent of India's branded snacks market since entering in 1990. How? Rather than tailoring its global, American-heritage brands such as Lay's potato chips to local tastes, the company created Kurkure, inspired by traditional Indian-style street food and Western-style potato chips. The product, which relies on simple, authentic ingredients used in any Indian kitchen, is now sold in countries such as South Africa, Pakistan, and Kenya.[38]
- Tingyi, a start-up founded by two Taiwanese brothers in China, became China's leading food and beverage vendor after it used local designers to shape its entire instant noodle product category, creating new flavors and launching brands such as Kangshifu ("Master Kong") and low-cost brands such as Fu Man Duo ("full of luck"). Tingyi's Master Kong brand is the most popular brand in China.[39] With its portfolio of food and beverage products, Tingyi generated revenue of $10.9 billion in 2013.[40]

- Wrigley, which has built its market share of the Chinese gum market to 40 percent, succeeded by tailoring its gum flavors to suit local consumer preferences and by investing in consumer education to emphasize chewing gum's health benefits.[41]

Pricing is another key decision in determining how much to customize. The amount a company is able (or willing) to charge its customers and relative positioning compared to its peers can have interesting nuances from market to market. In Brazil, Diageo capitalized on its understanding of affluent costumers when pricing its Johnnie Walker product. The company recognized that in Brazil retail price was a quality differentiator and that the spirits markets enjoyed lower price elasticity compared with other markets. Subsequently, Diageo repositioned Johnnie Walker into a higher premium category, and Brazil is now one of its most important markets.

For many players, however, the only way to be successful locally means rethinking their existing cost structures. Emerging-market companies have proven to be formidable competitors on cost. As we will allude to in Chapter 9, emerging-market players, particularly in capital-intensive industries, are increasingly capital light and inventive. That elevates the need for developed-market companies to innovate and localize research and product design, rethink supply-chain management and financing, and, in some cases, partner up to gain easier access to existing infrastructure.

- In India, General Electric has devised an electrocardiograph machine that can be sold profitably for $1,500, less than one-fifth the price of traditional electrocardiograph monitors in advanced markets. The new design not only helped General Electric make inroads in the rapidly growing Indian market, but also helped it figure out how to create a monitor it could sell for $2,500 in developed markets. Learning from this experience, GE now develops more than 25 percent of its new health-care products in India—with explicit intentions to deploy them both in emerging and advanced economies.[42]
- South Korea's LG Electronics is another example of successful innovation in the Indian market. LG had struggled in India until the 1990s, when a change in foreign-investment rules enabled it to heavily invest in local R&D facilities and in top-notch Indian design and engineering talent. Local developers knew that Indians

used their televisions to listen to music. So LG introduced new models with better speakers, while swapping flat-panel displays for cathode tubes in order to keep prices down. Today, LG's product innovation center in Bangalore is the company's largest outside South Korea, and LG has become India's market leader in televisions, refrigerators, air conditioners, and washing machines.[43]

- In China's ready-to-drink coffee market, Nestlé has been able to reduce prices by 30 percent by establishing a local low-cost supply base in Yunnan and relying almost entirely on Chinese sources.[44]

- VF Corporation, one of the ten largest fashion companies in the world, redesigned the way it manages its supply chains in response to an increasingly expanding footprint. Relying on an integrated IT system, VF designed "The Third Way," in which different brands in its portfolio aggregate their sourcing needs in order to create economies of scale. The company also works closely with manufacturers so that it can produce many different branded products in a single factory. From the mid-to-late 2000s, doing so allowed VF to reduce the production cost of jeans and other apparel by between 5 and 10 percent.[45]

- As Tingyi built its business in China, it set up new plants in every province, including rural areas like Qinghai, Sichuan, and Henan provinces. The strategy was to be local at the province level in order to take advantage of low-priced inputs, labor, and tax benefits, and to adapt product, sales, and distribution strategies to on-the-ground realities.

Learn to Market and Sell Through Multiple Channels

Businesses must meet customers where they are, where they prefer to shop, and where they prefer to make decisions. For example, our research underscores the importance of in-store interaction in emerging markets. In China, nearly half of consumers make purchasing decisions in-store, compared with just one-quarter in the United States. The in-store part of the consumer decision journey in emerging markets tends to be longer and more meaningful. Chinese consumers take two months and four store visits before making decisions about big-ticket consumer electronics.[46]

However, controlling that consumer in-store experience represents an enormous challenge for many executives. The Walmart in Optics Valley

Center in Wuhan, China, would be immediately recognizable to any Westerner, with its neatly organized and brightly lit aisles featuring clothes, diapers, electronics, snack foods, and household goods—plus the tub of croaking bullfrogs in the food section. But elsewhere, the retail landscape can be unfamiliar and bewildering. In markets such as India and Indonesia, retailing is highly fragmented, with small proprietors accounting for over 80 percent of sales. By comparison, in markets such as China and Mexico, modern trade already makes up over half of all sales. You must therefore prepare to simultaneously deal with global retailers, such as Carrefour and Walmart, and with local champions, such as CR Vanguard in China and Big Bazaar in India—as well as with a fragmented array of small proprietors.[47]

Many global companies get things wrong by relying on the key-account techniques and sales teams of third-party distributors that worked in home markets. As a result, multinationals should rethink their approach in these new locations and be prepared to build much larger in-house sales operations, segment sales outlets, and devise precise routines and checklists for monitoring the quality of the in-store experience.

Coca-Cola, which has been operating in emerging markets for decades, goes to great lengths in emerging markets to analyze and segment the range of retail outlets. For each category, it generates a "picture of success"—a detailed description of what the outlet should look like and how it should display, promote, and price Coke products. The company uses a direct-sales model for high-priority outlets and relies on distributors and wholesalers when that model isn't cost effective. Coca-Cola then scrutinizes everything from service levels and delivery frequencies to where the coolers are positioned in the store. In Africa, Coca-Cola has built a network of 3,200 microdistributors by recruiting thousands of small entrepreneurs who use pushcarts and bicycles to deliver Coke products to "last mile" outlets. In China, where the logistics infrastructure is more developed, Coca-Cola sells directly to over 40 percent of its two million retail outlets and monitors execution in 60 to 70 percent of all its retail outlets through regular visits by Coca-Cola salespeople and merchandisers. Coca-Cola is not an isolated example. In markets like India, Brazil, and Africa, long-established firms such as Unilever and Nestlé use everything from handcarts to bicycle carts to floating barges to get their products to consumers.[48]

In addition to distribution, companies must figure out how to position their brands and market in these new territories. Emerging-market consumers tend to have a smaller number of brands they initially consider and are less likely to switch to a new brand later. Our recent research indicates that Chinese consumers initially consider an average of three brands and purchase one of them about 60 percent of the time. The comparable figures for European and American consumers are four brands, with a purchase rate of 30 to 40 percent.[49]

The smaller and more important initial consideration set favors brands with high visibility and an aura of trust. In order to achieve awareness and consideration, testing of messages and geographically focused campaigns will be key. Locally focused campaigns tend to accelerate network effects and make it easier for new players to generate positive word-of-mouth, which is a critical prerequisite for emerging-market success. After all, many consumers reside in countries where trust in the media is at a relatively low level. For instance, in China, positive recommendations from friends and family are nearly twice as important as they are for consumers in the United States or Britain. In Egypt, the importance is nearly three times higher.[50]

You will need to rely on customer insight and local consumer testing to decide how much you need to adapt your brands and messaging. Acer's slogan "simplify my life" worked well with electronics customers in Taiwan. But when Acer China tested it in mainland China, the message didn't resonate. In focus groups, it became clear that Acer's intended message of simplicity and value was raising suspicion about the reliability and durability of the company's products. A change in Acer's message to stress reliability rather than simplicity and productivity helped the company to build a more relevant and trusted brand and to ultimately double its market share in less than two years.[51]

Adapt Your Organization and Talent Strategy

As global players grow bigger and more diverse, the costs of coping with complexity rise sharply. In a series of surveys and structured interviews with more than three hundred executives at seventeen of the world's leading multinationals, less than 40 percent of the executives said they were better than their local counterparts at understanding the operating environment and customers' needs. Many high-performing multinationals also suffered from a "globalization penalty," scoring lower than more geographically focused companies on key dimensions of organizational health. Managing tension between local adaptation and global complexity, setting a shared vision among employees, encouraging innovation, and building government and community relationships were among the commonly cited culprits.[52]

In order to increase agility in pursuing new opportunities, to maximize chances for success, and to reduce the globalization penalty, you may need to rethink your organizational structures and processes. For a company with most of its growth potential in emerging markets, does it still make sense for the board to be dominated by English speakers and even for the headquarters to be located in Europe or North America? Furthermore, would it be unthinkable to have the general manager of the São Paulo cluster hold a similar rank as the corporate head of the European market?

Increasingly, global players have started to move their core activities closer to priority markets. But "stickiness bias" toward existing strategy and resource allocation prevents many from acting in a timely manner. ABB, IBM, and General Electric are recent examples of organizations tilting toward emerging markets.

- ABB, the Swiss engineering giant, moved the global base of its robotics business from Detroit to Shanghai to pursue its "designed in China, made in China" strategy.[53]
- IBM, which gets 64 percent of its sales outside the United States, now runs human resources from Manila, accounting from Kuala Lumpur, procurement from Shenzhen, and customer service from Brisbane for its Japan business.[54]
- General Electric, which reaps more than half its revenues from overseas, in 2011 moved its X-ray business from Wisconsin to Beijing.[55]

"In some ways, capital is easier to reallocate than people—you can sit in Brussels, look at the annual capital flows of the different businesses, and act accordingly," said Jean-Pierre Clamadieu, chief executive officer of Solvay, the Belgian chemicals company. "With people, there is always a tendency to manage in geographic or business 'silos.' That's why we have recently established a new principle: that the top 300 people in the group are corporate assets."[56] In other words, the company's leading employees will be rotated across global operations based on local needs and growth rather than remaining at the company's headquarters.

In addition to rethinking organizational structures, companies need to decide on the right level of autonomy between headquarters and new markets. Many firms still operate with cumbersome reporting lines, in which international divisions oversee country-specific fiefdoms that don't collaborate and sometimes operate in their own languages, frustrating communication. This model often leaves C-level executives at headquarters too removed to understand the speed of change and the scale of the opportunity in emerging markets.

Our observation, however, is that companies experience success when they are able to break away from the "investing in a market" mentality and give local leaders sufficient freedom to chart their own path. When LG Electronics set about increasing its market share in India by building a local subsidiary, expatriate Korean managers acted only as mentors or advisors, without the authority to make decisions.[57] Tingyi's success in China stemmed in part from its strategy of giving local management full authority to make decisions and to tailor and develop new products that cater to the needs of Chinese consumers.

Attracting, developing, and retaining top talent to lead these new-growth markets is another crucial element of a successful emerging-market strategy. Based on a recent survey of leading global companies, only 2 percent of their top two hundred employees hail from key Asian emerging markets.[58] This is in part a reflection of a scarcity of supply, but also a result of stickiness bias to existing resource allocation or unclear "employer brand" proposition in new territories. Some global firms have tackled the issue by developing clear talent propositions that differentiate them from local competitors. In South Korea, L'Oréal became the top choice for female sales and marketing talent by creating greater opportunities for brand managers and by improving working hours and child-care infrastructure. In India, Unilever has attracted top Indian talent by creating a global leadership program that includes rotation and permanent placement programs.[59]

The rise of a new class of consumers around the world is imposing a tough new set of requirements on established companies. Advantages in a home market can't be easily replicated or taken for granted in far-flung markets. But the opportunities are too large to ignore. As impressive as recent growth has been, the process is just beginning. With each passing day, more people are moving from rural areas to cities, more people are going online and plugging in, and more people are joining the ranks of the world's consumers. As a result, more organizations may find, as Clarks

Village did, that the world is beating a new, entirely unpredicted path to their doorstep—at the same time that consumers in markets previously considered closed off are acquiring a taste for the types of products they make. Smart companies that systematically rethink the way they approach, manage, and serve *all* the world's promising markets can figure out how to meet customers where they are—and where they will be.

6

—

REVERSING THE CYCLE

Resource Opportunity

IN DECEMBER 2010, MOHAMED BOUAZIZI, A TUNISIAN STREET FOOD
vendor in the town of Sidi Bouzid, set himself on fire to protest harassment
by municipal authorities. This single act became the well-known trigger for
the protests that led to the ousting of Tunisian president Zine El Abidine
Ben Ali.[1] Tunisia was simply the initial opening act of the Arab Spring,
a long-running drama that gripped the Middle East and North Africa in
2011 and 2012. Analysts pointed to many causes of the unrest that swept
through the region: corrupt dictatorships, the rising expectations and frus-
trations of large populations of unemployed and underemployed youths,
and the catalytic role of social media like Twitter and Facebook.

But the root cause may have been a much older phenomenon: sharply
rising food prices. Just as the soaring cost of bread helped lay the ground-
work for the French Revolution of 1789, ballooning commodity prices may
have helped provide the kindling for the conflagration of the Arab Spring.

As events unfolded, analysts generally overlooked the fact that countries
in North Africa and the Middle East import approximately 50 percent of
their food supply.[2] This proportion, higher than that of any other major region in the world, makes the area extremely susceptible to global food-price
inflation. In 2007 and 2008, global food prices spiked, and the United
Nations Food Price Index doubled from earlier in the decade.[3] Local food
prices soared, sending a shock wave of bread riots across Bahrain, Jordan,
Yemen, Egypt, and Morocco. A month before the fall of the Egyptian and
Tunisian regimes in 2011, the UN reported record highs for dairy, meat,
sugar, and cereal prices.[4]

The toxic cocktail of inequality, rising food prices, and climate change continues to fuel civil unrest all over the world. In 2008 alone, more than sixty food riots occurred in thirty different countries. In the spring of 2014, the UN food price index remained above a "civil unrest threshold" as defined by the New England Complex Systems Institute, above the peak observed during the financial crisis.[5] The base level of food prices, in other words, is causing serious problems even in the absence of spikes, disruptions, crop failures, and more severe droughts.

The world has made astonishing progress in lifting hundreds of millions of people out of poverty in recent years. But expensive food bills hit poor households disproportionately. According to the World Bank, rising food prices drove forty-four million people back into poverty in the second half of 2010 alone.[6] The impact of rising food prices isn't just hitting the poor in developing economies. In Britain, one of the seven richest economies in the world, the Red Cross announced in 2013 that it would distribute food aid during the winter for the first time since World War II.[7] The Food and Agriculture Organization of the United Nations reported in 2012 that the number of undernourished people in developed countries increased 23 percent between 2004 and 2012, reversing a steady decrease.[8] In the United States, five years into the economic expansion, a near-record forty-six million people receive food stamps.[9]

The increase in resource prices wasn't restricted to food, and it doesn't only affect households. From 2000 to 2013, prices for commodities related to agriculture, metals, and energy have almost doubled.[10] The industrialization and urbanization of emerging economies has triggered soaring demand for energy, food, and natural resources, at a time of increasingly difficult and costly supply. The downsides for business are obvious. Sharply rising commodity prices can eat into consumers' discretionary spending, sap manufacturers' margins, and reduce the corporate appetite to invest in new projects. A world in which prices of key resources are more volatile is fraught with peril. But as is the case with other disruptive trend breaks, this development also presents an opportunity. The returns from investments, initiatives, and attitudinal shifts that allow for the more effective and efficient production, management, storage, and use of resources will yield higher returns, provide a competitive advantage, and form the basis for new businesses. We have already witnessed this phenomenon—the fracking revolution, enabled in part by higher oil prices, contributed (along with other factors such as slowing demand) to a 40 percent decline in oil prices between June and December 2014.

Rapid food price hike in 2000s hit many economies, causing higher household spending on food and beverages

Top ten countries with highest percent change of household expenditure on food and beverage

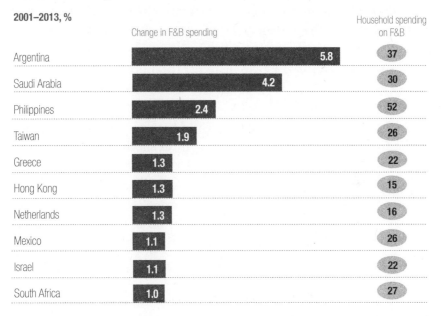

2001–2013, %	Change in F&B spending	Household spending on F&B
Argentina	5.8	37
Saudi Arabia	4.2	30
Philippines	2.4	52
Taiwan	1.9	26
Greece	1.3	22
Hong Kong	1.3	15
Netherlands	1.3	16
Mexico	1.1	26
Israel	1.1	22
South Africa	1.0	27

SOURCE: World Bank; International Monetary Fund; United Nations Conference on Trade and Development; UN; FAOSTAT; Comtrade; The Economist Intelligence Unit; McKinsey Global Institute analysis

TREND BREAK

A durable and powerful force entered the world stage at the dawn of the twenty-first century. The prices of a basket of key commodities—including energy, metals, food, and water—had fallen by almost half in real terms during the twentieth century. This remarkable development occurred despite the fact that the world's population quadrupled and global GDP per capita increased nearly fivefold.[11] The falling prices were all the more remarkable considering that rising standards of living and energy intensity helped push demand for commodities up by between 600 and 2,000 percent.[12] Significant advances in productivity—the application of steam power to mining, the widespread mechanization of agriculture, the construction of massive dams—helped humanity exert more effective control over the production, distribution, trade, and storage of commodities. Falling commodity prices served as a major tailwind, helping world economic output expand more than twenty times in the twentieth century. And with the exception of the oil crises of the 1970s, productivity in the use of resources was not a priority.

But this important trend has decisively ended. Thanks in large measure to sharply rising demand and to challenges to supply in key commodity sectors like oil and water, resource prices have doubled on average between 2000 and 2013.[13] The average price of a range of energy sources shot up by 260 percent in this period. Metals prices surged by 176 percent, copper by 344 percent, and steel by 167 percent. Food prices, which fell by an average of 0.7 percent a year during the twentieth century, rose by almost 120 percent between 2000 and 2013.

Since 2011, commodity prices have eased back a little from their peaks, prompting many observers to conclude that the supercycle is over. But reports of its death are greatly exaggerated. Between 2009 and 2013, in fact, resource prices rebounded more strongly than global economic output. On average, commodity prices in mid-2014 stood at levels that were close to 2008 peaks. We believe that four major drivers of rising prices, none of which is likely to be temporary or short lived, will keep them volatile in the years ahead.[14]

DEMAND

The first factor is sharply rising demand from the world's expanding number of middle-class consumers. As we've noted, urbanization and growth in emerging economies are bringing hundreds of millions of new consumers to the global table each year. The three billion additional people joining the global consuming class between 1990 and 2025 will have vast implications for all commodity sectors.[15] With each passing week, more people around the world are eating better. Rising discretionary incomes are driving demand for more expensive food, like beef. Beef prices jumped 117 percent from 2000 to 2013.[16] Or take demand for cars as an illustration of how nonagricultural commodities are booming. We expect the global fleet of passenger cars, which is approximately 1 billion today, to increase to 1.7 billion vehicles by 2030.[17] That means the world will need about 6.8 billion tires, give or take a few million. About 60 percent of natural rubber is used for tires. So it's no great surprise that rubber prices soared 350 percent between 2000 and 2013.[18] They are likely to climb further, especially if supply can't keep up with demand. Globally, steel production rose 82 percent

Resource prices have increased significantly since 2000

McKinsey commodity price index[1]

Real price index: 100 = years 1999–2001

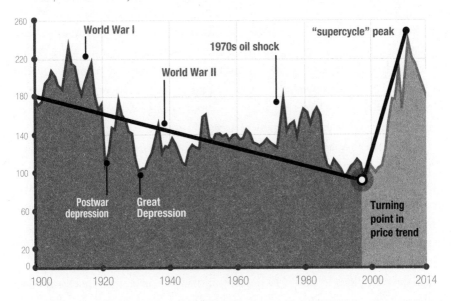

1 Based on arithmetic average of four commodity subindexes: food, nonfood agricultural items, metals, and energy.
SOURCE: Grilli and Yang; Pfaffenzeller; World Bank; International Monetary Fund; Organisation for Economic Cooperation and Development statistics; Food and Agriculture Organization of the United Nations; UN Comtrade; McKinsey Global Institute analysis

between 2000 and 2012.[19] But we expect demand for steel to increase by another 80 percent in the next twenty years, even as supplies remain limited.[20] Each year, both China and India annually add floor space equal to 3.5 times the entire residential and commercial footage of Chicago. This rapid expansion of buildings in turn fuels demand for resource-intensive infrastructure—utilities, roads, and transportation.[21] These trends are likely to power through any short-term reversals. "The integration of 2.5 billion people (China and India alone) into the global economy is producing a demand shift that is likely to put far more upward pressure on commodity prices than any technology gains are likely to offset," notes

Kenneth Rogoff, professor of economics and public policy at Harvard University. "So, for at least the next 50 to 75 years, and perhaps until humans start mining on Mars sometime in the coming centuries, prices for many natural resources are headed up."[22]

SUPPLY

Rising demand wouldn't be such a problem if supplies of commodities were increasing across the board at the same rate. But here, again, we're facing a trend break. Accessing the supply of resources needed to meet soaring demand is increasingly challenging. In many parts of the world, reserves of some resources are depleting at an accelerating rate. What's more, with the exception of shale gas, most new sources of supply are often found in places that are less easy and therefore more costly to access. For example, some reports have suggested that reserves of metals such as zinc and tin are expected to be depleted within twenty years, should current production rates continue.[23] The worldwide depletion rate of groundwater aquifers has more than doubled since 1960.[24] The boom in shale oil and natural gas drilling in the United States has captured numerous headlines—and rightly so. But in many places in the world, the oil industry is having a tough time tapping into new supplies. In 2005, 19 percent of offshore oil wells were classified as "deep water" and therefore more costly and complex. That proportion rose to 24 percent in 2009 and continues to rise.[25] In just the first ten years of the new millennium, the average price of bringing a new oil well onstream doubled.[26] (Of course, not all commodities are the same. In iron ore, for example, prices have been stable even as costs have risen. Compared with discovery-driven commodities like oil and copper, bulk commodities like iron ore and potash have shown greater elasticity in supplies.)

Other factors are helping to complicate the process of resource extraction. Historically, Chile—now a stable, relatively prosperous democracy—has been the world's leading producer of copper. But today, almost half of new copper projects are in countries with high levels of political risk.[27] Eni, ExxonMobil, Royal Dutch Shell, Total, KazMunayGas, and China National Petroleum Corporation have all been struggling for years to bring the vast Kashagan oil project in Kazakhstan online. More than 80 percent of the world's remaining unused available arable land is in countries that have either high political risks or limited infrastructure.[28] Low

Demand for many resources may rise sharply

**Additional supply needed over
twenty-year time frame**

■ Supply replacement
(at historical rates)

▨ Incremental supply

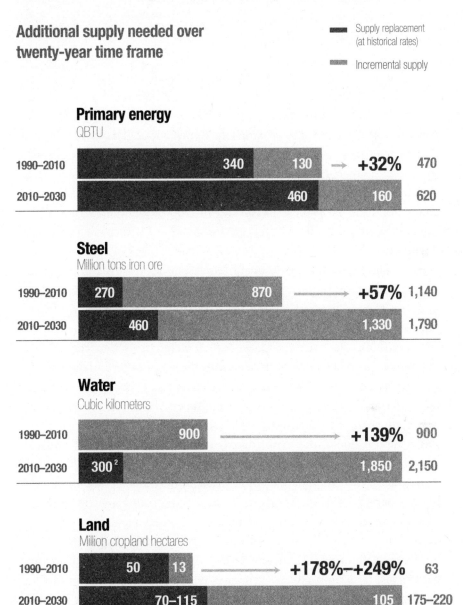

Primary energy
QBTU

1990–2010	340	130	→ **+32%**	470
2010–2030	460	160		620

Steel
Million tons iron ore

1990–2010	270	870	**+57%**	1,140
2010–2030	460	1,330		1,790

Water
Cubic kilometers

1990–2010	900	**+139%**	900
2010–2030	300[2]	1,850	2,150

Land
Million cropland hectares

1990–2010	50	13	**+178%–+249%**	63
2010–2030	70–115	105		175–220

1 Calculated as incremental supply plus replacement rate; does not tie to total demand.
2 Water supply will need to increase by a further 300 cubic kilometers to meet accessible, sustainable, reliable supply.
SOURCE: Resource Revolution report, McKinsey Global Institute

levels of spare capacity, long lead times, and costly extraction make short-term supply inelastic and drive resource price volatility.

INTERLINKING

As global interconnections rise, the world's resource markets become ever more closely linked. In many instances, rising demand for one type of commodity can lead to serious stresses on supplies of other commodities. Agriculture accounts for approximately 70 percent of global water use and 2 percent of global energy use. Feeding the world's rising population of middle-class consumers doesn't just require more beef, chicken, and grains. It requires more water, which in turns requires more energy. Energy accounts for 15 to 30 percent of the cost of crop production, 70 percent of the cost of groundwater extraction, and 50 to 75 percent of the cost of desalination.[29]

As recently as 2004, there was little relation between the prices of fuel and agricultural products. But today, thanks in part to the rising energy intensity of food production and in part to the rapid growth in the production of biofuels, oil prices can have a distinct impact on food prices. Through 2007, the prices of maize and oil were largely uncorrelated. But the two resource classes have shown a very strong positive correlation since then. When oil prices soar, farmers decide to plant more corn—and sell more of the corn to hungry ethanol producers. In effect, consumers are now competing with industry for plant-based fuel.[30]

Since oil is one of the main ingredients in plastics and other synthetic materials, higher oil prices tend to boost the prices of those products. And those prices, in turn, create upward pressure on the natural competitors, like rubber and cotton. Volatility in one market now swiftly results in volatility in others—especially as financial markets play a greater role in determining prices. Today, thanks to countless hedgers, speculators, and investors, the number of "virtual" barrels of oil, in the form of futures and derivatives, traded on global exchanges each day, exceeds the number of real barrels by an estimated ratio of 30 to 1.[31] This "market effect," enabled by the technologically advanced global financial grid, amplifies any market tremor. That's one of the main reasons oil prices collapsed in the immediate wake of the financial crisis, falling from almost $140 per barrel in 2008 to roughly $40 a barrel in 2009.[32] In March 2014, as a crisis unfolded in Ukraine, one of the world's great breadbaskets, global wheat prices soared nearly 6 percent in a single trading day.[33] The increased resource inter-connectivity in all aspects of our lives, from geopolitics to agriculture, is becoming a "new normal."

ENVIRONMENTAL COSTS

Many of the factors pushing up resource prices are internal ones—the dynamics of supply and demand and the availability of resources. But increasingly, we are seeing the impact of external factors on commodity and resource markets. For a century, the world essentially ignored the externalities and impacts of production. Now, governments around the world are taking the first steps to impose costs to compensate for environmental factors related to local resource production and for global issues such as increasingly frequent climate change events, ocean acidification, and deforestation.

The 2013 report from the Intergovernmental Panel on Climate Change concluded that its signatories were now 95 percent certain that humans are the main cause of climate change.[34] Climate-change-related damage to the environment is having a significant economic impact. Storms and drought that wreck harvests cause spikes in food prices; floods add huge costs; future-proofing infrastructure for a more extreme climate adds to an already large investment bill. Local environmental damage also creates health costs. A study commissioned by China's Ministry of Environmental Protection pegs the annual cost of damage to the country's ecosystem at $230 billion per year, or more than 3 percent of GDP.[35]

In order to prevent environmental destruction, governments are already raising taxes and imposing stricter environmental requirements on resource producers. In the summer of 2014, the United States promulgated new standards that would require the utility industry and power plant operators to cut emissions to 30 percent of 2005 levels by 2030.[36] In the future, governments may impose carbon taxes, higher emissions standards, and controls on water usage—all of which may drive up production costs.

For example, if the health and environmental costs associated with coal were embedded in the dark, powerful rock, the Brookings Institution expects that the price of coal would rise by 170 percent.[37] That would significantly alter utilities' business plans and push many companies to invest in wind production over coal. Since between 30 and 40 percent of copper and iron are mined in areas of moderate to high water scarcity—be it Chile's

Atacama Desert or Australia's parched Outback—boosting the price of water could have an impact on the cost and availability of these commodities.[38] Carbon-pricing schemes could have a similar effect on mining companies. According to Goldman Sachs, a hypothetical carbon tax of $10 per ton would have reduced mining profits by around 2 percent in 2011.[39]

Regardless of the course governments pursue in dealing with it, climate change is likely to make the supply and pricing of resources more volatile. Companies will increasingly find it necessary to build a higher level of resiliency to such changes into their business models.

How to Adapt

In the face of these pressures and powerful new trends, you'll need to rethink the nature of the challenge surrounding the production, use, and management of resources, not only as a problem to be dealt with but as an immense opportunity. Rather than taking a defensive posture and conducting business as usual until a crisis pops ups, consider the proactive, forward-looking measures you can take. Efficiency, recycling, and conservation have often been regarded as costly annoyances, especially when mandated by law or regulation. But in an age of volatile resource prices, these efforts are a competitive advantage and a requirement. As new business models and technologies proliferate, efficiency efforts can become important drivers of value and profits.

Double Down on Resource Productivity

Improving resource productivity is a large and complex agenda. Our experience and research have taught us that a host of high-potential opportunity areas lie before us, ranging from the energy efficiency of buildings to plugging water leaks and improving industrial processes. If the world were to take action on all fifteen opportunities enumerated below, it could meet nearly 30 percent of total demand for resources in 2030 and all demand growth between now and 2030—and save $2.9 trillion. Such efforts don't rely on futuristic and fanciful new technologies; all fifteen areas are achievable with the tools we have on our shelves now.[40] We do not claim that achieving these numbers will be easy, not least because they will require a lot of upfront investment, but we calculate that a capital investment of $1 trillion a year, equivalent to 1 percent of global GDP, could yield annual savings three times that amount.

Large resource efficiency opportunities exist

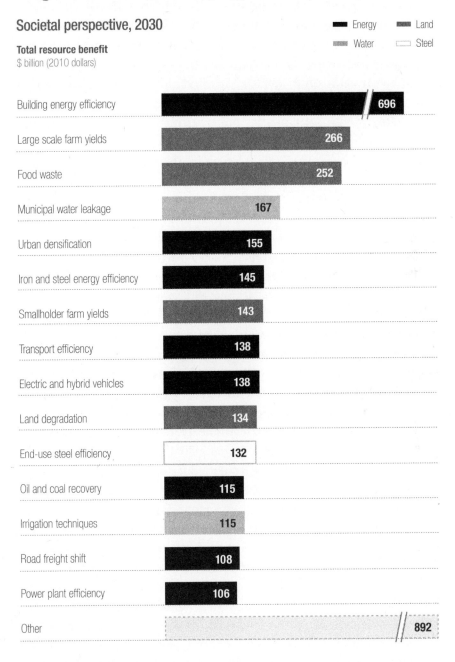

Societal perspective, 2030

Total resource benefit
$ billion (2010 dollars)

Legend: ■ Energy ▨ Land ▨ Water ▱ Steel

Building energy efficiency	696
Large scale farm yields	266
Food waste	252
Municipal water leakage	167
Urban densification	155
Iron and steel energy efficiency	145
Smallholder farm yields	143
Transport efficiency	138
Electric and hybrid vehicles	138
Land degradation	134
End-use steel efficiency	132
Oil and coal recovery	115
Irrigation techniques	115
Road freight shift	108
Power plant efficiency	106
Other	892

SOURCE: McKinsey Global Institute analysis

The biggest single opportunity is in making buildings more energy efficient through energy-management systems, heating that is sensitive to how many people are in a building, and smart water and energy meters. When Google came under fire for the amount of energy its data centers were using, the company took aggressive steps to ensure that its activities would be carbon neutral, investing in wind and solar farms, installing a seawater cooling system at its facility in Finland, covering its Mountain View campus with solar panels, and investing in efficient components. Google says that to provide its services to one typical user for a month, its servers use less energy than a light left on for three hours.[41] The market for energy-efficient buildings also represents a significant business opportunity. Enernoc, based in Boston, audits and controls the internal energy functions at hundreds of corporate offices and other institutions and enlists big users of power into demand-management schemes. Its website has a meter that tallies, in real time, how much money it has saved for consumers. In September 2014, the count stood at over $930 million.[42]

In the past, the first step in dealing with concerns over the supply of resources was to make more. That's still an important imperative. But new priorities have emerged—like figuring out how to use less and coming up with ways to make the most of current supplies. The cheapest and most available form of energy is the energy you don't use.

Reducing the amount of food already being produced that is wasted represents another immense opportunity that would both save money and significantly improve social welfare. In theory, more effective management of food resources could bring potential global saving of $340 billion by 2030. Put another way, doing so could reduce by sixty-five million hectares, or 300,000 square miles, the amount of agricultural land needed to feed the world. South Korea has been a pioneer. In 2012, South Koreans, who love *banchan* (small side dishes that diners pick at but do not always finish), wasted around 13,000 tons of food a day at a total annual disposal cost of $800 million.[43] For consumers in this wealthy country, throwing away food bore no significant financial or social cost, but the government cost of handling food waste kept increasing. When the government stepped in by charging households for food waste by weight in 2013, telecommunications company LG U+ developed a new garbage bin that can weigh waste to the nearest gram using radio-frequency identification technology. Users can only open the bins with a swipe card, and the cost of the waste disposed is charged instantly to their debit or credit card. In cities where these clever bins were piloted, food waste volume fell by 20 to 30 percent.[44] Nobody in South Korea is eating less, and food hasn't become more expensive. Rather, technology and smart incentives have nudged consumers to become more effective purchasers and managers of the food they buy.

It is common to hear investors complain about a lack of high-yielding investments. In an important trend break, efficiency efforts now have the capacity to produce significant returns quite rapidly. The scale of resource efficiency opportunities varies across sectors and businesses, but certain sectors such as consumer packaged goods show particularly large potential. Many manufacturers have saved up to 50 percent on their energy and water costs by raising resource productivity through tools that paid for themselves in less than three years. In Mexico, Walmart faced a food waste challenge, thanks to generally underdeveloped supply chains and a lack of cold-storage facilities at its suppliers. To tackle the issue, Walmart changed its unloading processes to prioritize perishables, extended credit financing to small suppliers so they could upgrade their own facilities, and invested to enhance its forecasting ability to minimize production waste. The combination of these measures helped the company significantly reduce the supply chain cost in its Mexican operations.

Move Toward a Circular Economy

In order to fully realize the benefits of resource productivity, you'll also need to reset your intuition about the life cycles of products. Rather than focus on how to divert materials from landfills, it would be far more useful to design products so that they don't have to be sent there in the first place. Every day, at factories and households around the world, over ten million tons of material are designated as waste, filling landfills, draining municipal budgets, and contributing to greenhouse emissions. Rather than continue to rely on a take-make-dispose model of material use in manufacturing, many smart companies are tapping into the rapidly developing circular economy. The circular economy creates value by better design and optimization of products for multiple cycles of disassembly and reuse. While it is hardly a new concept—people have been composting food scraps for centuries—the circular economy remains a relatively niche approach for most manufacturers. Often, such efforts may consist of only a few showcase products that constitute less than 5 percent of the overall portfolio.[45]

In order to succeed at building a circular economy, your business should focus on the logistics and economics of turning finished products back into materials: rethinking product design and creating new rent, lease, and take-back schemes that will resonate with customers and distributors. In order to truly spur the creation of robust circular economy value chains, new regulatory schemes, standards, and incentives that influence behavior beyond the factory floor may be required.[46]

The plant of French carmaker Renault in Choisy-le-Roi, near Paris, is one of the best-known examples of the circular economy in action. The factory remanufactures automotive engines, transmissions, injection pumps, and other components for resale and generates about $270 million in revenue annually. Renault redesigns certain components to make them easier to disassemble and reuse. It also targets components for closed-loop reuse, essentially converting materials and components from worn-out vehicles into inputs for new ones. To support these efforts, Renault formed joint ventures with a steel recycler and a waste-management company to bring end-of-use expertise into product design. Together, these moves help Renault save money by maintaining tighter control of its raw materials throughout vehicle life cycles. By focusing on remanufacturing used goods rather than creating new components, Renault is able to slash the energy used per unit production by 80 percent and water use by 88 percent.[47]

Companies are adopting a variant of this model in a range of industries. In an important trend break, many companies that originally kicked off recycling efforts for brand or image reasons, regarding them essentially as a kind of marketing cost, have come to consider them powerful investments. Ricoh, a global maker of office machines with annual revenues of $20 billion, designed its GreenLine series of office copiers and printers to maximize the reusability of products and components, while minimizing the use of virgin materials.[48] GreenLine products are now offered in six major European markets, where they account for 10 to 20 percent of Ricoh's sales by volume and generate margins that are as much as two times higher than those of the company's comparable new products—without a reduction in quality.[49]

The home and do-it-yourself retailer B&Q is piloting a take-back program for its power tools in a few of its stores. Customers can exchange used products for either cash or a charity donation. The company plans to refurbish the tools it collects in Europe for resale locally or to recycle them, and thus recover raw materials that could be used to make new tools.[50]

Focusing on reuse and recycling can create new businesses, especially when companies strike useful partnerships with companies in other industries. In 2013, global apparel retailer H&M launched a global garment collection initiative, encouraging customers to bring in old clothes in exchange for discount vouchers on new H&M clothing. The company then partnered with I:CO, a reverse-logistics provider, to sort the clothes for a range of subsequent "cascaded" uses—putting end-of-life material to use in other value streams and industries. Most of the shirts and socks collected are dispatched to the global secondhand-apparel market. Clothes no longer suitable to wear are used as substitutes for virgin materials in other applications—for example, as cleaning cloths and textile yarns, as inputs for damping and insulation materials in the auto industry, or for pipe insulation in the construction industry. When all other options are exhausted, the remaining textiles (1 to 3 percent, according to I:CO estimates) become fuel to produce electricity.[51] A year after the initiative began, H&M launched its first closed-loop denim capsule collection and collected more than three thousand tons of unwanted garments—the equivalent of fifteen million T-shirts.[52]

Bring Technology to the Rescue

The opportunity in resources doesn't lie only in efficiency efforts. Boosting supply aggressively can also help mitigate the downside of resource scarcity. Let's take energy as an example. Time and again in the twentieth century, technology played a vital role in overcoming logistical and geological difficulties. Today, three major areas of innovation in energy could transform the supply picture over the coming decade: oil and gas technologies, renewable energy, and advanced battery technology.

In oil and gas, hydraulic fracturing, or fracking, and horizontal drilling have enabled the large-scale extraction of gas and oil from shale rock and are already making a difference in global markets. Although fracking is controversial on environmental grounds, there is no doubting its extraordinary impact. In the United States, where natural gas production soared 25 percent between 2000 and 2013, winter gas prices have halved since 2008.[53] Driven by new technology, as we've noted earlier, the United States in 2013 surpassed Russia as the world's largest producer of hydrocarbons, and by 2020, it could become the world's largest producer of oil, according to the International Energy Agency.[54]

In addition to improving cost and access to new oil reserves, government efforts on researching and developing technology have also contributed to dramatic improvement in recovery rates of existing reserves. In effect, technology can help reset intuition surrounding acceptable and achievable benchmarks. Over the last three decades, Norway's government has heavily invested in research and technical understanding of oil-recovery issues and created monetary incentives for companies to conduct their own research. Today, Norway's industry-leading resource-recovery rate, at 45 percent, is almost twice that of Saudi Arabia.[55]

Renewable energy sources such as solar, wind, hydroelectric, and ocean power hold the promise of addressing the issue of constrained energy supply, without contributing to climate change or competing for scarce resources. Here, too, we are seeing an important trend break. For most of the second half of the twentieth century, renewable energy was viewed as a luxury or premium product, uncompetitive with traditional means of generating electricity. But the amplifying effects of globalization, technology, and scale have changed that calculus—decisively in some instances.

Thanks to competition, the rapid addition of manufacturing capacity, technological advances, and a massive increase in scale, the cost of installing solar power has dropped from nearly $8 per watt of capacity to one-tenth of that amount in the past two decades.[56] Solar and wind are increasingly being adopted at scale and by residential customers in advanced economies like the United States and the European Union. In addition, emerging-economy powerhouses such as China and India have aggressive plans for renewable energy adoption.

- In 2013, 37 gigawatts of solar capacity were installed around the world, up more than fourteenfold from 2007.[57]
- Between 2002 and 2013, the world's wind-generating capacity rose by a factor of ten, from 31 gigawatts to 318.[58] More wind capacity was installed in 2013 alone than existed in the world in 2002.

These cottage industries have become big businesses, creating large, integrated players and a network of suppliers and encouraging a host of service providers and smaller companies to enter the field.

Industrial trends are procyclical. The more renewable energy is installed, the more compelling a business it becomes. Prices are coming down, and a host of financial innovations—from solar leases to green bonds—are helping to increase the pace of rollout. If the current drive for large-scale renewable solutions continues, the sun could become the world's largest source of electricity by 2050, ahead of fossil fuels and hydro and nuclear power, according to the International Energy Agency.[59] In many parts of the developing world, the first supplies of electricity that consumers use will be carbon-free, generated by solar panels.

Building a system based on intermittent suppliers of electricity—like wind and solar—will place a higher premium on the storage and management of energy. Here, too, the combination of market forces and technology advances is presenting compelling opportunities. As energy storage technologies continue to improve, the price of batteries could rapidly decline by 2020, disrupting large sectors of the economy such as transportation, power generation, and oil and gas. Japanese conglomerate NEC is investing in a unit that supplies large-scale batteries to utilities, which can be deployed at substations or near solar plants to help maintain a regular flow of electricity into the grid.

Fuel cells provide a good example of the potential. Hydrogen can be converted to electricity with an energy efficiency rate of up to 60 percent in a typical hydrogen fuel cell. If this technology is applied in the residential sector for both heat and power, the rate can increase to 80 percent, as excess heat generated in the conversion is captured. And if fuel cells' production is scaled up, they could easily be used in cars, where they would prove far more efficient than combustion engines.[60]

Be Resilient by Design

Integrating energy storage into energy production is one way of building resilience into systems that can be rendered fragile by sudden shifts in resource supplies and prices. Adapting this mind-set in other areas will be a vital component of the intuition reset. With the exception of energy prices in the 1970s, the volatility of resource prices has never been higher. With higher correlation between the prices of oil and various commodities, many companies are trying to insulate themselves from price volatility. Companies are trying to mitigate resource price volatility by forging closer and more intelligent bonds with suppliers and customers, by engaging in more flexible product design, and by using financial instruments as a hedge. All of these approaches, which were conceived as essentially defensive moves, are useful levers for boosting profits.

A European food manufacturer was able to reduce volatility in corn prices by staggering contracting with its suppliers. Each year, the company set the price for one-third of its purchase volume over the next three years—regardless of its expectations on the evolution of the market price.

As a result, only one-third of the price that the company paid in any year was influenced by the currently prevailing market price; the other two-thirds reflected the price in the previous two years. The average price the company paid for its corn supplies remained almost constant over a fifteen-year period—but the price volatility it experienced fell by 50 percent.

Retailers and restaurant owners may be familiar with the idea of coordinating downstream to sustain resilience with a higher level of flexibility. One popular American restaurant chain decided to coordinate its procurement and marketing approach and introduced weekly specials that would change depending on the prevailing commodity price of beef or shrimp. The weekly special would be determined by whichever commodity was more advantageous to buy that week.

Financial hedging is another approach that companies have employed to gain some control over the price they pay for resources. One European dairy company found that when it was negotiating with a retail chain to sell its products, it did not know the price it would have to pay for milk at the time of future production to meet the retail contract. In fact, the price for milk could vary between 26 euros and 35 euros per ton—far too large of a swing to ignore. By purchasing milk futures on the futures market, the company could lock down the price it would pay—even if the future price was higher than the lower threshold of 26 euros—and thereby reduce its volatility effectively to zero.

Forward-thinking companies have also sometimes altered product design to account for volatility, by allowing inputs to be switched in and out at short notice—a tactic referred to as "design for switchability." Chevrolet manufactures a biofuel version of its popular Silverado 250 pickup truck. Containing a traditional gasoline tank and a container for compressed natural gas, the pickup allows users to toggle between different fuel sources, depending on availability and price. In a similar approach with "design for recyclability," another food manufacturer changed its packaging colors from lighter to darker colors to allow for more recycled plastic inputs, thereby reducing its exposure to raw plastics prices.

Plotting a resource revolution, at first blush, may seem to be a complex and costly endeavor. But as time goes on, our system will likely find that the costs of inaction are much higher. More significantly, even in the short term, businesses are discovering that the break in the trend of lower resource prices will present important opportunities—to defend against volatility and disruptions, but also to proactively improve operations, establish new lines of business, and build competitive advantages. Executives and leaders have to think deeply and ambitiously about the costs of resources, but also about how investments in better ways of producing and managing inputs like energy, water, and food can pay off. In our interconnected and growing world, many useful solutions and technologies are already being tested and proven. By taking existing technology and tools to scale, by devising new systems, and by embracing clever innovations and smart policies, you can position your organizations for success in a world of volatile resource prices.

7

—

END OF AN ERA

Farewell to Increasingly Cheaper Capital?

MUMBAI'S IMPOSSIBLY PACKED COMMUTER TRAINS ARE THE STUFF
of legend. Each day, more than 7.5 million passengers perform dangerous
acrobatics to latch onto one of the 2,300 train departures, which are often
the only viable means of transport during the monsoon season.[1] Every year,
an estimated 3,500 people—nearly 10 people every day—die in rail-related
accidents in Mumbai alone.[2] Even beyond the tragic human cost, this kind
of overcrowding, and the deficit in infrastructure spending it represents,
has the potential to derail India's impressive growth story.

And what a story it has been. Since 1991, India's GDP per capita has
increased nearly fivefold, the nation's foreign exchange reserves have increased nearly fiftyfold, and annual foreign direct investment inflows have
surged by a factor of 200.[3] Future prospects look no less bright. Estimates
are that India will rise from the tenth-largest economy in the world in 2013
to the third largest by 2030.[4] India's young and rapidly urbanizing population could become the country's "demographic dividend," fueling growth
and prosperity over the decades to come. By 2030, India could have an
urban population of approximately six hundred million, nearly twice that
of the entire United States as of this writing. India will be home to two of
the world's five most populous cities, along with sixty-eight other cities of
more than one million inhabitants each.[5]

But unless India significantly steps up investment in its cities, the infrastructure deficit may wipe out urbanization's productivity dividend. Before
the financial crisis, India's annual capital spending per capita was only 14
percent of China's and 4 percent of the United Kingdom.[6] Decades of

chronic underinvestment are evident in the country's strained infrastructure and the lack of basic services in its cities. The ranks of commuters in Mumbai are rising at three times the rate at which rail capacity is growing.[7] Power cuts are frequent, and electricity generation routinely falls about 15 to 20 percent short of peak demand. Waste and water infrastructure is sorely lacking, with over 30 percent of city sewage going untreated and one in four people living without access to piped water.[8]

Vibrant cities are an absolute necessity if India is to live up to its potential as a global economic powerhouse. But the country is suffering from a longstanding shortfall in capital investment. Just to meet urban demand, India needs to build between 700 million and 900 million square meters of residential and commercial space a year, construct between 350 and 400 kilometers of metros and subways every year, and pave 2.5 billon square meters of roads—twenty times what it has paved in the last decade. To do so, India would need to invest $1.2 trillion in capital expenditure—eight times the current per capita level—in its cities by 2030.[9]

India is by no means an isolated case. Amid a growth boom, the global investment rate as a percentage of GDP has paradoxically declined, falling from 25.2 percent in 1970s to 21.8 percent in 2009.[10] In large measure, the decline reflects the ebbing of the post–World War II investment in Japan and Western Europe. But looking ahead, weak global demand for capital is unlikely to continue. The world's major emerging economies—Brazil, China, and India—all need to increase infrastructure investment to keep up with demand being driven by urbanization and population growth. The world's low- and middle-income economies need to increase their rate of investment to meet economic and human development goals. Advanced economies need to address years of pent-up underinvestment if they are to improve the capacity and service levels of existing infrastructure. The global level of infrastructure investment needed to simply keep up with the pace of economic growth over the next two decades will rise to between $57 trillion and $67 trillion, or 60 percent more than the historical amount over the same period.[11] And rising demand for investment is but one of the factors that may conspire to push the price of capital higher.

TREND BREAK

Warning of more expensive capital in today's environment may seem like warning against drought as a monsoon rages. A simple look out the metaphorical financial window would suggest that there isn't much of a problem. Thirty years of declining interest rates have created an expectation that capital is cheap and will remain so. Our intuition also includes this expectation: most of us believed that asset prices, which are fueled in part by the ability to borrow, can only rise in the long term, volatility in the short term notwithstanding. Indeed, US home prices rose an average of 6.4 percent per year between 1968 and the mid-2000s, without a single year of decline.[12] In Brazil's two most populous cities, São Paulo and Rio de Janeiro, prices have more than doubled since 2008.[13] London home prices almost doubled in each of the last three decades.[14] Between 1980 and 2013, real house prices increased by 55 percent in Sweden, 85 percent in France, and 130 percent in Canada.[15] The combination of the weak demand for capital (driven by decades of low infrastructure investment rates) and an abundant supply of capital (driven by several years of unconventional monetary policy) have made capital today cheaper than it has ever been, a development that has underpinned rising asset prices.

But a big shift is underway, and it will require us to reset our intuition—along with our expectations about the future of capital costs and asset prices. However, while it is clear that a trend break is occurring, the direction is anything but clear. Will it be driven by the traditional view of supply and demand, in which interest rates rise? Or will it be driven by the central banks' unprecedented actions in the aftermath of the 2008 financial crisis, which have created an enduring new reality of suppressed rates? We have come through an era in which there was great certainty about interest rates—both their level (low) and general direction (down)—and about the level (high) and direction (higher) of asset prices. That trend is breaking, as experts such as Harvard economist Martin Feldstein have noted: "Long-term interest rates are now unsustainably low, implying bubbles in the prices of bonds and other securities. When interest rates rise, as they surely will, the bubbles will burst, the prices of those securities will fall, and anyone holding them will be hurt."[16]

As the emerging world continues to industrialize and urbanize, its need for investment is surging. From Kumasi to Mumbai, from Porto Alegre to Kuala Lumpur, capital-intensive building projects are being planned. As countries invest in infrastructure, the additional demand will be amplified by companies seeking to invest in new capacity, equipment, and upgrades in order to keep up with disruptive technologies. These demands on capital will coincide with an aging global population and long-term government

Central bank actions have come at the end of a thirty-year period of declining interest

Long-term interest rates in developed economies

Yield to redemption on long-term government bonds 1975–2012
%, GDP-weighted

▬▬ Nominal values
▬▬ Ex-post real values

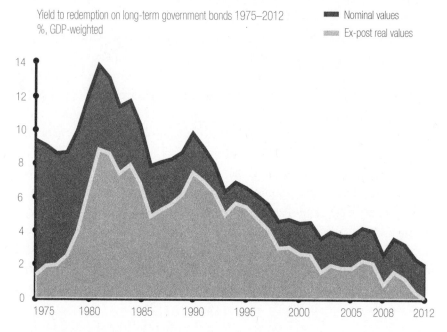

NOTE: Select advanced economies.
SOURCE: International Monetary Fund, McKinsey Global Institute analysis

deficits—which will put pressure on the world's pool of savings just as demand picks up. Based on the *traditional view* of macroeconomic fundamentals, the combination of rising demand and pressure on supply spells one outcome: *a world with tighter, more expensive capital.*

However, the unconventional monetary policy of recent years has taken us into *uncharted territory* and may have laid the foundations for a different, less easily comprehended world. It is one in which central banks and governments are always ready to step in and inject sufficient liquidity into the economy to keep it growing and keep interest rates low. Governments, of course, have been among the chief beneficiaries of these low rates. It is a world of *fragile equilibriums,* where periods of aggressive expansion of money supply may be followed by asset bubbles, inflationary challenges, and booms and busts of currencies. An increasing number of countries are exploring this new territory. In fact, we may be on the brink of transition into a world where expansive monetary policy and debt monetization—once considered taboo—become normal components of the central banks' repertoire. This version of the future could change the capital markets as we know them today and present us with a new set of challenges.

The power and fickleness of financial flows adds a further complicating factor. Global capital may be liquid, but it isn't distributed evenly. Some areas wither and suffer from a lack of capital, while others are flooded by it—with the same strange results. Consider two postmodern ghost towns. Detroit, the once-mighty industrial motor of the American Midwest, filed for municipal bankruptcy in 2012 and now finds it difficult to get financing for infrastructure on any terms. And so the vast city depopulates, with buildings falling into disrepair and weeds growing on residential blocks. Meanwhile, on the other side of the planet, Ordos, in Inner Mongolia, has attracted a surfeit of capital. The city, in the heart of a wealthy coal-mining region, has seen explosive growth in construction in the Kangbashi district—massive apartment blocks, parks, architecturally bold public edifices, two statues of humongous horses rearing up against each other. All that's missing are the projected one million people who would occupy this area. We can't always rely on the market to deliver capital precisely where and when it is needed in precisely the right amount.

Scenario 1: Higher Cost of Capital

The demand-side fundamentals paint a clear long-term picture. The global investment rate—global investment as a percentage of total global GDP—currently stands at just under 22 percent, up from the trough of 20.9 percent in 2009, at the depth of the global recession.[17] There is every reason to think that the rate of investment will continue to rise, with industrialization and urbanization of emerging economies fueling the boom.

Brazil, Indonesia, India, and China need a lot of bricks and mortar. The world's growing cities will need to double their stock of physical capital investment from nearly $10 trillion in 2013 to more than $20 trillion by 2025.[18] All the people moving to cities will need apartments to live in, roads to drive on, and schools to attend. Take Brazil's infrastructure as an example. Overall investment fell from 5.4 percent of GDP per year in the 1970s to only 2.1 percent in the 2000s. The limits of the country's infrastructure were on stark display during the 2014 World Cup, when rains flooded the sewers and streets of Recife. Brazil's transport infrastructure is decrepit—86 percent of roads remain unpaved. Compared to the United States, Brazil's rail network is less than 13 percent of the size, with about 90 percent of its landmass.[19] Even though it crashed out of the 2014 World Cup, losing to Germany in the semifinals, Brazil's soccer team retains a top ten FIFA ranking. But when it comes to quality of infrastructure, the World Economic Forum ranked Brazil 114th out of 148 countries.[20] To achieve its full economic growth potential, Brazil clearly needs to start investing in its roads, ports, and airports.[21]

Meanwhile, advanced economies around the world have pent-up demand for new infrastructure after decades of underinvestment. In developed countries, investment as a share of GDP has declined sharply since the 1970s. Between 1980 and 2008, total investment was $20 trillion less than it would have been if countries had maintained historical rates of investment.[22] That's roughly equivalent to the combined GDP of Japan and the United States.[23] The Acela, a high-speed train that connects Boston with Washington, is often slow, unreliable, and plagued by pokey Internet access. To eliminate current service deficiencies and expand capacity to keep pace with the growing demand, the American Society of Civil Engineers estimates that the United States needs to invest $1.6 trillion in infrastructure by 2020, on top of current levels.[24] The US Department of Transportation has estimated that spending on public transit will have to increase by approximately 40 percent per year to bring it to a state of "good repair" by 2028.

Overall, we calculate that through 2030, the world needs to spend an estimated $57 trillion to $67 trillion on roads, buildings, rails, telecoms, ports, and water just to enable expected economic growth.[25] That's more than the entire worldwide stock of infrastructure on the ground today—and nearly 60 percent more than the world invested between 1994 and 2012.[26] These investments, combined with the need to replace depreciated or outdated capital, will drive global total investment to $25 trillion by 2030 from $13 trillion in 2008, the peak before the financial crisis.[27]

Clearly, demand for capital is rising. What about the supply? Here, too, the potential exists for famine after years of strong harvests. In the absence of unconventional monetary policies, the long-term supply outlook is unlikely to mirror the reality of the past two decades. As the world continues to age, household savings will decline, causing a de-accumulation of assets. Age-related government spending is forecasted to increase by 4 to 5 percentage points as a percentage of GDP by 2030, further straining budget

Global investment will likely reach new postwar highs over the next decade, driven by emerging markets

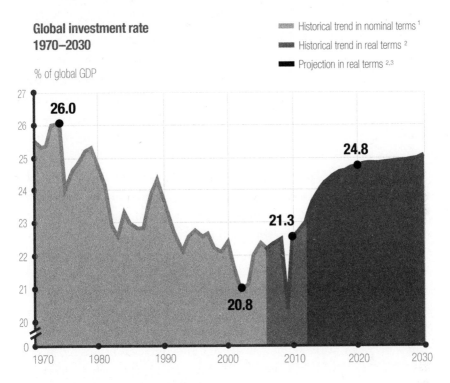

**Global investment rate
1970–2030**

% of global GDP

▨ Historical trend in nominal terms [1]
▨ Historical trend in real terms [2]
■ Projection in real terms [2,3]

26.0

24.8

21.3

20.8

1970   1980   1990   2000   2010   2020   2030

1 Based on actual prices and exchange rates of each year.
2 Shown in 2005 prices and exchange rates.
3 Forecast assumes price of capital goods increases at same rate as other goods and assumes no change in inventory.
SOURCE: Economist Intelligence Unit; Global Insight; McKinsey Global Economic Growth Database; Oxford Economics;
World Development Indicators of the World Bank; McKinsey Global Institute analysis

deficits and national saving levels.[28] Finally, emerging economies like China and India, the first- and sixth-ranked savers by total volume, may see savings rates decline as their economies rebalance toward consumption.[29]

One of the few phenomena more impressive than China's rise as an economic power has been its impressive propensity to save. The country has a relatively undeveloped safety net, and many Chinese live with fresh memories of the deprivation and desperate poverty of the 1960s and 1970s. This is one of the reasons that the Chinese people are world-champion savers, choosing to stow away their capital instead of spending it. China's savings rate rose from 37 percent of GDP in the early 2000s to more than 50 percent by 2008.[30] That year, annual savings totaled $2.4 trillion and made China the world's largest piggy bank.[31] Four years later, though the savings *rate* had not risen any further, rapid economic growth had pushed the total amount of savings still higher.

But China's savings rate seems unlikely to remain so high in the future. The government is trying to engineer a move away from relying on investment to relying more on consumption. It is encouraging citizens to spend a little more and save a little less. Should China follow the path of other Asian economies, such as Japan, South Korea, and Taiwan, its high savings rate could decline significantly. Taiwan's savings rate, for instance, dropped by 7 percentage points between 1995 and 2008 following efforts to improve public health-care and pension systems.[32]

As China's savings rate declines, the saving rates in advanced economies are likely to continue to disappoint. The rates in countries such as the United States, Australia, and the United Kingdom rose after the global recession. In the United States, for example, the personal savings rate jumped from 3 percent in 2007 to 6.1 percent in 2009, before trending downward again. But savings levels are still relatively low. And even if the current rate increases in advanced economies were to persist for twenty years, that would add only 1 percentage point to the global savings rate in 2030.[33]

By 2030, the supply and demand imbalances will lead to a $2.4-trillion tension between available global savings and the level of desired investments.[34] In the traditional macroeconomic view, such a gap between the world's desire to invest and the world's willingness to save will exert upward pressure on real interest rates and crowd out investment. That, in turn, could cause global GDP growth to slow down, unless it is offset by robust gains in capital productivity.

SCENARIO 2: A MORE VOLATILE SYSTEM

A challenge to the expected scenario of rising rates exists. In recent years, the world's central banks, led by the US Federal Reserve, have shown an increasing willingness to take interest rates into uncharted territory and to print money at an unprecedented rate. The ultraloose monetary policies triggered by the recession, the global financial crisis, and the slow recovery show no signs of being temporary. Since the start of the crisis, the central banks of the United States, the United Kingdom, the Eurozone, and Japan have injected more than $5 trillion of liquidity into their economies.[35] These actions no doubt prevented a catastrophic scenario from unfolding, but they also pushed interest rates to depths that have remained largely unexplored. And because rates have been held at such low levels for so long, they have helped created new habits that may be hard to shake. Governments across the globe became reliant on low interest rates to finance deficit spending and stimulus. For example, the combined deficits of countries around the world peaked at nearly $4 trillion in 2009.[36] But low interest rates held interest costs in check. Between fiscal year 2008 and fiscal year 2012, for example, the US government's net interest bill fell from $253 billion to $220 billion, a decline of 13 percent, even as the total gross federal debt outstanding grew 67 percent.[37]

Historically, expansive monetary policy has been a temporary measure deployed to boost consumer expenditure and corporate investments at times of slow growth. Most analysts agree that the central banks' efforts at quantitative easing over the past five years have boosted global aggregate GDP by 1 to 3 percent.[38] However, precisely *how* the central banks achieved this remains a point of debate. The impact of ultralow rates on consumer expenditure and corporate investment isn't clear. In the United States, for example, the personal savings rate in 2013 was 5 percentage points higher than the precrisis level, while the rate of business investment remains at its lowest levels since the end of World War II.[39] Did lower rates stimulate GDP growth? Rather, it appears that sharply higher government spending and a comparatively quick housing sector recovery were the main factors propelling growth. Between 2007 and 2012, the governments of the United States, the United Kingdom, and the Eurozone collectively saved nearly $1.4 trillion on lower interest payments on their debt, which allowed them to spend more.[40] Ultralow interest rates also helped the housing sector recover more quickly than anticipated.

In Japan, ultralow interest rates are nothing new. As the private sector deleveraged aggressively after the 1980s credit boom, the government ran large fiscal deficits to offset depressed demand and activity. At the same time, the central bank kept interest rates low and generally expanded its balance sheet. After two decades of low growth and continued debt monetization, Japan's annual fiscal deficit peaked in 2011 at just under 10 percent of GDP; the country's gross public debt is above 240 percent of GDP.[41] This level of debt has been sustainable because most Japanese debt is owned domestically.[42] However, Japan's demographic outlook means that the country is unlikely to be able to repay the debt traditionally, and it might need to monetize its government debt over the coming years. That is to say, the central bank will create new money in order to purchase the debt issued by the government.

Japan may not be alone. As governments struggle to find a way to deleverage in the face of increasing age-related spending and fragile growth rates, unconventional monetary policies such as quantitative easing and even permanent debt monetization may become less of a taboo among central banks and policy makers. In this new macroeconomic territory, a traditional view of supply and demand fundamentals may no longer be a sufficient indicator for the future cost of capital. As illustrated by the European Central Bank's move in the spring of 2014 to lower its benchmark deposit interest rate below zero, ultralow interest rates may remain the norm over the coming years.[43] As economists Carmen Reinhart and Kenneth Rogoff argued in a 2013 IMF paper, policy makers need to guard against overplaying the risks related to unconventional monetary support and limiting central banks' room for policy maneuvering.[44]

How to Adapt

As demand-supply dynamics change, business leaders need to be prepared to navigate both worlds. We have seen too many companies, households, and governments caught out by unexpected changes in the cost of capital.

Regardless of which scenario unfolds, you need to reset your intuition and develop more proactive and responsible ways of managing capital. Given the level of uncertainty over long-term capital costs, we've focused on five actions that will help companies emerge healthier, regardless of which scenario unfolds.

Double Down on Capital Productivity

With physical resources, it makes sense to focus on efficiency and productivity, regardless of market prices. The same holds with capital resources. You can create a better hedge for the future by improving capital productivity (the rate at which fixed capital generates output and returns). It can be done by defining explicit strategies for capital allocation, focusing on timely and efficient project delivery, reengineering products and processes, and adapting procurement, sourcing, and working capital terms.

Nowhere will the pressure to improve productivity be felt more than in capital-intensive industries such as mining, oil and gas, and real estate. Our analysis of more than 40 recent megaprojects (exceeding $1 billion in original capital expenditure investments) shows that over 80 percent wound up costing more than anticipated. On average, the capital ultimately invested was more than 40 percent higher than the original plan contemplated.[45] In recent examples, Gorgon, the huge Australian liquefied natural gas plant, and the mammoth Kashagan oilfield in Kazakhstan have proven to be huge headaches for their developers, with cost estimates for the latter rising to five times the originally budgeted amount.[46] If interest rates stay constant, cost overruns can quickly gobble up potential returns.

Should interest rates rise, overruns can prove fatal. Based on our experience across sectors, a combination of project reprioritization, shortening of project life cycles, and tight project execution can deliver as much as a 10 to 25 percent reduction in spending and a 20 to 50 percent reduction in delays.[47] A real estate company in the Middle East, for example, reduced cycle time by 30 percent for a $500 million tower project by taking advantage of lean management techniques—such as performance dialogues and war rooms—and prefabricating forms for beams and construction joints. These efforts allowed it to avoid $50 million in penalties for time overruns, while reducing the overall cost.[48]

When money becomes more expensive, not tying it up unnecessarily becomes more crucial. The just-in-time delivery processes pioneered by Asian manufacturers were, at root, efforts to avoid tying up capital unnecessarily in parts and supplies that would sit idle on factory floors. Today, Japanese and Korean automakers are increasingly adopting a "capital-light" approach to product design and processes. Already, product derivatives and capacity buildup in new markets account for 90 percent of capital expenditures by the typical carmaker. In the future, the demand for capital expenditures is likely to become even more important because of changes in the external environment. The fragmentation of customer demand is leading to a 30 to 50 percent increase in the number of new car models, particularly those that require local adaptation.[49] Innovation in PowerTrain Technologies is driving new R&D investments as well as spending for next-generation engine plants. Regulatory requirements for fuel efficiency are fostering the development of new technologies and materials (such as composites and aluminum) and driving new capital expenditures for plant and tooling upgrades. Competition sharpens these trends. In the five-year period ending in 2012, Asian carmakers reported a ratio of capital expenditures to revenue that was 30 percent lower than that of their European counterparts.[50]

Many companies can also seek to optimize their working capital productivity by adapting collection terms or cutting inventory. Take Tesla as an example. By requiring customers to pay $2,500 to $5,000 to make a reservation for purchase, the electric car manufacturer not only obtains a clearer view of the demand pipeline but minimizes the working capital necessary to run its operations.[51] In effect, Tesla has managed to get its customers to provide its working capital. In December 2013, Tesla held customer deposits in excess of $160 million.[52] Amazon, as another example, keeps only the fastest-moving items in stock in all of its distribution centers, carefully using advanced technology to pick the right items and stock levels. Taking immediate payments from customers and paying its suppliers with a month delay, Amazon operates with negative working capital. In the fourth quarter of 2013, Amazon reported accounts receivable of $4.77 billion and accounts payable of $15.133 billion, giving it a "float" of more than $10 billion of extremely cheap capital.[53] If the top 10 global retailers had Amazon's cash conversion cycle, they would collectively save over $150 billion in working capital.[54]

Tap into New Sources of Capital

Working on capital productivity enables you to make the most of the internal resources of your business, as does making the most of the widening array of external capital resources. Traditionally, getting access to capital meant having a good credit rating and nurturing relationships with major financial institutions in financial hubs such as London, Tokyo, and New York. Now, however, it means tapping into other large pools of capital, such as sovereign wealth funds (SWFs) and pension funds, and using digital platforms for peer-to-peer lending and funding crowd sourcing.

Given that the bulk of the increased demand for capital will be for long-term project financing in sectors such as infrastructure and real estate, executives and leaders will increasingly need to seek out pools of patient capital. Investors, such as pensions and sovereign wealth funds, could supply such capital. In doing so, they could capture higher profits than they could investing in government bonds, while maintaining hedges against inflation. Across all investor classes, SWFs have shown the fastest increase, with 10 percent annual growth and assets under management estimated at $3 trillion to $5 trillion in 2013.[55] The pension funds landscape is much larger, with roughly $32 trillion in assets under management in 2013, and more mature as well.[56] The growth outlook remains strong, driven by emerging economies and expected rises in interest rates.

Some entities, like Saudi Arabia's SWF, have kept a conservative profile, with the majority of their assets in secure government bonds and equities. Others, however, have embarked on surprisingly aggressive investment strategies. Many SWFs have participated in high-profile trophy deals in areas such as real estate, infrastructure, mining, retail, and entertainment. Two UK landmarks—the department store Harrods and the Shard, London's tallest building—are now part of the Qatar Investment Authority portfolio.[57] So, too, is the soccer team Paris Saint-Germain FC, which has acquired superstars like Sweden's Zlatan Ibrahimović and Uruguay's Edinson Cavani and has reemerged as one of Europe's leading powers.[58] Norway's SWF, with more than $800 billion in assets, directed more than 60 percent of its capital into equity markets with an increasing focus on high-profile real estate.[59] In 2013 alone, it bought 45 percent of Times Square Tower in New York and 47.5 percent of One Financial Center in Boston through a joint venture with MetLife.[60] It is considering moving investments to assets like wind and solar plants, as well as other infrastructure investments. Some SWFs are adapting investment strategies that more closely resemble those of private equity funds than passive index funds. Temasek, a Singaporean SWF that manages over $170 billion, in 2014 invested $5.7 billion in the A. S. Watson health and beauty group. Since its foundation in 1974, Temasek's portfolio has included everything from shares in shoemakers to a bird park.[61]

Digital platforms are also opening access to new sources of capital. These are often of particular interest for smaller companies that do not have access to more traditional capital sources such as public markets and bank loans. Peer-to-peer lending and fund-raising platforms such as Kiva and Kickstarter know no national borders. Kiva, a web-based platform that allows users to lend money to people around the world, has reached over 1.2 million lenders, intermediating more than $600 million in loans.[62] Since its founding in 2009, Kickstarter, a crowd-sourcing platform for creative projects—from movie documentaries to board games—has coordinated $1.3 billion in pledges from more than 6.9 million people.[63] Among the notable projects funded on Kickstarter was the *Veronica Mars* movie, a sequel to the television show, which raised $5.7 million from more than ninety thousand "backers."[64] Alipay, the payment processing company launched in China by e-commerce giant Alibaba, has a unit that provides financing to small businesses.[65]

Exploit New Commercial Opportunities

Companies with access to privileged sources of capital will have a clear competitive advantage. Considering that more than 70 percent of global growth—and associated new investment opportunities—will come from emerging markets, gaining exposure to these growth markets and understanding their capital restrictions and financial regulation is becoming essential for investors. Just as trade in goods and services is increasingly connecting nodes in the developing world to one another, so too is the trade in money. Companies can significantly benefit from embracing this "cosmopolitan capitalism" by seeking out new providers of capital, opening up to global markets, and adapting governance rules to international standards.

Interesting examples of cosmopolitan capitalism can be seen in both developed- and emerging-world companies. Between 2010 and 2012, India's second-largest telecom operator, Reliance Communications, sought and received about $3 billion in loans from several Chinese banks. The interest rates it paid, as low as 5 percent for portions of the debt, were significantly below the rates Reliance would have had to pay to Indian banks.[66] In 2011, private equity giant TPG reached a deal to sell 5 percent of itself to Kuwait and Singapore SWFs.[67] In 2010, a group of SWFs joined the Ontario Teachers' Pension Plan, one of Canada's largest pension funds, to invest $1.8 billion in BTG Pactual, one of Brazil's largest investment banks.[68] Firms with large balance sheets—and cash on hand—could become new investors of capital in these sorts of partnerships.

The benefits to borrowers of persistently low interest rates are obvious: companies and governments will be able to lock in cheap long-term borrowing. Those that act quickly can benefit by refinancing when interest rates fall. But a rise in the cost of capital can create other types of opportunities. Higher interest rates will offer higher returns on investments for many companies. Another benefit is likely to be reduced pension liabilities. As interest rates increase, the expected rate of return on investment increases because the short-term increase in interest payments is outweighed by the long-term appreciation in capital. This reduces the hurdle to funding defined pension plans. For instance, when interest rates increased in

2013 in the wake of the Fed's tapering announcement, Ford Motor Company was able to narrow its $9.7 billion pension plan funding gap by about $4 billion, dwarfing its increased interest expenses of $50 million.[69] In 2013, S&P 500 companies reported a collective pension funding gap of $355 billion, the largest on record so far.[70] Most of these large companies with unfunded defined benefit pension plans will see their funding gaps shrink as interest rates rise.

Retail banks can also adapt their business models to capture new opportunities. For long-term investments, banks can capitalize on existing corporate relationships and underwriting skills and can facilitate the syndication of loan deals on behalf of large institutional investors or partner with governments to create public-private lending institutions. For small and medium enterprises, banks can double down on services related to the provision of working capital or tap into the growing peer-to-peer lending space. Early moves are already taking place, with peer-to-peer lenders such as Lending Club and Funding Circle creating strategic alliances with Union Bank and Santander, respectively, to create new credit products for their customers.[71] In the summer of 2014, Lending Club, which was valued at $4 billion in a private fund-raising round, filed for an initial public offering of at least $500 million.

Cope with Risk Through Flexibility

The uncertain outlook and increased prospect of volatility means companies have to be more circumspect, agile, and opportunistic when it comes to making plans about capital. They have to think about it more like other resources or inputs. Since greater risk surrounds the direction of interest rates, companies may find it necessary to rely more on hedging as a form of insurance. In industries where volatile resources are a vital input, it is common for firms to engage in financial transactions that put both a floor and a ceiling on the price they'll have to pay. Airlines often hedge their jet fuel costs, Pepsi guards against fluctuations in the market price of sugar, and hog farmers use pork belly futures to mitigate their financial risk. Hedging may result in giving up some potential gains if prices of an input unexpectedly fall. But it also allows companies to protect themselves from being blindsided by unexpected changes, permits them to engage in rational planning, and provides peace of mind. More organizations will have to think about capital and money as an input with a potentially volatile price path—and consider ways they can hedge and control its cost.

Businesses must also be willing and able to pivot between the length of funding maturities and different sources. In May 2014, Caterpillar issued a fifty-year bond at a relatively high interest rate, while continuing to access shorter-term borrowing from banks and money markets. That same year, Électricité de France issued a one-hundred-year bond. While the rates for such ultralong-term debt are higher than short-term rates, they function as a form of near-permanent capital whose price will be fixed for several decades. Just as manufacturers are well served by diversifying and having redundancy built into supply chains, the same may hold for the supply of capital.

Change the Mind-Set

Regardless of the future direction of the cost of capital, there's a final way in which individuals, households, and companies will need to reset their intuition. Households that are used to seeing rapid asset price increases may need to increase their savings rate to account for slower increases.

One of the best ways for companies to prepare for short-term change is to plan for long-term trends. Companies that take a short-term view of the future of capital run the risk of being caught off guard if the cost of capital changes over time. A world in which 80 percent of companies feel pressure to demonstrate strong financial performance over a period shorter than two years is of particular concern for public companies, which tend to belong to large asset owners such as pension funds.[72] Outside investors and market pressures often drive publicly held companies into a "quarterly capitalism" rut. Given that companies borrow, invest, and make capital decisions over ten- and even thirty-year periods, this is problematic. Companies will need to revisit their mind-set for making investment decisions so they can create more value over the long run.

To lead these changes, asset owners will need to define long-term objectives and risk appetites more carefully and structure their portfolios accordingly. A probable consequence will be higher capital allocation in more illiquid assets that focus on long-term value creation, even if they suffer from temporary negative shocks. Singapore's sovereign wealth fund GIC, for instance, looks at a twenty-year horizon when it focuses on opportunities in Asian emerging markets, regardless of their short-term volatility.[73]

Companies can also help their investors to focus on long-term horizons by providing other metrics to analyze their performances. To bolster its strategy of a combined decentralized door-to-door sales force and higher quality, Brazilian cosmetics company Natura published data such as sales force satisfaction and training hours per employee. Sports retailer Puma decided to publish an analysis of its exposure to health and safety issues through subcontractors, addressing the demand for transparency on a risky dimension of the industry.[74]

———

As we've noted, the significant change surrounding the price of capital now lies in the uncertainty over its near-term path. To a large degree, the global economy is still navigating a body of water that has been transformed by significant additions of liquidity. It is difficult to be certain about whether the flood will quickly subside—pushing interest rates up—or will linger. Regardless, companies can reorient their thinking, practices, and competencies in ways that will help keep their ships watertight.

8

—

THE JOBS GAP

Overcoming Dislocation in the Labor Market

ABOUT THREE DECADES AGO, A CURIOUS TREND STARTED TO UN-
fold in the global labor market, especially in developed countries. The
trend was particularly striking in the United States, whose labor market,
with 155 million people, is the world's third largest and one of its most
flexible and dynamic.

In the 1950s and 1960s, the United States enjoyed a boom in prosperity
triggered by economic reconstruction, growing trade, and rising domestic
consumption. Millions of high school–educated American men found stable, well-paying jobs, many of them in an expanding manufacturing sector.
They were joined by American women, whose participation in the labor
force began to climb soon after the war and rose to a peak in the 1980s.
By and large, people finished high school (and occasionally college) and
joined the workforce with a steady job with decent pay and benefits. Their
careers often ended with the same companies where they started. During
recessions, layoffs tended to be temporary. Companies wanted to hold on
to well-trained workers so they'd be available when demand bounced back.

As a result, until 1991, the US economy displayed a fairly predictable
cyclical pattern. After every recession, once GDP had recovered to its prerecession level, the labor market would recover its prior peak employment
level in another three to six months. This happened following the frequent
recessions after World War II, in 1969, 1973, and 1981. But after the 1991
recession, which was relatively brief and shallow, the economy didn't recover the lost jobs until fifteen months after GDP regained its prerecession peak. Analysts and pundits wrung their hands and called it a "jobless

recovery," and the slow pace of jobs growth may have cost George H. W. Bush his chance at reelection. But 1991 turned out to be only a sign of things to come. After the next recession, in 2001, also quite shallow and brief by historical standards, recovering all the lost jobs took thirty-nine months. The jobless recovery had turned into a jobless expansion. Then came the financial crisis of 2008. Following the Great Recession and subsequent sluggish recovery, it took forty-three months after GDP had fully recovered for the labor market to restore all the lost jobs. Put another way, employment didn't regain its prerecession peak until June 2014—six and a half years after the recession began and five years after it ended.[1]

American-style jobless recoveries have been seen in other advanced economies during the past thirty years: Canada in the mid-1990s; Germany in the early 2000s; France in the mid-2000s; Australia, Sweden, and several other advanced economies since 2009. These are all examples of advanced economies that have struggled with jobless growth. In 2013, the European Commission announced that recovery in economic activity in the EU would "translate only gradually into job creation." In January 2014, the International Labor Organization warned that global unemployment was climbing despite an uptick in business activity. In the United States, the grinding years of low job growth have taken their toll on the dynamic American labor market. Real median household income has been essentially flat for twenty-five years.[2] Youth unemployment is at record levels. Lower-skilled workers have faced the brunt of these changes. Many have left the workforce altogether; America's labor force participation in 2014 was lower than at any time in the past thirty-six years.[3]

What happened? Armed with new technologies—information tools and machines that substitute for labor—and the ability to tap into the vast, newly engaged labor pools of China and India, companies in advanced countries have been able to maintain or even increase productivity during times of growth and in downturns. In the two most recent US recessions, in 2001 and 2008–2009, reduced employment accounted for 98 percent of the decline in GDP, while productivity was barely affected.

But labor markets have not proven to be as flexible as companies. We have witnessed a series of convulsions. Routine clerical and factory tasks have been automated. The labor market has steadily bifurcated, with menial low-wage jobs on one end and high-skill, high-wage careers on the other. Technology and competition from emerging markets have undermined those in the middle. Yet at the same time, companies report wide labor gaps in sectors ranging from health care to technology and fret about the future availability of workers with the necessary skills. The factors that have been creating widespread labor market dislocation have been around for some time. But the financial crisis and the ensuing recession exacerbated them and brought them into sharp relief for all to see.

TREND BREAK

Today we stand on the edge of another trend break. This one is driven by technological churn. The technologies that automated millions of routine transaction jobs (such as clerical work) and production jobs (such as assembly-line work) are now rapidly encroaching on high-skill interaction jobs as well—jobs that require personal interaction, problem solving, and a range of critical thinking skills. The information tools that helped improve productivity are now being used to disaggregate jobs into specialized tasks that can be scheduled down to the hour of a workweek with flexible labor and can increasingly be done remotely. And as technological churn renders new skills outdated at an ever-faster pace, new skill gaps are showing up more often and in more places, increasingly decoupling labor supply and demand.

Because technology is changing jobs across sectors and geographies, employers around the world need to reset their intuition about whom, where, and how they recruit; how they can use technology to substitute for skills, not just personnel; and how they adapt their ways of working. The jobs the US economy finally recovered in June 2014 are very different in nature from the ones that were lost, and they are part of a very different labor market. Technology is not only automating ever more jobs and worsening skill gaps for the jobs that remain; it is changing the very nature of work itself—and giving us an ever-shrinking window of time to adapt.

TECHNOLOGY CHANGING THE NATURE OF WORK

The use of technology to automate human work really took off when advanced machines started to replace many production jobs on the factory floor. In the second half of the 1990s, technology began to replace many routine transaction jobs as well. Jobs such as typist and switchboard operator, once significant sources of employment, have largely disappeared. Between 2001 and the peak of the recession in 2009 in the United States, more than three million production and transaction jobs disappeared. Production jobs have been impacted by the pressure to redesign processes to improve productivity; meanwhile, technology has automated many manufacturing processes and enabled the rise of lean operations. Advances in transportation and communication have enabled the outsourcing of manufacturing and assembly functions to low-cost locations. Transaction jobs, such as bank teller and retail cashier, have been streamlined, automated, and, wherever applicable, replaced with self-serve systems such as ATMs, kiosks, and self-service checkouts.

Today's most valuable workers undertake business activities that economists call "interactions"—the searching, coordinating, and monitoring required to exchange ideas, goods, and services. Specialization, globalization, and technology are making interaction work a critical element of success in developed economies. Interaction jobs range from relatively low skill (corrections officer, home health aide) to very high skill (surgeon, salesperson, lawyer). In the same period when nearly three million production and transaction jobs disappeared, nearly five million new interaction jobs were created in the United States. Many of these were in "nontradable" sectors, including health care, education, and government services—sectors that produce goods and services almost exclusively for domestic customers and thus are hard to export or import.

In addition to impacting job creation and job substitution, technology is increasingly allowing employers to redesign and disaggregate work and to reassign routine tasks to lower-skill employees. In every interaction job, there are hundreds of different tasks, many of which do not require interaction or do not require interaction by the most highly skilled talent. These tasks can be studied, captured, and standardized. Once routine, low-value-added tasks have been identified, they can be assigned to other workers—often to those who have lower skills or whose labor is less expensive. This trend is particularly visible in health care. Chronic disease management (such as counseling on lifestyle, diet, and exercise) can be assigned to middle-skill health workers like nurse practitioners rather than to physicians. Corporate human resources organizations are finding that basic calls on the specifics of coverage can be reassigned to an HR shared services center so that HR professionals can focus on tasks like talent development and building corporate culture.

The workplace itself is also being disaggregated. As the center of the labor force moves from production and transaction jobs to interaction jobs

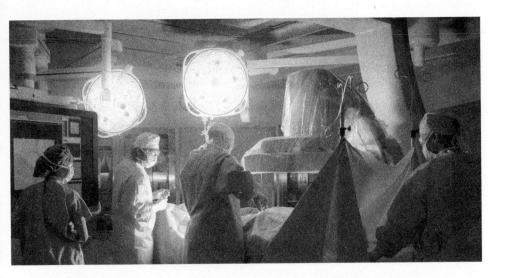

Most job growth in mature economies involves complex interactions. not routine production or transaction work

New jobs created in the United States, 2001–2009

Million employees

4.8

-0.7

-2.7

Interactions
Exchanges involving complex problem solving, experience, context
(e.g., lawyer, doctor)

Transactions
Exchanges that can be scripted, routinized, automated (e.g., bank teller, retail cashier)

Production
Process of converting physical materials into finished goods (e.g., factory worker, farmer)

SOURCE: US Bureau of Labor Statistics; McKinsey Global Institute analysis

that can be conducted remotely, companies are increasingly experimenting with ubiquitous telecommunication technologies and flexible work arrangements. Most of the reservation agents at JetBlue, the upstart airline that has evolved into an international player, work at home.

Powerful platforms, driven by technology and innovative business models, are changing the very definition of jobs for many people. Just as online platforms like Amazon and eBay have connected purchasers of consumer goods with manufacturers of consumer goods, new platforms, apps, and websites are connecting purchasers of services to service providers—in entirely new and disruptive ways. Lyft, a rival to Uber, allows people to transform themselves into professional drivers at their own convenience using their own vehicles. Airbnb, the wildly popular service that matches travelers with people who have spare rooms for rent in their homes, has allowed tens of thousands of people to work part-time as very small-scale innkeepers and hoteliers—on top of an existing job, or instead of it. Start-ups like oDesk, TaskRabbit, and Elance have established online marketplaces for a range of services from software development to basic cleaning and running errands. Increasingly, work is not a place people go to at the same time and place every day; it is something they do under an expanding array of new arrangements.

Shifting Goalposts and Skill Gaps Everywhere

The story of skill gaps is no longer a new one, but over the next decade, it will become a familiar one. Around the world, a shortage of approximately 40 million high-skilled workers and 45 million medium-skill workers may emerge, by 2020, alongside a surplus of 95 million low-skilled workers. If the previous era was defined by millions of workers in China joining the global labor force, the next era will see skill gaps emerge even in China—as its number of young workers shrinks by nearly 50 percent between today and 2030 and the country falls short of high-skilled workers by 23 million.[4]

"Skills security" also seems to be eroding. Continually and rapidly shifting job requirements are a feature of today's labor market, thanks to the influence of technological change. Twenty years ago, basic computer and Internet skills were an extra, not a base-level requirement. Today, it's difficult to find a job description that doesn't include proficiency in MS Word, Outlook, and PowerPoint, while many also require familiarity with more sophisticated accounting, database, and web-design software.

Even in science, technology, engineering, and mathematics, the so-called STEM fields, where quick churn in job requirements is common, companies and workers are struggling to cope. It's as if Moore's law applies to the technological requirements for employment. Every two years or so, workers must master a new set of tools: the web, e-commerce, social media, and so forth. As big data emerged as the next big opportunity in sectors ranging from finance to government, both the talent supply and employers' understanding of the skills they need struggled to keep up. "There aren't enough data scientists, not even close," said Sandy Pentland, a computer scientist and management thinker at MIT. "We tend to teach people that everything that matters happens between your ears when in fact it actually mostly happens between people." Pentland argues that the lack of data scientists makes it more difficult to fully apply the technology.[5] More than two-thirds of companies are struggling against limited or no capabilities in data analytics techniques.[6]

The story is not restricted to data analytics positions. In the United States, demand for skilled factory workers increased 38 percent between 2005 and 2012, according to The Conference Board.[7] As they recover from the hits they took during the Great Recession and preceding years, manufacturers can't simply rehire the employees they let go in those lean times. Because they have invested significantly in computers and technologically sophisticated production, they increasingly need factory workers who can operate computer-based machines.[8]

In a 2012 survey by the McKinsey Center for Government of more than 2,700 employers around the world, 39 percent said skill shortages were a leading reason for entry-level vacancies and more than a third said that a lack of skills was causing significant business problems in terms of cost, quality, and time.[9] It's not enough to simply encourage people to get a college degree. Rapidly growing China is having difficulty absorbing the seven million college graduates it produces each year.[10] While this is partly because the economy's growth rate is slowing, China is also not producing enough qualified people in high-demand majors such as information technology, finance, and accounting. So a paradoxical situation has arisen—a shortage of high-skilled labor amid a difficult job market for college graduates.[11]

The same contradiction can be seen in countries known for the flexibility and excellence of their higher education systems. In the United States, which is still suffering from chronic underemployment, there were 4.8

million unfilled job openings in October 2014. A survey of nearly five thousand US college graduates in 2013 found that about 45 percent said they were in jobs that didn't require four-year degrees.[12] Engineering majors may find themselves receiving multiple job offers while other college graduates might end up unemployed.

How to Adapt

The contradictions and gaps in labor markets won't resolve themselves. With physical resources, the blunt instruments of higher prices and incentives often help resolve the problems of supply. But human resources are more complicated. As technology further accelerates the decoupling of labor supply and demand, recurring skill gaps will become a norm. Governments, companies, and individuals will need to reset the way they think about labor markets, where to find workers, and the relationship between technology and work. They will need to focus on developing the skills and institutions needed to keep up with changing technologies. And in order to respond in an agile way, companies will also need to explore new pools of talent and keep recruiting and training practices up to date. The interaction between future employers and public-sector institutions also needs to intensify, to make sure all parties can spot and address imbalances early.

Tap New Pools of Talent

Nearly two-thirds of companies in the United States report having positions for which they often cannot find qualified applicants, with STEM fields topping the list. But only 15 percent of US graduates pursue majors in these fields. In China, STEM graduates account for 42 percent of degrees, while 26 percent of India's graduates major in STEM fields.[13] The two countries expect to add over two-thirds of the entire global increase in STEM graduates by 2030.

Such geographical disparities are increasingly common even on a regional and city basis. Pittsburgh, home to Carnegie Mellon University and a thriving technology industry, produces many more engineering graduates than does Philadelphia, a city in the same state less than 140 miles away. When making corporate location decisions, it is important to monitor education, aging, and wage trends so that companies can accurately assess the availability of talent. Private-sector firms like PayScale provide some of these services, but increasingly, local and regional economic development

The world is likely to have too few high-skill workers and not enough jobs for low-skill workers

Gap between supply and demand of
workers by educational attainment, 2020E

 % of supply of skill cohort
■ % of demand for skill cohort

Million workers **SHORTAGES**

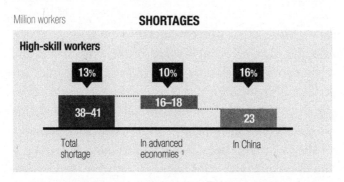

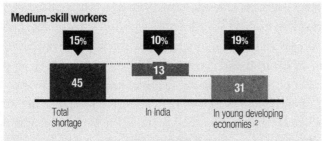

SURPLUSES

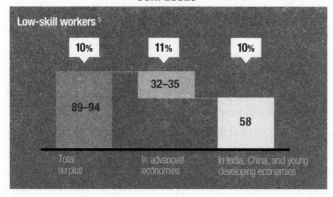

1 Twenty-five countries from the analyzed set of seventy countries, with 2010 GDP per capita greater than US$20,000 at 2005 purchasing power parity (PPP) levels.
2 Eleven countries from the analyzed set of seventy countries, from South Asia and sub-Saharan Africa, with 2010 GDP per capita less than $3,000 at 2005 PPP.
3 Low-skill defined for advanced economies as no post-secondary education; for developing economies, low skill is primary education or less.
NOTE: Numbers may not sum due to rounding.
SOURCE: McKinsey Global Institute analysis

agencies provide such data to attract potential investors. In addition to sizing the pools of appropriately skilled workers, it is necessary to assess the quality of local educational systems and the market dynamics that determine wage differentials. This analysis will become increasingly granular, down to knowing the number of college graduates and workers with specific training in cities around the world. Your business can gain an advantage by using this data to create maps of global skills supply, which will inform decisions about where to invest.

Business leaders are increasingly aware of these differences and tap into the global labor pool to address their needs. Many companies attract overseas talent through relocation incentives and progression opportunities, by establishing an attractive "employer brand," and by relocating parts of their organizations to places where the right talent is in abundant supply. In Silicon Valley, where the demand for STEM talent is soaring, executives are lobbying to expand quotas for temporary worker visas.[14] Some companies are aggressively considering establishing overseas offices so that they can import international talent more easily through internal transfers.[15] In the IT sector, global giants are increasingly turning their attention to technical talent in Central and Eastern Europe, which in 2011 topped India in the number of new outsourcing facilities set up. Wrocław, Poland, long dependent on heavy industry, is experiencing a renaissance in part because companies like HP have set up shop there. HP's Wrocław center, opened in 2005, now employs more than 2,300 workers, more than twice the number the company had expected.[16]

In addition to looking abroad, companies could tap into growing pools of underused talent at home: older workers, women, and youth. A lack of innovative work arrangements and cookie-cutter hiring practices means that these groups often remain overlooked by employers. Smart innovation with this labor pool could be a differentiator.

Companies like Etsy exemplify how technology can be used to tap into new labor pools, create viable businesses, and start to compensate for some of the traditional production and transaction jobs being lost to technological gains and globalization. An e-commerce platform founded in Brooklyn, New York, in 2005, Etsy seeks to replicate the concept of vintage markets. Profitable since 2009, it hosts one million active sellers. Sellers can get access to virtual storefronts for 20 cents per item and sell their handmade artisan products—hand-printed linen pillows, Tibetan leather Boho wrap bracelets—to customers across the globe. In 2013, it enabled transactions worth $1.4 billion, up 63 percent from 2012. More significantly, Etsy has

Graduation rates in science and engineering vary widely

College graduates with Science, Technology, Engineering or Mathematics
(STEM) degree

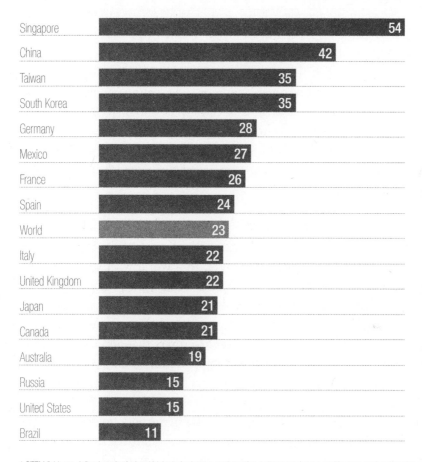

% of 2008 graduating class[1]

Singapore	54
China	42
Taiwan	35
South Korea	35
Germany	28
Mexico	27
France	26
Spain	24
World	23
Italy	22
United Kingdom	22
Japan	21
Canada	21
Australia	19
Russia	15
United States	15
Brazil	11

1 STEM fields are defined as physical and biological sciences, mathematics, computer sciences, architecture, and engineering.

SOURCE: National Science Foundation, Science and Engineering indicators 2012, First University Degrees by selected region and country/economy: 2008 or most recent; Singstat; McKinsey Global Institute analysis

found a way to utilize resources such as human ingenuity, crafting skill, and entrepreneurial energy that had previously lain dormant. About 70 percent of Etsy's sellers don't have full-time traditional jobs. In 2013, Etsy launched the Craft Entrepreneurship program, which helps chronically underemployed people turn their craft and manufacturing skills into supplemental income.

Etsy's growth is a testimony to the potential of underemployed talent. On its US site, some 88 percent of sellers are women; in the country more broadly, only 57 percent of women participate in the labor force.[17] Around the world, we can see similar efforts starting to work. In Japan, Toyota is recruiting retiring employees to work in part-time production roles. Diageo, the global beverage company, has worked for years with Tomorrow's People, now an independent UK-based charity, which targets disengaged youth and the long-term unemployed. Diageo's predecessor company, Grand Metropolitan, set up Tomorrow's People in 1984 as GrandMet Trust, with a goal of filling the space in between government, companies, and job seekers. The organization provides young people with sector-specific training, connects them with employers, and helps improve school performance. To date, it has helped more than four hundred thousand of the long-term unemployed find jobs, education, or training at Diageo and at other companies. Over three-quarters of those who find jobs remain employed after a year.[18]

Rethink Technology

Technology has traditionally been thought of as an effective way to substitute for labor and reduce labor costs. In a world with increasing skill shortages, the focus will need to shift to using technology to make the most of the skills that workers have and to improve their productivity. For instance, retailers that invested in bar-coding devices made their staff at checkout counters more efficient. Manufacturers that adopted computerized numerical control lathes for turning and milling eliminated the need for manual measurement and readjustment. Smart technology devices used by low-skill workers can equip them to perform higher-skill jobs. For example, as part of a financial inclusion program, introduction of technology allowed twenty thousand less-skilled workers in southern India to work as rural banking agents, processing payments with smart cards, cell phones, and kiosks.

Using technology to improve the productivity of professional and managerial work has traditionally not received as much attention as it has for more labor-intensive occupations. Research, however, is showing that organizations could realize improvements in knowledge-worker productivity by about 20 percent.[19] Using social platforms as a primary way to communicate and collaborate would vastly reduce the time it takes to write and answer e-mails, eliminate lengthy searches for internal knowledge and expertise, and reduce other tasks that consume the equivalent of a day's work per week. So far, few corporations have been willing to commit fully to social technologies, which require a level of open communication and information sharing that challenges existing norms. Atos, a French IT services company, is one of the few exceptions. The company has a vision to become a zero e-mail company, and it uses social community platforms to share information and knowledge instead. The company estimates that employees spent 25 percent of their time seeking information or expertise, and in the first weeks after the new social platform launch, it saw a 20 percent reduction in e-mail traffic volume.

Technology also has an exceedingly important role to play in educating and training future generations of workers. In South Africa, for example, the government and Nokia pioneered the MoMaths program, which allows thousands of students to do their math homework and revisions on Mxit, a mobile social networking platform used by millions of young people. The students receive immediate feedback on multiple-choice practice exercises and can compare results with classmates around the country. From a pilot involving 260 students in three provinces in 2009, the MoMaths program grew rapidly, to 14,000 students at 150 schools by the end of 2013.[20] Interim evaluations in 2010 showed that participants' math ability rose by 14 percent, and a very high proportion of students—82 percent—reported studying math after school.[21] In Pakistan, mobile operator Mobilink partnered with UNESCO and Bunyad, a nongovernmental organization, on a pilot in a rural area of southern Punjab that helps women and girls with basic literacy on a prepaid mobile phone. Users receive text messages on a variety of topics, including religion, health, and nutrition, and they practice reading and writing down the messages and responding to their teachers via SMS (short message service).[22]

Disaggregate and Cross-Train

Companies and workers alike must reset their intuition around what constitutes a job. The specific components and requirements of longstanding positions will be critical for both individuals and companies. Both have to understand the concept of disaggregation—the de-skilling and elimination of jobs, such as replacing a bank teller with an ATM. However, as the skill level required for high-skill jobs keeps rising, the disaggregation of very complicated positions may actually create new middle-skill specialties. For example, in health care, rising costs and the growing shortage of primary care physicians could be addressed by separating less technical parts, such as routine tests and flu shots, and reassigning them to nonphysicians. In the process, new health-care jobs are created and the higher-skill professionals have their time freed for more valuable work.

There are other potential benefits as well. Research in the United Kingdom found that reversing the current 60:40 ratio of doctors to other employees in primary care clinics would be more efficient and raise the quality of care. In the United States, disaggregating primary care could reduce growth in health-care spending while opening up new jobs for people with less than a four-year college degree—if professional practice regulations can be updated to allow such innovation. This type of shift has already occurred in the legal profession. In the 2000s, jobs for paralegals and legal assistants grew at 2.5 times the rate that jobs for attorneys did, shifting the overall composition of employment in the sector.

Disaggregation of more complex tasks can give rise to new businesses and recruiting models. Amazon's Mechanical Turk is a website where businesses can find workers to do simple tasks such as writing product descriptions or identifying people in photographs. Positions requiring higher skills can be filled on platforms such as InnoCentive's challenge platform and topcoder, where people compete for software development and digital asset creation work.

While disaggregation can help companies improve productivity, cross training and resisting the temptation to overspecialize can add a further edge, given the pace of change in demand and supply of labor. The Spanish grocer Mercadona cross-trains employees to perform a variety of small tasks, from ordering merchandise to performing inventory checks. When stores are crowded with shoppers, employees focus on customer-related tasks, and then spend their time on back-office efforts when traffic dwindles. The company recorded 18 percent higher sales per employee than other grocers in Spain in 2008. In 2011, as Spain reeled from a devastating economic downturn, Mercadona hired 6,500 additional employees, more than any other Spanish company. In a highly challenging economic climate, the company's sales and profits rose 8 percent and 20 percent, respectively, in 2011.[23]

Get More Involved in Education

The interaction between governments, companies, and educational institutions seems like an obvious step to address some of the ongoing skill shortages. Many people assume that putting up a sign or placing a help-wanted ad will attract the appropriate applicants with the appropriate skills. But that is not how it works in practice. Increasingly, companies have to take an interest in how their employees are prepared for the workplace. Seventy percent of employers that directly offer training and reach out to young people do not have difficulties in hiring the talent they seek, according to a survey conducted in 2012. In contrast, only a quarter of companies that fail to interact with job candidates continue to experience difficulty in finding people with the right skills.[24]

Brazil's oil and gas sector shows how it can be done. Even though it is sitting on rich deposits of oil and gas, this country of more than two hundred million people does not have enough talent to exploit its resources to their fullest potential. To address this problem, Petrobras, the state-owned energy giant, and Prominp, a coalition of dozens of government agencies, private companies, trade associations, and labor unions, work together to develop a five-year personnel projection in specific skill areas such as shipyard welding, pipefitting, and petroleum engineering. Prominp then identifies the best providers to codevelop a curriculum with selected companies to meet those needs. Petrobras pays the majority of the costs, while the government covers the rest. Prominp has trained more than 100,000 people since 2006, and more than 80 percent of those who have gone through its programs are employed. The auto, tourism, advanced manufacturing, and shipbuilding industries all offer examples of employers "prehiring" young people—essentially guaranteeing them a job if they complete a rigorous program.

In the United States, a consortium of companies and community colleges has engaged in a similar effort. Under the Automotive Manufacturing Training and Education Collective, auto manufacturers and educational institutions designed a series of programs. Automakers listed every task they needed performed and the competencies associated with them and ranked them by importance. Together with community colleges, they designed a curriculum of sixty study modules, spanning three to eight weeks, focused on specific skills. Employers can choose to have workers they hire get training from providers in all or some of the 110 competencies.

To meet these needs, governments clearly need to ensure that education systems are producing people with the skills they need to find jobs. As governments look for ways to respond to labor market needs, new opportunities come up for industry to partner with the public sector. In the United Kingdom, the National Career Service is a centralized hub of labor-market information published by the Commission on Education and Skills and the Sector Skills Councils. The website features comprehensive job profiles with information on salaries, hours required, qualifications, industry trends, and training programs. Since its launch in April 2012, it has received more than a million visits and enabled 270,000 face-to-face sessions. Colombia's Labor Observatory, set up in 2005, collects data on the graduation and employment rates of every education provider in the country. Young people can view this information at the national, regional, state, and city level and can see the performance of previous students—whether they went on to further training, which institution they attended, what they studied, when they found employment, what their starting salaries were. A teenager in Medellín, for example, can look up the economics course at the local university and have a well-informed view of his future prospects.

The changes in the labor market are among the most difficult to manage for both corporate leaders and individuals. Most adults were brought up to believe that their schooling would provide them with the credentials and skills needed to get started and advance in the workplace. But that's no longer true. Many people over forty already work in companies, and even industries, that didn't exist when they graduated from college. And none of us can say with certainty that we will be working in the same industry, the same position, or the same company ten years from now. The industries that are being created will require skills and capabilities that we may not even comprehend today. And simply staying current on the latest trends and technology will require constant education and skills maintenance. Indeed, the very definition of a job as we understand it today may change beyond recognition as machines produce more goods and services. The scale of technological change, the disruption in the way we work, and the mismatches between skills and jobs are all daunting challenges in the new global labor market. But they're not insurmountable. Every time a new technology revolution has unleashed its powerful forces, humans have figured out a way to adapt, find new endeavors, and prosper. That, at least, is one long-term trend that is not breaking.

9

—

FROM MINNOWS TO SHARKS

Rise of New Competitors and a
Changing Basis of Competition

SINCE ITS FOUNDING IN 1995, EBAY, THE ONLINE MARKETPLACE FOR the sale of goods and services, has been at the epicenter of changes in the global competitive landscape. A platform that started out allowing people to trade used Beanie Babies and baseball cards has evolved into an international bazaar where everything from small cities (Bridgeville, California, has been auctioned three times since 2002) to a $28,000 partially eaten grilled cheese sandwich bearing an image of the Virgin Mary changes hands.[1] The $2,642 worth of goods that trade on eBay every second symbolizes the peer-to-peer business opportunities it has enabled for small businesses.[2]

By 2002, when eBay grew to become a $1 billion revenue business, many believed it to be unstoppable.[3] With its low transaction costs and overhead, eBay forged a business model that could scale rapidly—and posed a threat to a host of retailers. In 2003, eBay, fresh off its success in the United States, plunged into the nascent Chinese e-commerce market. By 2005, according to *Forbes*, eBay had one-half of the country's $1 billion e-commerce market. "A bunch of small competitors are nipping at our heels," said Meg Whitman, then the chief executive officer.[4] Among them was Alibaba, started in the apartment of a former teacher named Jack Ma. Worried that eBay might encroach on its core business-to-business market, Alibaba in 2003 launched a competing consumer-to-consumer auction site named Taobao ("digging for treasure").[5] Since those early days, China's e-commerce market has evolved into a vast ocean, and Alibaba is now the great white shark at the top of the food chain. In 2006, Taobao overtook eBay's EachNet and became the leader in the Chinese consumer-to-consumer market, and the company has rolled from strength to strength.[6] Alibaba's blockbuster $25 billion initial public offering, on the Nasdaq in September 2014, attracted hordes of investors.[7] According to its IPO filing, Alibaba boasts 231 million active buyers and earned $6.5 billion in revenues in the last nine months of 2013 alone.[8] At the end of November 2014, Alibaba's market capitalization stood above $270 billion, above Facebook's and quadruple eBay's.[9]

Disruptive forces are combining to transform the very nature of global competition in virtually every sector. Online players are no exception, and disruptors such as eBay often find themselves disrupted before they enter adolescence. The industrialization and urbanization of emerging economies is powering a new breed of formidable corporate giant that is rapidly gaining prominence on the world stage. As the world becomes more interconnected, the speed at which emerging-market companies can mount their assault on world markets is accelerating. Technology is shifting the balance of power between large, established companies and smaller, nimbler start-ups, moving value from sector to sector and blurring the boundaries between them, mandating a redefinition of whom you view as competitors. Rather than focus on local rivals you know intimately, start becoming familiar with upstarts you've never heard of, based in towns and cities you've never visited, working on platforms on which you've never stepped, and deploying advantages that may be difficult to replicate.

TREND BREAK

For large parts of the twentieth century, the global competitive landscape resembled a steady, slow-moving game. The terrain was dominated by developed-world giants—especially North American and European companies—that had dueled with their well-known competitors for decades. In those days, it was Ford versus General Motors, Coca-Cola versus Pepsi, Nestlé versus Hershey, Burger King versus McDonald's, *Time* versus *Newsweek*, Barcelona versus Chelsea. Year after year, titans slugged it out for dominance, and the rosters didn't change much. Roughly two-thirds of the companies listed on the Fortune 500 in the 1960s were still there fifteen years later.[10] When a new entrant did come onto the scene, it was most likely a well-known competitor from an adjacent region or country or from an adjacent sector. GM and Ford had long anticipated Volkswagen's entry into the US market during the 1950s. In Brazil, for example, GM, Ford, Fiat, and Volkswagen together held more than 90 percent of the domestic car market during the 1960s and 1970s.

During the last few decades of the twentieth century, however, the dynamic began to change—with a definitive trend break in the first decade of this century. First, emerging-market companies began to grow with the industrialization in their domestic economies, gaining scale and mass. The global ascendance of Japanese firms like Sony, Toyota, and Panasonic in the 1970s preceded the rise of companies from South Korea and Taiwan in the 1980s and China in the late 1990s.[11] After holding steady at just over twenty companies between 1980 and 2000, the number of Fortune Global 500 companies headquartered in emerging markets rose 50 percent by 2005, doubled by 2010, and doubled again by 2013, reaching 130.[12] MGI's projections suggest that emerging economies will be home to half of the Fortune Global 500 by 2025. Walmart, IBM, Coca-Cola, and Exxon-Mobil are still on the list. But so, too, are CNOOC, Cemex, and Petronas. The growth of global trade and financial interconnections is enabling these emerging-market giants to grow and enter new markets around the world.

Secondly, technology is fueling competitive churn and shortening the life spans of established companies. Life at the top of the corporate food chain increasingly resembles the bleak way in which Thomas Hobbes memorably defined human existence without organized communities: "nasty, brutish, and short." The average company's tenure on the S&P 500 fell to about eighteen years in 2012, down from sixty-one years five decades earlier.[13] It's no longer sufficient to regard large firms as potential competitors; start-ups with access to digital platforms can be born global, scale up in the blink of an eye, and disrupt long-standing rules of competition in markets ranging from taxi services to hotels and retail. Many of these micro-multinationals are upending competition by bringing about a new "sharing economy" in hospitality (Airbnb), transportation (Lyft), and even home Wi-Fi rentals (Spain's Fon). Technology has leveled the playing field between large and small players and increased companies' willingness to enter new markets and expand into new sectors. Microsoft took fifteen years to reach $1 billion in sales.[14] Amazon reached that mark in fewer than five years.[15] Netflix is no longer merely disrupting content distribution, but is also becoming a formidable force in original content production. Zipcar and other car-sharing upstarts are not only disrupting the car-rental business, they are also challenging traditional car ownership models. This raises an important point about the changing basis of competition. In previous decades, companies didn't just know their competitors intimately; they recognized the *way* they did business. At root, General Motors, Volkswagen, and Ford were engaged in the same endeavor—using assembly lines to turn steel, plastic, and rubber into vehicles. Today, however, as technology continually allows for the creation of entirely new platforms, incumbents may not have any familiarity with the mechanics, business models, and competencies of their new competitors.

The acceleration of emerging-economy growth, technological change, and global interconnections since the early 2000s has created a trend break in the world of competition. It is no longer a slow-moving board game played by large firms in adjacent sectors and regions. It now more closely resembles a fast-moving video game in which new competitors emerge, seemingly instantaneously, from any part of the world and any sector of the economy, and can gain mass and scale in a heartbeat. Established firms, long used to the old rules of competition, will need to reset their intuition to compete effectively.

THE RISE OF EMERGING-MARKET COMPETITORS

The first wave of global competitors to Western firms rose out of the ashes of postwar Japan. In the 1960s and 1970s, many US and European incumbents faced the rise of Japanese companies. By 1965, Japanese companies in chemicals, plastics, and other industrial sectors were listed in international rankings of the largest sector participants. By 1980, South Korean groups such as Hyundai and Samsung joined the ranks of global industrial conglomerates.

As companies from Japan and then Korea began to move up the value chain, a second wave of emerging-market competitors entered the global scene, following the early stage of industrialization in these countries. Large companies in natural resources, construction, manufacturing, and commodities appeared on the global playing field during the late twentieth century from China, Brazil, and other emerging countries. Oil and gas companies such as China National Petroleum, Sinopec, Gazprom, and Petrobras took their place alongside giants like ExxonMobil, Shell, and Total. These emerging-markets giants offered a taste of how global the competition in other sectors could become. In mining, basic materials,

By 2025, emerging regions are expected to be home to almost 230 companies in the Fortune Global 500, up from 130 in 2013

Evolution of the Fortune Global 500 [1]
Number of Fortune Global 500 companies

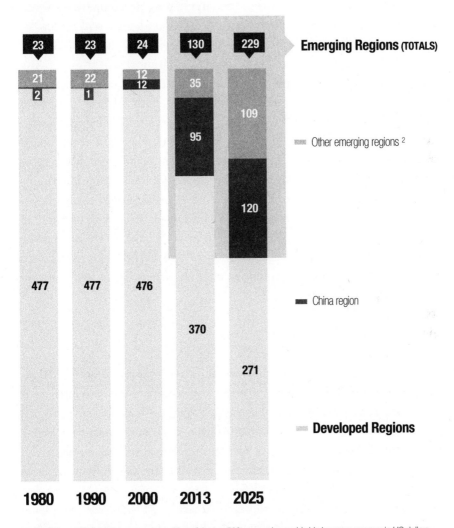

Emerging Regions (TOTALS)

Other emerging regions [2]

China region

Developed Regions

1980 1990 2000 2013 2025

1 The Fortune Global 500 is an annual ranking of the top 500 companies worldwide by gross revenue in US dollars.
2 Shares of emerging regions excluding China and Latin America combined until 2000.
NOTE: Fortune Global 500 share in 2025 projected from revenue shares of countries in 2025.
SOURCE: Fortune Global 500; MGI Company Scope; McKinsey Global Institute analysis

and minerals, emerging-market companies such as Brazil's Vale, Russia's Norilsk Nickel, and China's Shenhua Group already control about half of worldwide sales. The comparable figure is approximately 40 percent for the global construction and real estate industry.

Next came the current, third wave, bigger and fiercer than ever before. Emerging-market companies that grew to dominate hugely populous local markets have already long surpassed the scale of their developed-world counterparts. Bharti Airtel, the largest telecom company in India, has roughly 275 million mobile customers in South Asia and Africa. By contrast, AT&T, the largest telecommunications company in the United States, has 116 million wireless customers.[16] Mumbai's Tata Group employs more than 580,000 people worldwide and is now one of the largest private-sector employers in the United Kingdom, with nineteen companies and over 50,000 workers.[17] Our research suggests that emerging-market companies are growing more than twice as quickly as their counterparts in developed economies.[18] Over the coming decade, the GDP of emerging markets may increase by a factor of 2.5, which will reset the global competition landscape. Seven out of ten of the new "billion-level" companies—firms with annual sales of more than $1 billion—are likely to be based in emerging regions. The number of large companies based in these countries could increase from 2,200 today to around 7,000. If that holds true, China alone will house more large companies than either the United States or Western Europe by 2025.[19]

MINNOWS AND SHARKS

Technology is also shifting the balance of power from large, established incumbents to small businesses, start-ups, and entrepreneurs. In global markets, size has typically not only been an advantage—it has been a necessity. In the 1990s, it was virtually impossible for small enterprises to compete in markets around the world or to scale up operations to a global level immediately. In the vast commercial ocean, the sharks would easily mow down the minnows. Today, however, minnows are increasingly chasing and getting the better of sharks, thanks in large part to the rise and power of new technological platforms such as Alibaba and the UK government's procurement portal.

In an important trend break, technology has allowed small, nimble attackers to compete with large, established companies. Start-ups today can

Emerging market companies are growing faster across the board

Revenue compound annual growth rate 1999–2008, percent

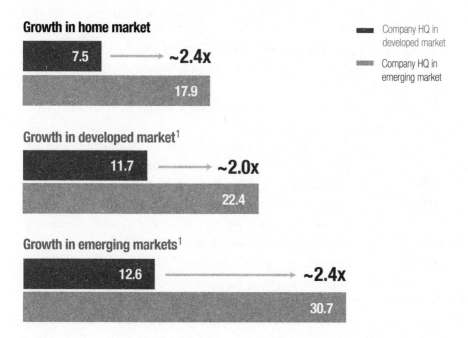

Growth in home market

7.5 ····▷ ~2.4x

17.9

■ Company HQ in developed market

▨ Company HQ in emerging market

Growth in developed market[1]

11.7 ····▷ ~2.0x

22.4

Growth in emerging markets[1]

12.6 ····▷ ~2.4x

30.7

1 Other than home.

plug into enormously powerful global platforms with the same ease as a large corporation and can expand to millions of customers in a matter of a few years, if not months. The success of "sharing economy" start-ups such as Airbnb and Lyft exemplifies the way technology is removing barriers to entry and scale, allowing part-time individuals to compete with established players. Waze, an Israeli community-based navigation mobile app, grew from zero to more than fifty million users in less than five years.[20] In June 2013, Google—the ultimate shark in the app and mapping space—paid a reported $1 billion to acquire Waze. Another example is TransferWise, a UK start-up offering a peer-to-peer money-transfer service in seventeen different currencies.[21] TransferWise grew from zero to over $1 billion in transactions in less than four years, threatening the established business model of currency exchanges and money-transfer providers.[22]

Large institutions often find themselves caught off guard and unable to pivot fast enough. Many find themselves paralyzed by complicated processes and large legacy IT systems that often delay execution for months, if not years. New competitors can buy state-of-the-art systems off the shelf and install them in a matter of weeks. Three-D printing allows start-ups and small companies to "print" highly complicated prototypes, molds, and products in a variety of materials with no tooling or setup costs. Cloud computing gives small enterprises IT capabilities and back-office services that were previously available only to larger firms—and cheaply, too. Indeed, large companies in almost every field are vulnerable, as start-ups become better equipped, more competitive, and able to reach customers and users everywhere.

Because it is so easy for minnows to take on sharks, companies that not that long ago disrupted entire industries must constantly pay attention to other disrupters. Expedia, which launched in 1996, grew to become the largest travel company in the world, reaching $4.8 billion in revenues in 2013.[23] By aggregating prices, data, reviews, and payment options, the web-based start-up constituted an important new platform that changed the basis of competition in the industry. But Expedia and its peers now face disruption from a new type of business model represented by Airbnb, the peer-to-peer hospitality site. Airbnb's millions of customers can research, reserve, pay for, and review lodging at hundreds of thousands of locations without needing to interact with Expedia's platform. Technology giants such as Facebook and Google must also be aware of new entrants. Snapchat, a photo-messaging app that enables senders to set a time limit for how long receivers can view their "snaps" (pictures), was started in 2011. By 2014, its users had proved more prolific snappers than those on Facebook and Instagram, with four hundred million pictures shared every day.[24] WhatsApp reached five hundred million active users and handled over ten billion messages per day in 2014, prompting a $19 billion acquisition by Facebook, a move that was as much defensive as it was a strategic expansion.[25]

BLURRING LINES

Technology has long blurred the boundaries between physical and online consumption, shifting value from books to Kindles and from CDs to iTunes to Spotify, where users can stream music without ever formally taking ownership of it. As information technology has given consumers an ever-greater ability to compare prices and products, companies have been forced to cut margins in their traditional businesses—and search for new opportunities. Companies are increasingly expanding into new sectors to exploit their privileged access to technology, data, or customers or to simply reinvent themselves in the face of disruption. The endless and rapid disruption imposed by technology is leading to some unlikely pairings. As Carlos Ghosn, the chief executive officer of Nissan, has perceptively noted, "Business schools may prepare people to deal with internal crises. But I think we need to be more prepared for external crises, where it's not the strategy of the company that is in question; it's the ability of leaders to figure out how to adapt that strategy. We are going to have a lot more of these external crises because we are living in such a volatile world—an age where everything is leveraged and technology moves so fast. You can be rocked by something that originated completely outside your area."[26]

In the early 2000s, UK auto insurers were caught off guard by the rise of price-comparison websites such as Confused.com. By tilting the balance of power away from traditional insurers, the aggregator sites grew their market share from zero to over 50 percent of new insurance policies in a decade.[27] With increased price transparency and consumers shopping around, many traditional players have struggled to make money on core underwriting in UK motor insurance ever since. In response to the success of online aggregator sites, nontraditional players such as Google have started to take notice and experiment in the space. In a live poll at a recent Digital Insurer Event in the United Kingdom, 75 percent of responders worried about the likes of Google representing the biggest threat to the industry.[28]

In addition to the new online players, traditional insurers now also have to worry about car manufacturers encroaching on their playing field. As smart car technology advances, car manufacturers such as Citroën are announcing plans to fit black boxes into all new vehicles of certain models. The use of telematics technology allows companies to monitor driving habits such as distance traveled, speed, and braking behavior—and better understand customer behavior as a result.[29] Whether car manufacturers will become major insurance players remains to be seen, but insurers such as Allianz have already entered into partnerships to mitigate the threat.

In media, technology has long shifted value between players and blurred boundaries between adjacent sectors and distribution channels. Netflix is an example of a company that has managed to thrive as the basis of competition shifts quickly. Originally a subscription service sending DVDs of movies through the mail, Netflix quickly pivoted to a content-streaming company when online video caught on. Then, as competition arose in online video distribution, Netflix decided it needed to get into the content creation business. In 2012, eager to give its twenty-four million customers reason to keep subscribing, Netflix partnered with director David Fincher and production firm MRC to air *House of Cards,* a deeply cynical, high-quality drama series starring Kevin Spacey as an immoral politician. The show, an adaptation of a British series of the same name, attracted audiences that rivaled those of popular cable television shows, with viewership of about three million in the United States alone.[30]

How to Adapt

Adapting to the changing nature of competition isn't easy, particularly for companies that built their culture, strategy, and processes in the old world of global competition. The question for most executives today isn't *if* they will get disrupted but when, by whom, and how severely. It is of paramount importance that your business expands its thinking beyond the traditional competitor set, monitors the growth of new competitors, and strives to understand the economics and business models of new industries. In addition, spend the time and mental energy to develop a new clarity about your own assets, core competencies, and competitive advantage. The most successful executives will choose the right allies and be prepared to take decisive action—even if it means disrupting their own businesses.

Understand and Monitor the New Ecosystem

You'll need to track up-and-coming business hubs in emerging regions. Small- and medium-sized cities across the emerging world pose a particular blind spot. But they are the ones that give rise to the most dangerous future competitors. For example, Hsinchu, in northern Taiwan, may not be a household name, but it is already the fourth-largest advanced electronics and high-tech hub in the China region, home to thirteen large company headquarters. Similarly, Santa Catarina is not yet on the radar of most executives. But the prosperous state in southern Brazil has incubated and housed the biggest chicken processor in the world (BRF), the world-leading maker of refrigeration compressors (Embraco), the leading Latin American clothing textile company (Hering), and the largest Latin American electric motor manufacturer (WEG Indústrias).

Technology-based start-ups pose unexpected challenges to some industries that need to be monitored. But what's the best way to keep tabs on young upstarts and the revolutionary ways in which they are doing business? Some large companies are using the accelerator model to stay close to potential disruptions. General Electric's GE Garages is a pop-up lab incubator that provides start-ups with access to high-tech equipment such as 3-D printers, computerized numerical control machines, and laser cutters. The start-ups get access to equipment and GE's technical and managerial expertise, and GE can move quickly when new technologies reaches maturity.[31]

GE is not alone. Samsung runs accelerators in Silicon Valley and Tel Aviv. In July 2014, Disney invited eleven technology and media start-ups to join its accelerator program. BMW's iVentures incubator houses companies such as Life360 and ParkatmyHouse.com. Microsoft Ventures supports start-ups through a community of mentors, providing funding to early stage firms and using seven accelerators around the world to speed up successful launch and scale.

Tap the Power Within

The disruptive nature of the new competitive landscape means that traditional players need to deploy all assets at their disposal. As a result, it is crucial for incumbents to take another look at their assets and unique positions.

In an environment of increased competition in the automotive industry, German premium car manufacturers have relied on a multifaceted approach—strong brand heritage, superior car quality, strong organization skills, and accelerated innovation in materials, software, and connectivity.

BMW, for instance, enhances the customer experience through features such as remote-control services, including a mobile app that lets users set the interior temperature of the car, find where it's parked, and check if the doors are locked remotely. The company is the first major OEM (original equipment manufacturer) to produce carbon-fiber cars on a large scale for its i series. The BMW i3's technical capabilities include a parking assistance feature that allows the car to park itself at the push of a button.[32] Daimler's Mercedes-Benz E- and S-class cars have steering assistance and "stop & go" features that enable the cars to autonomously navigate traffic lights, roundabouts and other vehicles on the road.[33] In 2014, Audi introduced Audi Connect—a state-of-the-art software package with 4G connectivity, picture navigation, and multimedia functionality—in its Audi

A3 models in 2014, partnering with AT&T in North America to do so.[34] Such product enhancements, added to an already powerful brand heritage, have allowed premium German automakers to ward off rising competition, with Mercedes, Audi, and BMW all hitting record sales in 2013.[35] Put another way, in an era when automakers around the world can make solid, functional vehicles at a relatively low cost, German automakers have decided to compete on the basis of information technology, apps, software, and customer experience—rather than relying solely on the superiority of their chassis and power trains.

Form Alliances

Finding partners is crucial to thriving in an era in which the basis of competition is shifting rapidly and traditional business models may quickly become uprooted. Smart alliances that can provide a hedge for the future, quick access to new capabilities, or help pivoting the existing business model will be increasingly vital.

The traditional telecommunications industry faces uncertainty, as new competition cuts into margins and new technology brings both challenges and opportunities to existing business. While WhatsApp and similar message mobile apps are increasingly capturing the SMS market, traditional players are struggling to survive. Increasingly, they are seeking to change the basis of competition by viewing their expansive mobile networks and customer bases as platforms for providing other services. This mind-set of traditional players places a higher premium on striking smart partnerships.

In emerging markets, mobile reach often exceeds banking access. In countries like Argentina, Colombia, and Ukraine, for example, virtually everybody has a mobile phone, but less than half the population has bank accounts. As messaging apps threaten to disintermediate their core business, telecommunication companies have partnered with banks to offer new payment channels. In Kenya, Safaricom, East Africa's largest mobile telecommunications provider, partnered with Commercial Bank of Africa to launch m-pesa, Afric'a first SMS-based money transfer service, in 2007. (The *m* is for mobile, and *pesa* is Swahili for "money.") In its first eigtheen months of existence, m-pesa gained four million users, many of whom don't have bank accounts and rely on a network of agents they can visit to deposit and withdraw cash in exchange for virtual money. In 2013, m-pesa had fifteen million users, and the company is recognized as one of the most successful financial services innovators in the world.[36] In Brazil, the country's largest telecom player, Oi Telecom, partnered with UK-based data analytics firm Cignifi to generate credit scores for customers based on mobile phone behavior. The information was then used to extend lending services to unbanked customers in Brazil through Paggo, Oi Telecom's SMS-based virtual credit card system.

In developed markets, health-care players have turned into valuable partners for telecom incumbents. Orange began to offer mobile health services, such as remote monitoring systems for diabetics and cardiac patients, to gain a stake in health-care growth by addressing consumer demand for home care with mobile solutions. Deutsche Telekom teamed up with Germany's largest health insurance company, Barmer, to develop mobile fitness solutions that track data like heart rates and the distance traveled during workouts and send it to the company's health portal, which generates new training programs.

Engage the World's Talent

As new competitors emerge, all businesses will find themselves increasingly competing for the skills they need. According to a survey of senior executives, 76 percent believe their organizations need to develop global-leadership capabilities, but only 7 percent think they are currently doing so very effectively.[37] About 30 percent of US companies say they haven't exploited international opportunities sufficiently because they have too few people with international competencies.

Offering executives from emerging markets global career opportunities is one powerful way to get the best talent. In 2010, Unilever assigned about two hundred managers from its Indian subsidiary to global roles with the parent company, and two of them are now part of the top leadership team. Other companies are finding that the traditional single headquarters model no longer fits their needs. Some have set up secondary headquarters or split head-office functions to align more closely with markets outside their home territory. General Electric and Caterpillar Group have split their corporate centers into two or more locations that share decision making, production, and service leadership. Unilever, whose main headquarters and incubator for executive talent is in London, created a second leadership center for global development in Singapore, aiming to attract and retain leadership talent with a global mind-set. After all, Unilever derives 57 percent of its revenues from emerging markets.[38] "Singapore sits at the nexus of the developed and emerging world. It is a leading hub for leadership and innovation and a gateway to the rapidly growing Asian economies," as Unilever CEO Paul Polman put it. "When our future leaders come here, whichever part of the world they come from, we know they will gain exposure to new insights and perspectives."[39]

Avoid Inertia

It's a point we've stressed in earlier chapters, but business leaders will have to become more agile in this new era of competition. They will have to be wary of maintaining the status quo and build new skills, particularly when it comes to capital allocation and technology.

Beyond expanding and monitoring their competitors, business leaders have to train themselves to become more agile in the way they allocate and deploy their capital. In fact, we've found that companies that perform well on measures of agility, such as changing their capital reallocation from year to year, post significantly higher performance with lower risk. Based on data from more than 1,600 companies, we found that total return to shareholders of the top one-third most agile companies—those with the highest capital reallocation year over year—was 30 percent higher than that of the least agile companies, whose capital allocation remain fixed year after year.[40]

In a world where technology is allowing sharks to fall prey to minnows, business leaders have to become fluent in information technology. As companies seek to negotiate the new landscape, as they eye potential rivals and partners, they have to elevate technology to the core of strategic thinking in every business unit. In addition to employing a chief information officer, who generally tends to the nuts and bolts of the technology a company uses, there is a strong argument for having a chief digital officer, who oversees technology as a strategic issue. Technology is becoming the lever through which companies can disrupt their own business models and adapt to the changing basis of competition. Burberry, a British fashion company, rebuilt itself from the inside out to become a technology leader.[41] Developing the concept of "democratic luxury"—the strategy of providing universal access to its brand—Burberry launched a cross-platform digital strategy. It integrates its website, social media, other social applications— such as Burberry Acoustic, a YouTube project promoting unknown British musicians—and its technologically innovative flagship stores.[42] As then-CEO Angela Ahrendts put it, "walking through the doors [of the Regent

Street flagship store] is just like walking into our website."[43] By going digital, Ahrendts said, Burberry "nearly tripled the business in seven years."[44]

———————

Competing in the global economy in some ways resembles the quadrennial soccer World Cup. It's a high-profile, high-stakes, high-tension tournament in which a team's fortunes can rise and fall very quickly. A squad may spend years qualifying and building a base that enables it to compete on the world stage, only to falter at an important moment or crash when an unexpected source scores a goal. While upstarts occasionally make a run, the established powers tend to win most of the time. The 2014 semifinalists—Germany, Argentina, Brazil, and the Netherlands—have won eleven of the twenty championships between them. But there's an important difference between soccer and business. At the 2014 World Cup in Brazil, thirty-two teams competed. All of them used the same ball, played on a field the same size, and had to abide by the same rules. Thanks to the rapidly changing basis of competition, however, the economic World Cup is more like a free-for-all. Competitors can show up from any corner of the earth with skilled strikers and unbeatable goalkeepers, and they bring their own rules with them. Some may field eighteen players at the same time instead of the standard eleven, while others may use a ball that can be manipulated by remote control. To compete, your organization must deploy effective networks of scouts, redouble its training efforts, and mine your culture and workforce to develop the most effective strategy.

10

POLICY MATTERS

Challenges for Society and Governance

IN THE LATE 1990S, GERMANY WAS OFTEN DUBBED THE NEW "SICK man of Europe."[1] And with good reason. Seven years after reunification with the impoverished east, Chancellor Helmut Kohl's administration was struggling with unemployment near 10 percent, slowing GDP growth, an aging population, and a strained welfare system. The situation worsened over the next several years. Economic growth was less than 0.5 percent a year, the economy went through two brief recessions, and by 2005 unemployment stood at 11 percent.[2] Yet less than a decade later, Germany is being hailed as an economic wonder. By 2008, the unemployment rate had fallen to 7.5 percent. As the global recession took hold and millions of workers lost their jobs around the world, Germany's unemployment rate held steady, then fell further, to 5.4 percent in 2012—despite an even sharper contraction in the country's GDP.[3] World leaders from Barack Obama to Xi Jinping have sought inspiration from Chancellor Angela Merkel and the "German miracle." How did the sick man recover so quickly?

Between 2003 and 2005, the German government enacted a series of aggressive labor market reforms as part of its Agenda 2010 program. Under the so-called Hartz reforms, Chancellor Gerhard Schröder revamped the German labor market by improving vocational education, creating new job types, and changing unemployment and welfare benefits. The wide-ranging reforms were deeply unpopular. More than one hundred thousand people marched in the Monday demonstrations of 2003 to protest cuts to social welfare benefits.[4] Older workers—whose labor force participation rose after the reforms—were not always interested in extending their careers. Chancellor Schröder's party lost the 2005 elections to Merkel, who subsequently benefited from the German miracle.

In the era of trend breaks, the primary challenge for policy makers is the one Germany's government faced in the early 2000s. How can governments respond faster and develop the political maturity and leadership needed to help societies navigate changes and ensure their own survival in the process? Those who govern will need to reset their intuition, just as business leaders will. In this chapter, we discuss the political leadership challenge these trend breaks present, and we highlight ways that government is rising—or not—to meet this challenge.

The Case for Change

Global competition and technological change have sped up creative destruction and outpaced the ability of labor markets to adapt. Job creation is a critical challenge for most policy makers even as businesses complain about critical skill gaps. Meanwhile, graying populations are starting to fray social safety nets—and for debt-ridden societies in advanced economies, the challenge can only get more pressing as the cost of capital starts to rise. Much-needed productivity growth continues to elude the public sector. Income inequality is rising and causing a backlash, in some cases targeted at the very interconnections of trade, finance, and people that have fueled the growth of the past three decades. The disruptive forces and trend breaks discussed in this book pose a unique set of challenges for policy makers, affecting several domains—labor, fiscal, trade and immigration policy, and resource and technology regulation.

Labor Policy in a Time of Global Competition and Technology Disruption

In the aftermath of the 2008 recession, job creation remains among the greatest policy challenges in both advanced and emerging economies. At the same time, continued advances in technology that are now encroaching on knowledge work make it easier for machines to replace human work in a range of new fields. Young workers and low-skilled workers are bearing the brunt of the impact on job creation and skill demand in OECD countries.*

---

*Thirty-four mostly high-income countries, including the United States, Japan, and Western European nations, plus Mexico, Turkey, and Hungary.

At the same time, counterintuitive as it may seem, both advanced and emerging economies are struggling with labor shortages. Faced with an aging workforce, some companies are already worried about the impact of retirement. Many are wrestling with growing skill gaps, particularly in the scientific, technical, and engineering fields.[5] Labor market imbalances are worsened by the much lower participation rates of women. In Middle Eastern and North African countries, among the fastest-aging populations in the world, less than a quarter of women participate in the labor force. Such imbalances are evident in some advanced economics as well. In Japan and Korea, for example, while 70 percent of men are in the labor force, less than half of working-age women participate.[6]

Should these trends continue without major intervention, labor imbalances will, we estimate, lead to a shortage of nearly eighty million high- and medium-skilled workers and a surplus of roughly ninety-five million low-skilled workers by 2020. To close the gap, advanced economies will need to accelerate the number of young people completing post–high school education to 2.5 times the current rate. In addition, they will need to provide better incentives to promote training in job-relevant disciplines. In the United States, where there are typically four to five million job openings every month, only 14 percent of college degrees are in STEM fields. For emerging economies, the challenge is to find creative ways to train hundreds of millions of young adults and catch up on secondary graduation rates. In 2012 it was estimated that in order to meet government targets, India would need to hire twice the number of secondary school teachers and add 34 million secondary school seats by 2016.[7]

Fiscal Policy in a Time of Aging Populations and Rising Capital Costs

From the United States and Europe to Japan and China, many of the world's largest economies are dealing with the challenge of an aging population and impending retirements. Social safety nets constructed in the last century will be put to the test as the proportion of people over the age of sixty-five years rapidly increases (to one in four) by 2040 in advanced economies, while the share of children stays at a virtual standstill. China is expected to see public pension expenditures rise from 3.4 percent of GDP today to 10 percent in 2050. Thanks to the amplifying forces of the aging population and health-care inflation, public health-care costs are expected to rise even faster. In the United States, where Medicare and

Youth unemployment is high and rising, putting an entire generation at risk

Youth unemployment rate

DEVELOPED COUNTRIES[1]

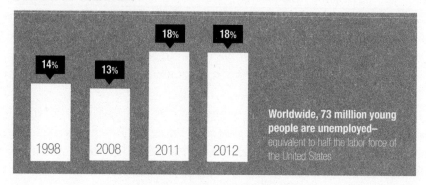

1998	2008	2011	2012
14%	13%	18%	18%

Worldwide, 73 milllion young people are unemployed– equivalent to half the labor force of the United States

Select countries

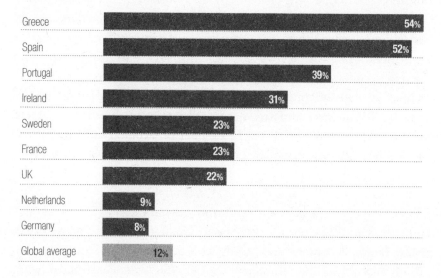

Greece	54%
Spain	52%
Portugal	39%
Ireland	31%
Sweden	23%
France	23%
UK	22%
Netherlands	9%
Germany	8%
Global average	12%

1 Includes the EU-27 and other wealthy economies, such as Australia, Canada, Japan, and the United States.
SOURCE: ILO Global Employment Trends for Youth, 2013; McKinsey Global Institute analysis

Medicaid already cover a huge swath of the population, public expenditures on health care are expected to more than double, to nearly 15 percent of GDP, by 2050.[8]

The timing of the impending public sector expenditure "bomb" doesn't help. As the era of historically low interest rates ends, the cost of capital could start to rise. That spells trouble for governments that are presiding over massive pools of floating-rate debt that constantly needs to be rolled over and refinanced. The combined balance of global fiscal deficits was at an unprecedented $4 trillion in 2011, and total government debt stood at 120 percent of GDP, putting pressure on the ability of governments to provide services.[9] The European Commission projects that the graying population will impose an additional "off-balance-sheet commitment" of 3 percent of GDP by 2030. Should a higher level of growth fail to materialize, this added debt would require tough fiscal tightening.[10]

Trade, Immigration, and Monetary Policy in a Time of Global Integration

Rising global prosperity and increased digitization have combined to accelerate the flow of trade, finance, people, and data across borders. And as we've noted, the more a country participates in these inflows and outflows, the greater the economic benefit. Growth in economic activity between countries contributes up to 25 percent to global GDP growth each year.[11] Yet the public—and certain elements of the business and governing elites—is often wary of participating in such activities, in part because they create obvious dislocations. Global trade is routinely blamed for job losses. Capital flows can be volatile and difficult to manage. Anti-immigration sentiment is high in many countries, developed and emerging alike, and can target legal as well as illegal immigrants. And many policy makers highlight the dark side of increased connectivity in the form of higher exposure to global shocks.[12]

The strain of the recession, austerity, and the fragile recovery have combined to stretch social safety nets and given rise to anti-immigration sentiment not just in Europe but also in countries traditionally built around migrant workforces. Singapore has historically been friendly to immigrants, and one-third of its residents are born elsewhere, but it is reducing national quotas for foreign workers.[13] "What we are doing is to put in place measures to nudge employers to give Singaporeans—especially our young graduates and professionals, managers and executives—a fair chance at

Declining budgets and high levels of government debt are stretching government resources

Countries' sum of fiscal balances

USD Trillions

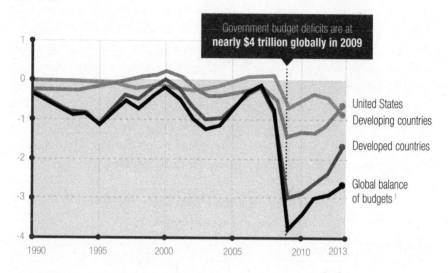

Government budget deficits are at **nearly $4 trillion globally in 2009**

United States
Developing countries
Developed countries
Global balance of budgets [1]

1 Sum of developing and developed countries' fiscal balances.
SOURCE: EIU World Database; McKinsey Global institute analysis

both job and development opportunities," Tan Chuan-Jin, then acting minister (now minister) of manpower, said in 2013. "Even as we remain open to foreign manpower to complement our local workforce, all firms must make an effort to consider Singaporeans fairly."[14] History suggests that these sorts of preferential policies, which are difficult to unwind once established, are likely to reduce potential growth in these locations by hampering immigration of skilled workers.

Inequality in a Time of Productivity Growth

Global inequality between countries is shrinking as China and other emerging economies grow rapidly. With their newfound prosperity, they continue to reduce the income gap between themselves and advanced economies by increasing productivity. At the same time, however, income inequality within countries is widening. Since the mid-1980s, in all but four of the countries in the OECD, incomes have risen significantly faster for the top decile of households than for the bottom decile. The handful of exceptions that had faster income growth in the bottom decile include Portugal, Ireland, Greece, and Spain, each of which has suffered a remarkably deep recession.[15]

Advanced economies are not the only ones facing this challenge. The Gini coefficient (a measure of income distribution within a nation) for China and India has also increased in the last two decades, in part due to a wide and growing disparity between rural and urban areas. In China in particular, the cities most connected to global trade and financial flows— Shanghai, Beijing, Guangzhou, and Shenzhen—have far outpaced less connected cities in the interior.[16] Christine Lagarde, the managing director of the International Monetary Fund, summed up the issue: "Put simply, a severely skewed income distribution harms the pace and sustainability of growth over the longer term. It leads to an economy of exclusion, and a wasteland of discarded potential."[17]

Debate rages about the source of the growing inequality and indeed about whether there is even a single source. One thing is certain, however. Productivity plays an often-overlooked role. According to some research, productivity growth confined to a small segment of the population tends to worsen inequality. When only the wealthy become more productive, they reap a disproportionate share of the benefits. Consequently, greater and more widely distributed productivity growth could then be a solution to rising inequality. And yet at a time of weak demand growth, economic policy makers everywhere often face a public perception that productivity kills jobs. History teaches otherwise. In every rolling ten-year period except one since 1929, job growth and productivity growth have gone hand-in-hand in the United States.[18] Unfortunately, conventional wisdom that comes to the opposite conclusion has proven difficult to dispel.

The demographic trends discussed in earlier chapters makes the productivity imperative even more critical over the next fifty years. The rapid global GDP growth of the previous half century, about 3.6 percent annually on average, was driven by growth in both the world's labor force and in its productivity. For instance, an analysis of twenty countries, including the G19 and Nigeria, shows that there are 2.3 times more employed workers today compared to fifty years ago and that each worker generates 2.4 times more in output than he or she did fifty years ago. Today, however, the demographic trends fueling growth are weakening and even reversing in some countries. The rate of global employment growth could drop to just 0.3 percent annually thanks to declining fertility rates and aging populations, and the world is likely to hit peak employment at some point in the coming half century. As a result, productivity gains will be instrumental in driving GDP growth. To sustain the recent growth trajectory, productivity will need to accelerate to nearly twice its historical rate. Simply maintaining the fifty-year historical rate of productivity growth over the coming fifty years will cut the global economic growth rate from 3.6 percent annually to 2.1 percent annually. Rather than expand sixfold, as it did in the past fifty years, the global economy would only expand threefold in the coming fifty years.

Where will this productivity growth come from? In our research, we find that about three-quarters of the needed growth can come simply from "catch-up" improvements, that is the broader adoption of existing best practices. The remaining one-quarter will come from technological, operational, or business innovations that go beyond today's best practices. But capturing this potential is not easy, as it requires broad and relentless change across industries and countries. Without a supportive environment—flexible labor markets, sufficient investments in skill development—productivity alone won't overcome the substantial demographic headwinds. We have identified ten enablers required to foster strong productivity growth: the removal of barriers to competition in service sectors; a focus on efficiency and performance management in public and regulated sectors; investment in physical and digital infrastructure, especially in emerging markets; fostering demand for, and R&D investment in, innovative products and services; regulations that incentivize productivity and support innovation; exploiting data to identify improvement opportunities and catalyze change; harnessing the power of new actors in the productivity landscape through open data and digital platforms; encouraging labor-market participation among women, the young, and older workers; adjusting immigration systems to help bolster skills and the labor pool; improving education and matching skills to jobs; and making labor markets more flexible.[19]

The productivity imperative applies especially to government, and in particular to its impact on the consequences of inequality. In many developed countries, public spending makes up 50 percent or more of GDP, while government employment accounts for between 15 and 20 percent of the total labor force.[20] Yet when it comes to productivity gains, the public and quasi-public sectors such as education and health care are laggards. In the G8 countries (Canada, France, Germany, Italy, Japan, Russia, the United Kingdom, and the United States), improvements in government performance could unlock annual value of $650 billion to $1 trillion by 2016.[21] In India, roughly 50 percent of public spending on basic services, including up to two-thirds of spending on health care, family welfare, drinking water, and sanitation, does not reach its intended beneficiaries because of inefficiencies, corruption, and diversion to other projects.[22] Public-sector productivity is critical to simultaneously tackle cost inflation in health care, rising public-sector costs, the emerging labor skill gap, and other societal challenges.

Standards in a Time of Technology and Resource Disruption

Major technology disruptions are occurring with increasing frequency. At the same time, new technologies are being adopted faster than before, whether in software, Internet services, or hardware. Companies and individuals are not the only ones involved. Governments play an important role in supporting research and development and in creating basic enablers for the private sector. However, the uncertainty and speed of technological change make it difficult to decide what R&D to support and how and what sort of talent and infrastructure to invest in. Policy makers who understand technology can harness it to improve societal outcomes in a range of ways—from providing health care, education, and other public services to improving productivity and making governance more transparent and accountable.

In addition, governments need to constantly revise legal and regulatory frameworks to ensure their relevance. California legislators are now trying to prepare for advances in self-driving cars; officials from several state departments meet routinely to try to understand all of the ways in which the technology requires legislative changes—such as in liability insurance, drivers' licenses, safety requirements, and infrastructure needs. They understand that the benefits of being early—especially the potential jobs that could be created in related businesses—are sufficiently large to offset the difficulties of being early.[23]

Governments around the world are also facing new challenges from increasing global connectivity in data and communication flows. In the wake of the recent NSA scandal in the United States, many countries are rethinking data privacy and protection laws. In Germany, the backlash has been particularly strong, with plans for resuming counterespionage measures and rising enthusiasm for a secure Euro-link network.[24] Angela Merkel, the German chancellor, pointedly stated, "We'll talk with France about how we can maintain a high level of data protection. Above all, we'll talk about European providers that offer security for our citizens, so that one shouldn't have to send emails and other information across the Atlantic."[25]

The regulatory frontier extends to resources as well. Some technology disruptions directly affect the resource sector. Fracking technologies have unleashed a shale gas revolution in the United States, attracting regulatory attention to the environmental effects of methane emissions, water contamination, and related issues. Globally, resource prices between 2000 and 2013 more than doubled, as a response to demand in emerging economies and rising supply and exploration challenges. At the same time, average annual resource price volatility over the last thirteen years has been roughly three times that witnessed in 1990s.[26] The impact of technology disruptions in concert with high and volatile resource prices is increasing pressure on governments to act as efficient regulators.[27]

Implications for Future Governance

The political leadership challenge triggered by these trend breaks is made even more urgent by the growing number of outlets for public expression and participation. Citizens around the world demand that governments deliver public services in shorter time frames, of consistent quality, and often at lower cost. In times of tightening budgets, short election cycles, and instant feedback loops, the room for error by public-sector leaders is small. From Hong Kong to Ukraine, from Egypt to Brazil, it is common to see large groups of citizens, impatient for change, taking to the streets. After a thirty-year decline, sovereign debt in default has been rising (as a share of global debt and global GDP) since 2011, indicating that we may be at the start of yet another default cycle; emerging-market debt crises triggered the last one, in the 1980s.[28]

Often, the challenge for public sector officials isn't lack of vision, but short time frames, competing priorities, and flawed delivery. Many governments have risen to the occasion; an Asian country reduced street crime by 35 percent in the first year of a transformation program. A South American government reduced hospital waiting lists by 80 percent and increased by more than 50 percent the number of top graduates choosing to become teachers. An emerging-market government introduced a social-security scheme to hundreds of thousands of workers in two months. In each of these cases, policy makers used what McKinsey calls a Delivery

2.0 approach—a well-designed program with appropriate metrics, experimental "delivery labs," small and high-powered execution teams, visible support from leaders, and a culture of performance accountability.[29] Beyond delivering results, communicating them effectively is vital. Publicly available dashboards that document performance in real time can establish transparency and instigate conversations about how to improve services.

Just as trend breaks have forced many businesses to reassess their strategy and reimagine their business assumptions, government has to do the same. As policy makers try to adapt, these trend breaks raise three interesting questions about the nature of government in the future: the size of government, the degree to which it should be centralized or localized, and its overall role.

Size: The first question relates to the size of government in the future. For the OECD, average government spending is about 45 percent of GDP. But there is wide variation, with government spending accounting for more than 55 percent of GDP in countries such as Denmark, Finland, and France and 30 percent or less in South Korea and Mexico. In Norway, the public sector employs 30 percent of the workforce; in Japan, the proportion is less than 10 percent. Most countries have seen government employment remain the same or shrink marginally over the past decade, and most of the jobs are in general administration—even in countries with large public-sector companies.[30] Ultimately, the effectiveness of government matters more than its size. But as policy makers think about the impact of trend breaks, it is worthwhile to ask the question: Is there a "right" size for their government? This matters even for policy makers looking to e-governance as a way to improve delivery. The economies and central government employment of the United Kingdom and Italy are roughly the same size, but the United Kingdom spends four times more per government employee on information technologies than does Italy.[31]

Centralization: The second fundamental question relates to the organization of government and whether policy should become more local, more national, or, indeed, more global. In Ireland, the central government accounts for 76 percent of all government spending and 90 percent of public-sector employment. But in Germany and Switzerland, which have more robust state and regional governments, the central government accounts for less than 20 percent of spending and 15 percent of employment. A great deal of decision making has devolved toward cities and states, whether it is for infrastructure project selection in the United States or workforce training in Germany. In the United States, individual states are responsible for nearly 85 percent of all government investment. Spain has become more decentralized in the past decade, Norway has become more centralized—at least as measured by public employment—and most other OECD nations haven't seen a change.[32] Furthermore, as global connections have grown, we have also seen the rise of more global or multilateral decision authorities, such as the European Union's monetary regulator, the International Criminal Court, and ASEAN's trade officer. Governments are also increasingly cooperating on knowledge sharing and policy design. The Alliance for Financial Inclusion, now one of the largest developing-world organizations, was founded in 2008 and designed specifically for policy makers from developing countries to share knowledge and discuss policy options for financial inclusion.[33] With increasing interconnectivity, the question of which government policy decisions should become more local and which ones more national or supranational is becoming very pertinent.

Role: The third question relates to the future role of government. In general, central governments focus on funding major outlays such as social protection and defense; local governments focus on funding and delivery of education, housing, and other community-related activities. Will we see government getting out of many of its current activities (such as infrastructure construction) and plunging into new areas (such as resource efficiency)? Overall in the OECD, the largest spending category is social protection—pensions, unemployment, disability—which makes up more than 35 percent of total spending. But large emerging economies such as China and India, which have yet to construct robust safety nets, only spend 15 to 20 percent on such social welfare programs. Korea spends only 13 percent of its budget on social protection, while it spends more than 20 percent on economic efforts to promote domestic industry—four times the share in the United Kingdom. The US government spends 21 percent of its budget on health care, but Switzerland spends only 6 percent. Greece spends 8 percent of its budget on education, while Israel and Estonia each spend nearly 17 percent.[34] Given these large variations, is there a "right" mix of policy priorities, and how should a government achieve this mix?

Funding is only one way to measure what a government actually does. Broadly, policy actions geared at achieving desired outcomes tend to fall into one of three categories: incentives, regulation, and information. Around the world, governments are employing all three approaches to navigate the changing landscape with agility, innovation, and best-in-class implementation.

Using Incentives to Accelerate Change

Typically, we think about incentives as carrots and sticks that the government provides to the private sector. But government can often craft incentives that induce government itself to work more intelligently. Germany's Hartz labor reforms used incentives to retool Germany's labor agency, such as changing performance goals for caseworkers and more targeted placement and training programs. Along with incentives for companies to hire the long-term unemployed and retain workers in periods of weak demand, these efforts played a crucial role in changing the country's labor market condition.[35] Other job-creation initiatives underway that utilize incentives in both advanced and emerging economies range from export promotion to infrastructure, providing social services, and entrepreneurship. The US government's National Export Initiative seeks to promote job creation in domestic services and advanced manufacturing industries by making it easier for companies to access export markets.[36]

China, which has the world's largest diaspora and largest overseas student population, is using incentives to lure high-skilled professionals back home as part of its National Talent Development Plan 2010–2020. The Thousand International Talents Program targets Chinese engineers and scientists living abroad, offering inducements such as large research grants, housing assistance, and tax-free education allowances for the children of those who return and work full-time in China for at least three years. Such incentives, combined with China's formidable economic momentum, encouraged nearly three hundred thousand students to return in 2012 alone.[37]

Several countries are using incentives to cope with the demographic and economic challenges of an aging population. One key effort toward bolstering the ranks of the employed is to include more women. In 2012, only 51 percent of working-age women participated in the labor force globally, compared with 77 percent of men.[38] Denmark has instituted a host of incentives, including the provision of a child-care facility within three months of a parent's request, such as day care, kindergarten, or leisure time centers and school-based centers. As a result, over 80 percent of Danish infants and toddlers and over 90 percent of Danish children between the ages of three and five years are in regular child care.[39] By 2009, Danish women aged fifteen to sixty-four had a labor participation rate of 76 percent, one of the highest in the OECD.[40] Of those women in the labor force, more than 95 percent are employed.[41]

Conditional cash transfer incentives have proven particularly effective in poverty reduction efforts. In Mexico, Oportunidades has been credited with a 10 percent reduction in poverty within five years of its introduction,[42] in part because the program is designed to provide cash payments for families who meet certain conditions such as health clinic visits and school attendance. More significantly, it has created strong financial incentives for families to invest in efforts that boost human capital over the long term.

Government can also provide incentives in the form of forward-looking procurement policies and standards. From the telegraph and railroad to semiconductors and mobile phones, governments have long played a direct role by providing critical early demand for unproven technologies. The US Navy has been a customer of energy-saving technologies, including fuels; it led the shift from coal to oil in the 1900s, then to nuclear in the 1950s. Faced with persistently high oil prices, the Navy is now spurring demand for biofuels and energy-efficient technology. But incentives must be carefully designed to avoid the risk of unintended consequences and creating market distortions, as agricultural subsidies often do.[43]

Using Regulation to Direct Response to Change

Government's power to regulate—to set standards and define the rules of conduct and markets—can play a vital role in modernizing economies and preparing for the future. Regulation can prove a particularly effective tool in places where market failures are obvious and structural issues inhibit adoption of best practices. Shareholders of large financial institutions can't effectively ride herd on the risk-taking actions of executives, so regulators must impose capital standards and supervise them carefully. Making buildings more energy efficient requires owners to make upfront investments that they may not be able to pass along directly to renters. As a result, smartly designed industry-wide standards can be useful.

To address the problem of aging populations, some countries have extended the legal retirement age, in some cases by up to two years. That's a start, but it's not nearly sufficient to keep pace with the demographic changes the world is seeing. A recent analysis of forty-three mostly developed countries found that between 1965 and 2005 the average legal retirement age rose by less than six months.[44] In the same period, male life expectancy rose by nine years. In graying Europe, Danish legislation recognized the impending pension time bomb early, and the country decided to index the pension age to life expectancy and place restrictions on early retirement. As a result, Denmark's population of people aged fifty-five to sixty-four has a higher labor participation rate (58 percent) than the average EU country (less than 50 percent) and will have the highest retirement age (sixty-nine years) among all OECD countries by 2050.[45] In response to the demographic tide, Japan's government introduced compulsory long-term care insurance contributions by citizens over age forty in the early 2000s.[46]

Countries—particularly countries with underdeveloped financial institutions or specific risk exposures to global flows—use the regulatory approach to manage their vulnerability to global participation. For instance, governments have crafted various regulatory responses to rising capital inflows, ranging from short-term, high-intervention measures to systemic longer-term changes to their financial markets. Regulation is usually most intrusive when markets are least developed.

Chile, whose economy is relatively modern but disproportionately reliant on copper exports, maintained its openness to foreign capital but maintained a conservative fiscal policy stance. In 2007, the government set up the Economic and Social Stabilization Fund with an initial contribution of $2.6 billion. The fund was set up specifically to reduce Chile's dependency on global business cycles and revenue volatility from copper price fluctuations.[47] It invests primarily in government bonds, and a portion of its assets can be used to finance deficit spending or pay down government debt. The fund's assets have grown to about $15 billion, and Chile has become one of the most financially deepened* countries in the region. The IMF recently nominated Chile as a representative example of resilience to fluctuations from global flows.[48]

Governments have used regulation to mandate social, environmental, and other broad outcomes in response to global trends, while letting industries sort out the technologies needed to meet the targets. In these cases, there is a social consensus about what needs to happen but no agreement

---

Financial deepening is a term that indicates that financial services and access to capital (along with banks, financial institutions, and capital markets) are becoming more accessible in a country.

on how to get there. And getting there is most of the battle, because market participants may be wedded to technologies linked to whatever environment preceded the trend break. For example, the advent of sharply higher energy prices caused the promulgation of sharply higher automobile mileage requirements in the United States. This, in turn, has spurred a host of innovations—electric vehicles, hybrid power trains, replacing steel with aluminum, and integrating start-stop engine technology. New regulatory requirements on food safety and tracking in the EU and the United States are generating industry interest in data platforms and advanced analytics throughout the supply chain.

Examples of regulation abound in the policy response to resources. In the United States, Ohio, Texas, and Pennsylvania allowed the deployment of fracking, which the state of New York bans.[49] In Europe, public concerns about the environmental impact of shale gas have led to drilling bans in Bulgaria, France, and Germany.[50] To encourage recycling, Sweden has used landfill taxes and the inclusion of recycling costs in the price of goods. As a result, about 99 percent of household waste is either recycled or burned to create electricity and heat.[51] The German government is using regulation to hasten the transition to renewables and has mandates for electricity efficiency.[52]

Harnessing Information to Improve Productivity

Big data isn't just for apps and e-commerce. Information is a critical tool to improve public-sector productivity, especially in an environment where there is pressure to continually improve productivity and quality of service. Governments are starting to prioritize information as an effective tool for better management of the resources and tasks they steward, such as education, health care, matching labor supply and demand, and even defense and security. And government is supporting industry in providing information that consumers can then use to make better decisions. Central European countries—Austria, Germany, and Switzerland in particular—have long been models of industry-based vocational education. There, vocational programs target over two hundred different occupations and are intended to ensure a match between labor supply and demand. The Swiss government oversees certification, and potential employers help define needed skills and shape curricula. Other countries have similar models, but on a smaller scale and targeting specific sectors. Brazil's government is taking the lead via Prominp (National Oil and Natural Gas Industry

Mobilization Program) to convene firms, universities, and unions to improve education and keep Brazil's oil and gas sector competitive.[53]

Under President Nicolas Sarkozy, France launched the General Review of Public Policies. Dubbed "do more with less," it is aimed to reduce the country's public expenditure and provide better service quality for citizens as well as promoting a "culture of results." Among other actions, the review promoted service improvements in high-visibility areas leading to greater citizen satisfaction, such as the introduction of fifteen quality-of-service indicators, including waiting times in accident and emergency departments.[54]

Another step is identifying and monitoring the economy's main productivity drivers. Even among the best-performing countries, a wide distribution of performance exists within sectors. Within the quasi-public sector, countries have both excellent and poorly performing hospitals and schools. The best performers have usually understood and implemented practices honed in the private sector—lean principles, data analytics, smart procurement and performance management—to great effect.

Technology and big data provide another avenue for policy makers to unleash productivity improvements across all public services. In Kenya, the national government launched an open data portal to share previously difficult-to-access information spanning realms such as education, health, and energy. This data publication has led to the development of over one hundred mobile applications and an estimated potential savings of $1 billion in procurement costs.[55] Estonia's 1.3 million residents can use electronic ID cards to vote, pay taxes, and access more than 160 services online, from unemployment benefits to property registration; even private-sector firms offer services through the state portal.[56] The Brazilian Transparency Portal publishes a wide range of information that includes federal-agency expenditures, elected officials' charges on government-issued credit cards, and a list of companies banned from contracting work with the government.[57]

New Opportunities for Businesses

As policy makers reset their intuitions and change their approach to governance, the private sector will be affected as well. The rules of the game may change in some areas; in others, new opportunities will present themselves. Already we are seeing examples of companies benefiting from the policy response to deepening global engagement, collaborating on infrastructure and education initiatives, and addressing resource and technology issues.

The government response to technology trends determines the opportunity for new markets for everything from real estate portals to consumer finance. Government regulations on e-commerce and data exchange—and the willingness to share public data with private companies—allow these new markets to develop. Take real estate as an example. Location selection can be optimized through use of geospatial, commuter traffic, and infrastructure data. Portals that aggregate real-time information on property availability, prices, recent transactions, and taxes with other relevant nonfinancial information can help match buyers and sellers effectively. Aggregators such as Zillow are substituting for traditional brokers; they allow users to search for properties based on custom preferences and then generate automatic valuation estimates. Consumer finance is another interesting example. Many new players are emerging and harnessing the power of open data to help consumers better navigate increasingly complex and proliferating financial products. Wallaby, a venture-backed US firm, recommends which credit card to use for different types of purchases in order to maximize rewards. BillGuard pulls together information from all its users' credit card transactions to highlight transactions and payments that are unwanted or even fraudulent to its users.

The global smart city technology market—smart energy, water, transportation, buildings, and government—is expected to grow from $9 billion in 2014 to $27.5 billion by 2023.[58] Companies are already working with pioneering cities such as San Francisco, Barcelona, and Amsterdam. The growth in the global smart city technology market has fueled growth in adjacent sectors, such as video surveillance.

An opportunity also exists to capitalize on the search by governments for partners to provide public services. Such partnerships span countries and sectors. In some of the world's most water-stressed areas, including parts of Africa and Latin America, Coca-Cola has partnered with international agencies such as the World Wildlife Fund and the United Nations Development Programme to improve access to water and sanitation, protect watersheds, provide water for productive use, and raise awareness about water issues. In the United States, private sector partners are playing a role in high-profile infrastructure projects, including Miami's port tunnel, Washington, DC's streetcar line, and Atlanta's multimodal transport hub. In India, a massive project to train a five-hundred-million strong workforce by 2022 is taking shape under the auspices of the National Skills Development Corporation, a public-private partnership in which the private sector holds 51 percent of equity—including representation from companies in sectors as wide ranging as construction, aerospace, retail, and life sciences.

Danish firms provide a good example of the opportunities resulting from policy changes in resources. As Denmark successfully transitioned from oil to renewables, government demand and clear policy goals allowed Danish companies to make early investments that helped them become world leaders in the sector. Wind turbine maker Vestas capitalized on its home market experience to expand globally—initially in important markets such as the United States, then ramping up across Europe and Asia. The market for renewables has grown in these parts of the world over the past decade, and Vestas has recorded over 20 percent annual revenue growth through the 2000s. Today, the company's global revenue exceeds €6 billion.[59] Other domestic beneficiaries of the Danish government's energy initiative include Grundfos, the world's largest pump manufacturer, and Danfoss, a producer of energy-efficient components.[60]

The trend break era is imposing uncertainties and pressures on governments and policy makers that are as significant and meaningful as those it is placing on companies and executives. Increasingly, public leadership will be judged by its ability to marshal resources and build consensus to face these challenges head on. Ultimately, it is difficult to prescribe a specific regimen for the appropriate size and shape of government. Each country must make these decisions for itself. But regardless of a government's situation—expanding or contracting, developed or developing, in surplus or in deficit—it must strive to respond quickly and with agility. Doing so will allow governments to insulate and protect themselves from some potentially threatening trends. More significantly, it will allow the public sector to take advantage of the enormous opportunities being presented. The intelligent deployment of incentives, regulations, and data is a requirement for success.

CONCLUDING THOUGHTS

If much of the intuition you have built up over your life is wrong—or, at least, seriously questionable—how should you go about managing your investments, your career, and your business?

In the previous chapters, we've laid out some examples of how the twenty-first-century business and economic climate could be different. It is typical, even compulsory, for how-to books in diet, nutrition, exercise, investment, remodeling to end with a snappy, ten-item to-do list that guarantees life-altering success within a matter of weeks. Simply check off the items, and you're golden. As readers will have surmised by now, this is not that kind of book. The transformations we describe are far too complex and powerful to be broken down so simply. The trend break era is too swiftly changing, too full of opportunity, and too fraught with peril for us to boil down a menu of action items and takeaways that the generic global executive can latch onto, matrix out, and execute. Despite our most diligent efforts, the world we see in our work every day cannot always be reduced to a bunch of bullet points or a few PowerPoint slides.

Any one of the great disruptive forces discussed in this book and the trend breaks they are creating has significant implications for organizations—whether they be companies, governments, or nonprofits—and the people who lead them. Together, they will be profound. The coming decades will redefine who runs the world economy: which countries, which companies, and which individuals.

The global economy is poised at a set of historical, technological, economic, political, and social inflection points. The transformation we're living through has sometimes been likened to the Industrial Revolution. In fact, the Industrial Revolution pales in comparison to today's convulsions, because the shifts today are happening much faster and on a much bigger scale. Because they are so interlinked—urbanization and consumption, technology and competition, aging and labor—and because they amplify one another, the changes are harder to anticipate and more powerful in their impact. And they challenge our imaginations as much as they do our competencies and skills. One of the factors that makes managing today so difficult is the ever-present potential for second- and third-order effects of the changes we're witnessing.

Consider one example. Several companies, including Google, are working on self-driving cars. Equipped with wireless communications technology, these vehicles will theoretically be able to navigate effectively while avoiding collisions. Should self-driving vehicles become standard, that would likely lead to fewer accidents and road deaths. This indisputably desirable outcome would have a series of effects on other industries and sectors. It might reduce the need for professional drivers, sap demand for emergency response workers, or bolster the bottom line of health insurance companies. But we might also expect to see a growing and urgent demand for artificial hearts. Why? Thanks to the growing number of people who check the "organ donation" box on their driver's licenses, fatal automobile accidents have become a significant source of donor organs used in transplants. Should they work as advertised, then, driverless cars might indirectly disrupt the brilliant system through which a tragic accident winds up saving a life.

How many of us would be able to make the link between the technology behind driverless cars and the fourth-order impact on the need for artificial hearts, and then plan for the scenario? It may seem far-fetched, but this is how our world works. Like a stone tossed into a placid pond, a breakthrough or innovation in one sector will create ripples that spread outward.

Readers may feel an overriding sense of alarm and confusion as old certainties evaporate and established economic relationships break down; as volatility increases, necessitating a speed of decision making beyond most current capabilities; and as challenges come at them on all fronts. Executives report that dealing with uncertainty can be overwhelming and any solution can feel like it costs too much or takes too long. Uncertainty can breed paralysis. This is particularly true for incumbents with established market positions. Those who have already made it have the most to lose.

But the trend break era should also be a time for great optimism—and not just from the upstarts who are storming the palisades. Even in this complex and challenging age, some trends are clear. The world is getting richer, and countries are becoming less unequal. We are generally living longer and healthier lives. "The context has changed, without a doubt—and I think it will continue to evolve," said Daniel Vasella, the chief executive officer of Novartis. "So you've got longer life spans, expanding populations, and more wealth in emerging economies; all of those imply opportunities and risks."[1] An ever-larger universe of products and services is becoming available to us as consumers. The miracles of modern life that so many of us take for granted—electric lights, vaccinations, freedom from hunger, the ability to communicate freely—are become more widely available with each passing day. In the years to come, hundreds of millions more people in emerging countries will rise from poverty and enter the middle classes in a democratization of global wealth. Technology is opening economic opportunity to millions of people, enabling a new wave of entrepreneurs, and transforming the building blocks of society, from education to health. What's more, these developments are providing executives with a new set of tools that will help them stay on top of breaking new trends, develop new approaches, and drive them through complex organizations. "The world has always been a complicated and volatile place," Alan Mulally, then the chief executive officer of Ford, said in 2013. "[I]t is just that we now have the tools to recognize it, to try to make sense of it, and to respond to it."[2]

The question, of course, is how to surf the wave without getting wiped out by it. In the preceding ten chapters, we have laid out the types of tactics, strategies, and mind-sets needed to thrive in this new, emerging world. In some instances, that is easier said than done, especially to the extent that it involves resetting our intuition. Intuition is a product of life experience, knowledge, and a hard-earned, time-consuming understanding of the world. It builds up over the course of decades or a career. People who have succeeded and risen to levels of responsibility trust a great deal, explicitly and implicitly, in their intuition. Asking a veteran leader to reset her intuition on a range of subjects quickly is like asking a courier whose horse has crossed a continent—through storms, wind and cold, over high mountains and through deep valleys—to swap it for an entirely new, untested, unfamiliar form of transportation. Like, say, an automobile. Doing so may be counterintuitive, difficult, bewildering, and alienating at times. But the rewards—for individual couriers, for their customers, for the economy at large, and even for horses—can be significant.

Even so, it is difficult to shift gears. Social scientists and behavioral economists find that human beings are biased toward the status quo and resistant to changing their assumptions and approaches even in the face of the evidence. In 1988, William Samuelson and Richard Zeckhauser, economists at Boston University and Harvard, respectively, highlighted a case in which the German government needed to relocate a small town in order to mine lignite, which lay beneath it. The authorities suggested many options for planning the new town, but its citizens chose a plan that looked "extraordinarily like the serpentine layout of the old town—a layout that had evolved over centuries without (conscious) rhyme or reason."[3] Faced with the opportunity to design an entirely new, rationally laid-out living space, the burghers chose to replicate the familiar. Similarly, businesses, which often pride themselves on their ability to make and execute far-reaching initiatives, suffer from a surprising degree of inertia, especially when it comes to backing up strategy with hard cash. McKinsey found that, between 1990 and 2005, US companies had almost always allocated resources on the basis of past, rather than future, opportunities. A third of the companies actually allocated almost exactly the same as they had in previous years.[4] This passive behavior persisted even during the global recession of 2009.

So what *can* leaders do to reset the intuitions of their organizations?

One fundamental realization is that to drive the necessary change, leaders must first develop the capabilities to reset their own intuition. McKinsey research and client experience suggest that 50 percent of all efforts to transform companies fail either because senior role models fail to drive change or because of the inherent tendency to defend the status quo. Many leaders react to a changing landscape by focusing on a technical solution. They will concentrate on changing policies, processes, or organizational models, which is necessary but hardly sufficient. If the sea level rises by three feet, traditional thinkers are inclined to add another three feet to the existing seawall, pipe in new sand, or put beachfront homes on stilts, rather than fundamentally rethink the logic of building, insuring, and protecting properties that face the ocean. The first step for all leaders is self-awareness. Understanding their own tendencies and biases, and recognizing the factors that drive their decision processes, is fundamental if they are to effectively respond to change.[5] And they must invest the time and effort necessary to change the mind-sets and behaviors of those tasked with carrying out solutions.

Another key to survival is to embed curiosity and learning in an organization. In an era of rapid change, full of examples of companies that have become casualties of stasis, successful leaders must adapt to "be students in a way that maybe we haven't been before," as management guru Tom Peters puts it.[6] The ability to understand, monitor, and navigate a sea of ever-changing trends will be greatly rewarded. At our firm, the McKinsey Global Institute functions as an internal think tank and research arm, taking deep dives into big trends and producing useful analysis and perspective. Simply setting aside time each day to keep up with the changing external environment—and encouraging others to do the same—can make the difference between responding to a new trend and allowing it to leave you irrelevant. When he ran Microsoft, Bill Gates would famously disconnect for a week or two in a lake house where it was difficult to reach him and spend his time reading on a wide range of topics. Larry Fink, CEO of BlackRock, one of the world's most powerful asset management firms, claims he still learns as much each day now as he did when he started in the investing business: "Here I am running this company not quite 25 years. And I still spend an hour a day studying the world and the markets," Fink said. "In my view, if you don't believe you're learning, if you're not a student, you're probably going backward."[7]

It is also essential to surround yourself with the right people, those who are able to act as "reset catalysts" for an entire organization. Large organizations and groups of people don't simply respond with alacrity to commands and edicts issued from on high. The twenty-first-century corporation does not function like a nineteenth-century military unit. Rather, people tend to respond to the actions and inspiration of peers, competitors, and colleagues. We rethink what is possible and desirable based more on what we see and less on what we are told. For many years, running a mile in under four minutes was believed to be impossible. But that was largely because no one had done it yet—there was no immutable law of physics that would prevent a human from moving 1,760 yards in 240 seconds. In 1954, Roger Bannister broke the four-minute barrier in a race in Oxford, upending decades of conventional wisdom almost instantly. Bannister went down in history as the first sub-four-minute miler, but he wasn't the last. Indeed, by 1957, sixteen more runners had broken that once-insurmountable barrier.

By demonstrating what was possible, Bannister had acted as a catalyst for the running community, which quickly reset its collective intuition surrounding the limits of distance runners. We have seen this happen time and again—in mountain climbing, the speed of computer processing, and vehicle fuel efficiency. Resetting the intuition of a large organization can at times feel similarly impossible, but often all it takes is for one person to embrace a new perspective and actively discredit the old way of thinking.[8]

Agility is another vital attribute necessary to thrive in the trend break era. In professional sports, training regimens that once relied on brute strength and speed have come to include yoga, stretching, and other exercises aimed at boosting flexibility and balance. Why? It turns out that athletes who develop greater agility, be they 300-pound defensive ends, 200-pound tennis players, or 100-pound gymnasts, tend to avoid injury and react more effectively during competition. This analogy translates to business. As changes unfold in the external environment, companies that can adapt nimbly will be able to grab new opportunities. But they can do so only if their leaders prioritize agility instead of dismissing it as too expensive, too defensive, or too difficult because of all the "unknown unknowns." Unfortunately, the only alternative to agility is a wait-and-see approach that does nobody any favors. In the twenty-first century, agility does not always require expensive capital investment up front. A satellite sales office instead of a new headquarters, a pop-up store instead of a big box, a food truck instead of a large restaurant, even the basic "lean" skill of continuous improvement are all ways that companies can respond quickly to disruptions and experiment, even while delivering ongoing improvement in a stable environment. Agility is hardly a defensive posture—successful firms have used technological flexibility, build-to-order capabilities, and even dynamic labor arrangements as ways to build agility in their organization.

Lastly, and most importantly, all leaders will have to resist the temptation to focus on the hazards of the period ahead instead of the opportunities it presents. Looking around the world today, there is ample reason for pessimism, especially when it comes to geopolitics. Living through a searing experience like the financial crisis of 2008 or high youth unemployment can leave significant scar tissue. But while pessimists have surely had their share of days in recent years, it's important to note that the long-term trend of so many indicators points up and to the right. In 1930, as the Great Depression spread around the world, the great British economist

John Maynard Keynes boldly predicted that, one hundred years on, progressive countries' standard of living would be between four and eight times higher than it was at the time. Despite the Great Depression, an enormously destructive world war, and the Cold War, the higher end of his optimistic expectation has turned out to be our reality today.

We believe that optimism will still win the day, even in the trend break era. Thanks to the forces at work, the world we inhabit ten or more years from now will be a better one. Those who understand the magnitude and the permanence of the changes that we are now witnessing, reset their intuitions accordingly, and see the opportunities will shape this new world—and they will thrive.

ACKNOWLEDGMENTS

Since 1990, the McKinsey Global Institute (MGI), the business and economics research arm of the global management consulting firm, McKinsey & Company, has sought to provide leaders in the commercial, public, and social sectors with facts and insights on which to base management and policy decisions. MGI has conducted detailed research on productivity, competitiveness, the impact of technology, capital markets, natural resources, labor markets, and urbanization. In MGI's twenty-fifth year, we have stepped back from these individual research streams to take a more holistic view of the global economy and the areas of interconnection between these research areas. In doing this, we are building on current and previous MGI and McKinsey research and the experience that comes from our colleagues and our own service and conversations with clients around the world.

One of the most gratifying aspects of being part of McKinsey is the opportunity it affords us to learn from our work with clients and colleagues around the world. The experiences and trends we describe in the book aren't abstract or academic concepts. They are issues we are grappling with every day, in every market, in every sector, and in virtually every country in the world. We are fortunate to be part of a firm that has committed to invest in MGI's research with a simple mission to understand how our world works and is changing and to help inform the decision making of business leaders and policy makers. And we also are grateful for the lessons we have been able to draw from our colleagues and our own work and conversations with clients.

The leadership of McKinsey has been behind this effort from the beginning. We'd like particularly to thank Dominic Barton and Ian Davis, the firm's current and former managing directors, along with Eric Labaye, the chairman of MGI, members of the MGI Council—Jacques Bughin, Toos Daruvala, Heinz-Peter Elstrodt, Acha Leke, Scott Nyquist, and Shirish Sankhe—and other leaders of the firm, including Peter Bisson, Peter Child, Martin Hirt, Tomas Koch, Gordon Orr, and Seelan Singham.

Much of the fundamental research that served as a framework for this book was conducted under the auspices of MGI. We are enormously grateful for the work of MGI's partners Jaana Remes, Michael Chui, Susan Lund, and senior fellows, including Alan FitzGerald, Anu Madgavkar, Jan Mischke, Jeongmin Seong, Fraser Thompson, and Sree Ramaswamy. We also want to acknowledge the advice of a group of leading economists and practitioners, including Nobel laureates, who act as MGI research advisors. In particular, we would like to thank several friends and advisors who reviewed this book and provided important guidance. They include Martin Baily, Richard Cooper, Howard Davies, John Manzoni, Michael Spence, and Adair Turner. We would also like to thank the previous leaders of MGI, Diana Farrell, Fred Gluck, Ted Hall, Herb Henzler, Bill Lewis, Lenny Mendonca, Ken Ohmae, and Charles Roxburgh.

For anecdotes, pointers, guidance, and constant reality checks, we turned to our colleagues in industry and functional practices. The contributions of several of our colleagues went above and beyond. We would particularly like to thank Patrick Viguerie, Elizabeth Stephenson, and Yuval Atsmon from McKinsey's Strategy and Corporate Finance Practice and Paul Wilmott from the Business Technology Office for their input throughout the process.

On its journey from a collection of ideas and observations to a coherent book, the manuscript went through several iterations and a meticulous internal editorial and review process. Janet Bush, David Gasca, Sree Ramaswamy, Andrea Zitna, and João Leite led this effort, working closely with a team of McKinsey consultants, which included Renan Andrade, Nathan Kaplan, and Wonhoe Koo.

Our colleagues at McKinsey Publishing run an operation that continually refines the raw materials of economic and industrial research into accessible final papers and reports. Rik Kirkland shepherded this project from conception to completion and helped us negotiate the publishing world. The team at *McKinsey Quarterly* enabled us to air portions of the arguments in this book. We'd like in particular to thank Allen Webb, Frank Comes, and Mike Borruso. And as is the case with all our publications, MGI's editorial and communications team—Tim Beacom, Janet Bush, Marisa Carder, Geoff Lewis, Julie Philpot, Lisa Renaud, and Rebeca Robboy—have provided support and advice to help ensure our research reaches the broadest possible audience.

We also relied on some key editorial professionals to polish the manuscript and its exhibits. Our special thanks goes to Daniel Gross, whose elegant editing and first-rate instincts contributed enormously to the final shape of the book. Sari Sapon helped bring the exhibits to life. Marie Morris copyedited the manuscript.

PublicAffairs is a publisher whose standards and ambitions align with our own. Founder Peter Osnos and publisher Clive Priddle saw the potential for this book from the outset. John Mahaney provided early insights and advice on the thrust of our argument and expertly edited the book. The manuscript was copyedited by Kate Mueller, and Timm Bryson worked diligently to create a visually appealing book.

Finally, much of this book was written on weekends. We would like to thank our families for putting up with this intrusion into family time.

James, San Francisco
Jonathan, Shanghai
Richard, London

NOTES

AN INTUITION RESET

1. Adobe Digital Index, December 1, 2014, www.adobe.com/news-room/press releases/201412/120114AdobeDataShowsCyberMondaySalesUp.html.

2. Adam Jourdan, "Alibaba reports record $9 billion Singles' Day Sales," Reuters, November 11, 2014; www.nytimes.com/2013/11/12/business/international /online-shopping-marathon-zooms-off-the-blocks-in-china.html?_r=0. Note that the etymology of Singles Day is also interesting. In Chinese, November 11 is "yao yao yao yao," and *yao* also means "me," so the day is all about "me."

3. "North Dakota field production of crude oil," Energy Information Administration, www.eia.gov.

4. Amit Chowdhry, "WhatsApp hits 500 million users," Forbes.com, April 22, 2014, www.forbes.com/sites/amitchowdhry/2014/04/22/whatsapp-hits-500 -million-users.

5. PRNewswire, "Facebook reports third quarter 2014 results," October 28, 2014, http://investor.fb.com/releasedetail.cfm?ReleaseID=878726.

6. Gardiner Harris, "On a shoestring, India sends orbiter to Mars on its first try," *New York Times,* September 25, 2014.

7. James H. Stock and Mark W. Watson, "Has the business cycle changed and why?," National Bureau of Economic Research working paper no. 9127, August 2002, www.nber.org/papers/w9127.

8. Richard Dobbs, Jaana Remes, Sven Smit, James Manyika, Jonathan Woetzel, and Yaw Agyenm-Boateng, *Urban world: The shifting global business landscape,* McKinsey Global Institute, October 2013.

9. Dominic Barton, Andrew Grant, and Michelle Horn, "Leading in the 21st century," *McKinsey Quarterly,* June 2012.

10. Richard Dobbs, Sven Smit, Jaana Remes, James Manyika, Charles Roxburgh, and Alejandra Restrepo, *Urban world: Mapping the economic power of cities,* McKinsey Global Institute, March 2011.

11. Richard Dobbs, Jaana Remes, James Manyika, Charles Roxburgh, Sven Smit, and Fabian Schaer, *Urban world: Cities and the rise of the consuming class,* McKinsey Global Institute, June 2012.

12. MGI Cityscope database. For more detail, you can explore the evolving urban world though the free Android and Apple iOS app Urban World.

13. International Telecommunication Union, *World Telecommunication Development Report 1999,* October 1999, www.itu.int/ITU-D/ict/publications/wtdr _99/material/wtdr99s.pdf.

14. eMarketer, "Smartphone users worldwide will total 1.75 billion in 2014," eMarketer.com, January 16, 2014, www.emarketer.com/Article/Smartphone -Users-Worldwide-Will-Total-175-Billion-2014/1010536; "The state of broadband 2012: Achieving digital inclusion for all," Broadband Commission for Digital Development, September 2012, www.broadbandcommission.org/Documents/bb -annualreport2012.pdf.

15. Jay Winter and Michael Teitelbaum, *The Global Spread of Fertility Decline: Population, Fear, and Uncertainty* (New Haven, CT: Yale University Press, 2013).

16. European Commission, "The 2012 ageing report: Underlying assumptions and projection methodologies," Economic and Financial Affairs, April 2011, http://ec.europa.eu/economy_finance/publications/european_economy/2011/pdf /ee-2011-4_en.pdf.

17. United Nations, "World fertility patterns 2013," Department of Economic and Social Affairs, Population Division, January 2014, www.un.org/en/ development/desa/population/publications/pdf/fertility/world-fertility-patterns -2013.pdf.

18. United Nations, "South-South Trade Monitor," No. 2, UNCTAD, July 2013; James Manyika, Jacques Bughin, Susan Lund, Olivia Nottebohm, David Poulter, Sebastian Jauch, and Sree Ramaswamy, *Global flows in a digital age: How trade, finance, people, and data connect the world economy,* McKinsey Global Institute, April 2014.

19. Dambisa Moyo, "China helps Africa to develop," *Huffington Post World Post,* March 31, 2014, www.huffingtonpost.com/dambisa-moyo/china-is-helping -emerging_b_5051623.html.

20. Manyika et al., *Global flows in a digital age.*

21. Richard Dobbs, Jeremy Oppenheim, Fraser Thompson, Marcel Brinkman, and Marc Zornes, *Resource revolution: Meeting the world's energy, materials, food, and water needs,* McKinsey Global Institute, November 2011.

22. Richard Dobbs, Jeremy Oppenheim, Adam Kendall, Fraser Thompson, Martin Bratt, and Fransje van der Marel, *Reverse the curse: Maximizing the potential of resource-driven economies,* McKinsey Global Institute, December 2013. As measured by the McKinsey Global Institute's Commodity Price Index of

forty-three key commodities broken into four subgroups: energy, metals, food, and nonfood agricultural materials; Angus Maddison, *The World Economy: A Millennial Perspective,* vol. 1 (Paris: OECD Publishing, 2001).

23. Richard Dobbs, Susan Lund, Charles Roxburgh, James Manyika, Alex Kim, Andreas Schreiner, Riccardo Boin, Rohit Chopra, Sebastian Jauch, Hyun Kim, Megan McDonald, and John Piotrowski, *Farewell to cheap capital? The implications of long-term shifts in global investment and saving,* McKinsey Global Institute, December 2010.

24. "10 year treasury rate by year," www.multpl.com/interest-rate/table.

25. Richard Dobbs, Anu Madgavakar, Dominic Barton, Eric Labaye, James Manyika, Charles Roxburgh, Susan Lund, and Siddarth Madhav, *The world at work: Jobs, pay, and skills for 3.5 billion people,* McKinsey Global Institute, June 2012.

26. Ibid.

27. Grigory Milov, "Smart computers, skilled robots, redundant people," *Vedomosti,* May 28, 2013, www.mckinsey.com/global_locations/europe_and_middleeast/russia/en/latest_thinking/smart_computers.

28. Dobbs et al., *The world at work.*

Chapter 1. Beyond Shanghai

1. Based on Tuesday flight schedule, www.google.com/flights/#search;f=KMS;t =ACC;d=2014-09-02;r=2014-09-07;tt=o;q=kumasi+to+accra+direct+flights; based on Africa World Airlines advance promotional fare of GHS 75.

2. "2010 population and housing census: Summary report of final results," Ghana Statistical Service, May 2013, www.statsghana.gov.gh/docfiles/publications/2010_PHC_National_Analytical_Report.pdf; "The composite budget of the Kumasi Metropolitan Assembly for the 2013 fiscal year," Kumasi Metropolitan Assembly, Republic of Ghana, www.mofep.gov.gh/sites/default/files /budget/2013/AR/Kumasi.pdf.

3. "GNI per capita, PPP," World Bank database, http://databank.worldbank .org/data/download/GNIPC.pdf.

4. Richard Dobbs, Jaana Remes, James Manyika, Charles Roxburgh, Sven Smit, and Fabian Schaer, *Urban world: Cities and the rise of the consuming class,* McKinsey Global Institute, June 2012.

5. World Bank Database, http://data.worldbank.org/indicator/NY.GDP .MKTP.CD.

6. World Bank database; James Manyika, Jeff Sinclair, Richard Dobbs, Gernot Strube, Louis Rassey, Jan Mischke, Jaana Remes, Charles Roxburgh, Katy George, David O'Halloran, and Sreenivas Ramaswamy, *Manufacturing the future: The next era of global growth and innovation,* McKinsey Global Institute, November 2012.

7. Paul Hannon, "Emerging markets take largest share of international investment in 2013," *Wall Street Journal*, January 28, 2014, http://online.wsj.com/news/articles/SB10001424052702303553204579348372961110250; *Global Investment Trends Monitor* no. 15, United Nations Conference on Trade and Development, January 28, 2014, http://unctad.org/en/publicationslibrary/webdiaeia2014d1_en.pdf.

8. Yuval Atsmon, Peter Child, Richard Dobbs, and Laxman Narasimhan, "Winning the $30 trillion decathlon: Going for gold in emerging markets," *McKinsey Quarterly*, August 2012.

9. Dobbs et al., *Urban world: Cities and the rise of the consuming class*.

10. Exhibit E2; Dobbs et al., *Urban world: Cities and the rise of the consuming class*.

11. Ibid.

12. Richard Dobbs, Sven Smit, Jaana Remes, James Manyika, Charles Roxburgh, and Alejandra Restrepo, *Urban world: Mapping the economic power of cities*, McKinsey Global Institute, March 2011.

13. Bloomberg News, "Li Keqiang urges more urbanization to support China's growth," *Bloomberg News*, November 21, 2012, www.bloomberg.com/news/2012-11-21/li-keqiang-urges-deeper-urbanization-to-support-china-s-growth.html; UN Department of Economic and Social Affairs, World Urbanization prospects 2014 revision, http://esa.un.org/unpd/wup/CD-ROM/Default.aspx.

14. Daniel Gross, "The real China: Urban wealth, rural poverty," Yahoo Finance, November 7, 2011, http://finance.yahoo.com/blogs/daniel-gross/real-china-urban-wealth-rural-poverty-124416045.html.

15. Stephen S. Roach, "Generating 'next China,'" *China Daily USA*, September 1, 2012, http://usa.chinadaily.com.cn/opinion/2012-09/01/content_15725888.htm.

16. Ian Johnson, "China releases plan to incorporate farmers into cities," *New York Times*, March 17, 2013, www.nytimes.com/2014/03/18/world/asia/china-releases-plan-to-integrate-farmers-in-cities.html.

17. Dexter Roberts, "China wants its people in the cities," *Bloomberg Businessweek*, March 20, 2014, www.businessweek.com/articles/2014-03-20/china-wants-its-people-in-the-cities.

18. Richard Dobbs and Shirish Sankhe, "Comparing urbanization in China and India," McKinsey & Company, July 2010, www.mckinsey.com/insights/urbanization/comparing_urbanization_in_china_and_india.

19. *The Millennium Development Goals Report 2013*, United Nations, 2013, www.un.org/millenniumgoals/pdf/report-2013/mdg-report-2013-english.pdf.

20. Dobbs et al., "Urban world: Cities and the rise of the consuming class."

21. Exhibit 1; Yuval Atsmon, Peter Child, Richard Dobbs, and Laxman Narasimhan, "Winning the $30 trillion decathlon," August 2012.

22. Anne-Sylvaine Chassany, "Danone expands in Africa with 49% stake in dairy," *Financial Times* (London), October 24, 2013, www.ft.com/cms/s/0 /7da59ec2-3cbe-11e3-86ef-00144feab7de.html#axzz3alaccule.

23. Shirish Sankhe, Ireena Vittal, Richard Dobbs, Ajit Mohan, Ankur Gulati, Jonathan Ablett, Shishir Gupta, Alex Kim, Sudipto Paul, Aditya Sanghvi, and Gurpreet Sethy, *India's urban awakening: Building inclusive cities, sustaining economic growth*, McKinsey Global Institute, April 2010.

24. Shirish Sankhe, Ireena Vittal, Richard Dobbs, Ajit Mohan, Ankur Gulati, Jonathan Ablett, Shishir Gupta, Alex Kim, Sudipto Paul, Aditya Sanghvi, and Gurpreet Sethy, *India's urban awakening: Building inclusive cities, sustaining economic growth*, McKinsey Global Institute, April 2010.

25. Department of population and economic affairs, "*World urbanization prospects, Highlights*," 2011, revision.

26. Department of population and economic affairs, "*World urbanization prospects, Highlights*"; Dobbs et al., *Urban world: Cities and the rise of the consuming class*.

27. Dobbs et al., *Urban world: Cities and the rise of the consuming class*.

28. Luís M. A. Bettencourt et al., "Urban scaling and its deviations: Revealing the structure of wealth, innovation, and crime across cities," *PLOS ONE*, November 10, 2010, www.plosone.org/article/info:doi/10.1371/journal.pone.0013541.

29. Scott Burnham, "Reprogramming the city: Can urban innovation meet growing needs?" *Guardian* (Manchester), September 28, 2013, www.theguardian .com/sustainable-business/reprogramming-city-urban-infrastructure-changes.

30. Ibid.

31. Scott Burnham, "Existing city infrastructure can be 'reprogrammed,'" *Green Futures Magazine,* September 26, 2013, www.forumforthefuture.org/ greenfutures/articles/existing-city-infrastructure-can-be-%E2%80 %98reprogrammed%E2%80%99.

32. "Visual explorations of urban mobility: Traffic origins," Senseable City Lab, Massachusetts Institute of Technology, http://senseable.mit.edu/visual -explorations-urban-mobility/traffic-origins.html

33. Raoul Oberman, Richard Dobbs, Arief Budiman, Fraser Thompson, and Morten Rossé, *The archipelago economy: Unleashing Indonesia's potential,* McKinsey Global Institute, September 2012.

34. Mercer, "2014 cost of living survey rankings," July 2014, www.mercer.com /newsroom/cost-of-living-survey.html.

35. "Panasonic to pay China workers pollution compensation," BBC.com, March 12, 2014, www.bbc.com/news/business-26555874.

36. "Ghanaian city to get a skytrain," *African Review of Business and Technology,* March 14, 2014, www.africanreview.com/transport-a-logistics/rail/kumasi -metropolis-to-get-a-skytrain.

CHAPTER 2. THE TIP OF THE ICEBERG

1. "The Knowledge," The London Taxi Experience, www.the-london-taxi
.com/london_taxi_knowledge.

2. Brendan Greeley, "Cabsplaining: A London black car driver on the Uber
protest," *Bloomberg Businessweek,* June 11, 2014, www.businessweek.com/articles
/2014-06-11/cabsplaining-a-london-black-car-driver-on-the-uber-protest.

3. "Uber: Why London cabbies hate the taxi app," *The Week,* June 11, 2014,
www.theweek.co.uk/uk-news/58491/uber-why-london-cabbies-hate-taxi-app.

4. Juliette Garside and Gwyn Topham, "Uber taxis face legal battles from
London black-cab drivers," *Guardian* (Manchester), May 29, 2014, www
.theguardian.com/uk-news/2014/may/29/uber-taxis-legal-battles-london-black
-cab-drivers.

5. John Alridge, "Fare fight: It's Uber v Hailo v Addison Lee in London's taxi
wars," *London Evening Standard,* January 17, 2014, www.standard.co.uk/lifestyle
/esmagazine/fare-fight-its-uber-v-hailo-v-addison-lee-in-the-londons-taxi-wars
-9064289.html.

6. "TripIndex Cities 2013," TripAdvisor United Kingdom, www.tripadvisor.co
.uk/infocenter-a_ctr.tripindex_Cities_2013_UK.

7. "Hailo arrives in Cork" (press release), July 1, 2013, https://hailocab.com/
ireland/press-releases/hailo-cork-release.

8. www.uber.com/cities.

9. Evelyn M. Rusli and Douglas MacMillan, "Uber gets an uber-valuation,"
Wall Street Journal, June 6, 2014, http://online.wsj.com/articles/uber-gets-uber
-valuation-of-18-2-billion-1402073876.

10. Ian Silvera, "Uber CEO Travis Kalanick: We will have 42,000 London
drivers in 2016," *International Business Times,* October 2014, http://www.ibtimes.co
.uk/uber-ceo-travis-kalanick-we-will-have-42000-london-drivers-2016-1468436.

11. "Angry London cabbies attack Hailo taxi app office," BBC.com, May 22,
2014, www.bbc.co.uk/news/technology-27517914.

12. Rhiannon Williams, "Uber adds black cabs amid claims taxi strike 'could
cost lives,'" *Telegraph* (London), June 11, 2014, www.telegraph.co.uk/technology
/news/10891442/Uber-adds-black-cabs-amid-claims-taxi-strike-could-cost-lives
.html.

13. "2,500,000 BCE to 8,000 BCE timeline," Jeremy Norman's HistoryofIn-
formation.com, www.historyofinformation.com/expanded.php?Id=4071.

14. W. Brian Arthur, "The second economy," *McKinsey Quarterly,* October,
2011.

15. www.mooreslaw.org.

16. "Innovation in Cambridge: Human Genome Project," www.cambridgehistory
.org/discover/innovation/Human_Genome.html.

17. James Manyika, Michael Chui, Jacques Bughin, Richard Dobbs, Peter Bisson, and Alex Marrs, *Disruptive technologies: Advances that will transform life, business, and the global economy,* McKinsey Global Institute, May 2013.

18. Ibid.

19. Exhibit E3; Manyika et al., *Disruptive technologies.*

20. Ashlee Vance, "Illumina's DNA supercomputer ushers in the $1,000 human genome," *Bloomberg Businessweek,* January 14, 2014, www.businessweek .com/articles/2014-01-14/illuminas-dna-supercomputer-ushers-in-the-1-000 -human-genome.

21. Manyika et al., *Disruptive technologies,* and accompanying slideshow "A Gallery of Disruptive Technologies."

22. Ibid.

23. Joseph Bradley, Joel Barbier, and Doug Handler, "Embracing the Internet of everything to capture your share of $14.4 trillion," Cisco Systems, February 12, 2013.

24. Manyika et al., *Disruptive technologies.*

25. HowieT, "The big bang: How the big data explosion is changing the world," Microsoft UK Enterprise Insights Blog, April 15, 2013, http://blogs.msdn .com/b/microsoftenterpriseinsight/archive/2013/04/15/the-big-bang-how-the-big -data-explosion-is-changing-the-world.aspx.

26. James Manyika, Michael Chui, Brad Brown, Jacques Bughin, Richard Dobbs, Charles Roxburgh, and Angela Hung Byers, *Big data: The next frontier for innovation, competition, and productivity,* McKinsey Global Institute, May 2011.

27. As data proliferates, larger units of measurement are needed to describe storage space: 1,024 gigabytes = 1 terabyte; 1,024 terabytes = 1 petabyte; 1,024 petabytes = 1 exabyte; John Gantz and David Reinsel, "The digital universe in 2020: Big data, bigger digital shadows, and biggest growth in the Far East," IDC, EMC Corporation, December 2012, www.emc.com/collateral/analyst-reports/idc -the-digital-universe-in-2020.pdf.

28. James Manyika, Jacques Bughin, Susan Lund, Olivia Nottebohm, David Poulter, Sebastian Jauch, and Sree Ramaswamy, *Global flows in a digital age: How trade, finance, people, and data connect the world economy,* McKinsey Global Institute, April 2014.

29. James Manyika, Michael Chui, Diana Farrell, Steve Van Kuiken, Peter Groves, and Elizabeth Almasi Doshi, *Open data: Unlocking innovation and performance with liquid information,* McKinsey Global Institute, McKinsey Center for Government, and McKinsey Business Technology Office, October 2013.

30. "Innovation in government: Kenya and Georgia," McKinsey & Company, September 2011.

31. Blair Claflin, "Employees use skills to reduce traffic congestion in Pune," Cummins Inc., www.cummins.com/cmi/navigationAction.do?nodeId=219&siteId =1&nodeName=Reducing+Traffic+in+Pune&menuId=1050.

32. "Haiti," Humanitarian OpenStreetMap Team, http://hot.openstreetmap .org/projects/haiti-2.

33. Michael Chui, James Manyika, Jacques Bughin, Richard Dobbs, Charles Roxburgh, Hugo Sarrazin, Geoffrey Sands and Magdalena Westergren, *The social economy: Unlocking productivity and value through social technologies,* McKinsey Global Institute, July 2012.

34. Drew DeSilver, "Overseas users power Facebook's growth; more going mobile-only," Pew Research Center Fact Tank, February 4, 2014, www .pewresearch.org/fact-tank/2014/02/04/overseas-users-power-facebooks-growth -more-going-mobile-only.

35. Josh Ong, "Tencent's WeChat messaging app passes 300m users, adding its latest 100m in just 4 months," The Next Web, January 16, 2013, http://thenextweb.com/asia/2013/01/16/tencents-wechat-tops-300-million-users -days-before-its-second-birthday/1.

36. MG Siegler, "App Store now has 150,000 apps. Great news for the iPad: Paid books rule," TechCrunch, February 12, 2010, http://techcrunch.com/2010 /02/12/app-store-numbers-books-ipad.

37. Seth Fiegerman, "Apple App Store tops 75 billion downloads," Mashable, June 2, 2014, http://mashable.com/2014/06/02/apple-app-store-stats-2014.

38. Manyika et al., *Disruptive technologies,*; Nirmalya Chatterjee, "Global industrial robotics market (products, functions, applications and geography)—global analysis, industry growth, trends, size, share, opportunities and forecast—2013–2020," Allied Market Research, May 2014, www.alliedmarketresearch.com /industrial-robotics-market.

39. "Cisco Visual Networking Index: Forecast and methodology, 2013–2018," Cisco Systems, June 10, 2014.

40. Matthieu Pélissié du Rausas, James Manyika, Eric Hazan, Jacques Bughin, Michael Chui, and Rémi Said, *Internet matters: The Net's sweeping impact on growth, jobs, and prosperity,* McKinsey Global Institute, May 2011.

41. Jacques Bughin and James Manyika, "Measuring the full impact of digital capital," *McKinsey Quarterly,* July 2013.

42. Richard D. Kahlenberg, *Broken Contract: A Memoir of Harvard Law School* (NY: Hill and Wang, 1992).

43. "Creative destruction whips through corporate America," Innosight Executive Briefing, winter 2012, www.innosight.com/innovation-resources/strategy -innovation/upload/creative-destruction-whips-through-corporate-america_ final2012.pdf.

44. Ibid.

45. Ibid.

46. Bill Gurley, "A deeper look at Uber's dynamic pricing model," Above the Crowd, March 11, 2014, http://abovethecrowd.com/2014/03/11/a-deeper-look-at -ubers-dynamic-pricing-model/; Matthew Panzarino, "Leaked Uber numbers, which we've confirmed, point to over \$1B gross, \$213M revenue," TechCrunch, December 4, 2013, http://techcrunch.com/2013/12/04/leaked-uber-numbers -which-weve-confirmed-point-to-over-1b-gross-revenue-213m-revenue.

47. Salvador Rodriguez, "Lyft surpasses 1 million rides, expands to Washington, D.C.," *Los Angeles Times,* August 9, 2013, http://articles.latimes.com/2013/ aug/09/business/la-fi-tn-lyft-1-million-washington-dc-20130808.

48. "AHA statistical update: Heart disease and stroke statistics—2013 update," American Heart Association, *Circulation* 2013:127:e6–e245, December 12, 2012.

49. "Medtronic launches CareLink Express™ Service" (press release), Medtronic, August 14, 2012, http://newsroom.medtronic.com/phoenix.zhtml?C=251324&p =irol-newsarticle&ID=1769548.

50. Amy Dockser Marcus and Christopher Weaver, "Heart gadgets test privacy-law limits," *Wall Street Journal,* November 28, 2012, http://online.wsj .com/news/articles/SB10001424052970203937004578078820874744076.

51. Kiva website: www.kiva.org/about.

52. Kickstarter website: www.kickstarter.com/help/stats?ref=footer.

53. Martin Hirt and Paul Willmott, "Strategic principles for competing in the digital age," *McKinsey Quarterly,* May 2014.

54. Amit Chowdhry, "WhatsApp hits 500 million users," Forbes.com, April 22, 2014, www.forbes.com/sites/amitchowdhry/2014/04/22/whatsapp-hits-500 -million-users.

55. Darrell Etherington, "Snapchat accounts for more photo shares than Instagram as pic sharing set to double in 2013," TechCrunch, May 29, 2013, http://techcrunch.com/2013/05/29/snapchat-accounts-for-more-photo-shares -than-instagram-as-pic-sharing-set-to-double-in-2013.

56. Jacques Bughin, Michael Chui, and James Manyika, "Ten IT-enabled business trends for the decade ahead," *McKinsey on Business Technology* 33, spring 2014; Panzarino, "Leaked Uber numbers"; Rodriguez, "Lyft surpasses 1 million rides."

57. Francesco Banfi, Paul-Louis Caylar, Ewan Duncan, and Ken Kajii, "E-journey: Digital marketing and the 'path to purchase,'" McKinsey & Company, January 2013.

58. http://uk.burberry.com/store-locator/regent-street-store.

59. Matthieu Pélissié du Rausas, James Manyika, Eric Hazan, Jacques Bughin, Michael Chui, and Rémi Said, *Internet matters: The Net's sweeping impact on growth, jobs, and prosperity,* McKinsey Global Institute, May 2011.

60. www.linkedin.com/mnyfe/subscriptionv2?displayProducts=&trk=nav_ responsive_sub_nav_upgrade.

61. *2013 Annual Report,* LinkedIn, April 2014, http://investors.linkedin.com/annuals.cfm.

62. "Glossybox flogs 4 million boxes within two and a half years," deutsche-start-ups.com, July 9, 2013, www.deutsche-start-ups.com/2013/07/09/glossybox-flogs-4-million-boxes-within-two-and-a-half-years.

63. Graham Ruddick, "Families snack on graze boxes," *Telegraph* (London), November 10, 2013, www.telegraph.co.uk/finance/newsbysector/retailandconsumer/10439490/Families-snack-on-graze-boxes.html.

64. Doni Bloomfield, "New York Times drops after forecasting decline in ad revenue," Bloomberg, October 2014, www.bloomberg.com/news/2014-10-30/new-york-times-beats-earnings-estimates-as-online-ads-increase.html.

65. "Paywalls open doors," *The Economist,* March 27, 2014, www.economist.com/blogs/babbage/2014/03/start-ups-slovakia.

66. Rick Edmonds, "Slovakian Piano Media acquires Press+ and aims to take paid digital content global," Poynter.org, September 8, 2014, www.poynter.org/latest-news/business-news/266839/slovakian-piano-media-acquires-press-and-aims-to-take-paid-digital-content-global.

67. Misty White Sidell, "Is this the future of make-up? New 3-D printer lets you create unlimited lipstick and eyeshadow at home—for $200," *Daily Mail* (London), May 6, 2014, www.dailymail.co.uk/femail/article-2621837/Is-future-make-New-3-D-printer-lets-create-unlimited-lipstick-eyeshadow-home-200.html.

68. Ben Elgin, "Google buys Android for its mobile arsenal," Bloomberg BusinessWeek, August 16, 2005, www.businessweek.com/stories/2005-08-16/google-buys-android-for-its-mobile-arsenal.

69. Stephen Baker, "Google-YouTube: Was it worth $1.6 billion?," *Bloomberg BusinessWeek*, May 21, 2008, www.businessweek.com/stories/2008-05-21/google-youtube-was-it-worth-1-dot-6-billion.

70. Larry Page, *Larry Page at Zeitgeist Americas 2013*, YouTube video clip, September 20, 2013.

71. Christina Farr, "Tech IPOs in 2013: Enterprise rules, and a watershed e-commerce moment," VentureBeat, December 26, 2013, http://venturebeat.com/2013/12/26/tech-ipos-in-2013-enterprise-rules-and-a-watershed-e-commerce-moment.

72. www.gegarages.com.

73. http://digital-accelerator.com.

74. "Walgreens appoints Sonia Chawla to newly created role as president of digital and chief marketing officer" (press release), Walgreens, November 21, 2013, http://news.walgreens.com/article_display.cfm?Article_id=5823.

75. "Walgreen to buy drugstore.com," Dealbook, *New York Times,* March 24, 2011, http://dealbook.nytimes.com/2011/03/24/walgreens-to-buy-drugstore-com.

76. Brian T. Horowitz, "Walgreens opens API for mobile prescription scanning to developers," eWeek.com, February 13, 2013, www.eweek.com/developer/walgreens-opens-api-for-mobile-prescription-scanning-to-developers/?Bcsi-ac-e9597abe29b9070f=225a122e000000051s0pg2wbcqfx1kzbtjdvptjxtbqmaaaabq aaaitsggdaqaaaaaaakxbcqa=; Adam Pressman and Deepika Pandey, "Chains need to go beyond multichannel, omnichannel," *Chain Drug Review,* October 28, 2013, www.chaindrugreview.com/inside-this-issue/opinion/10-28-2013/chains -need-to-go-beyond-multichannel-omnichannel.

77. Michael Zennie and Louise Boyle, "Billion dollar deal makes 26-year-old America's next tech tycoon: High school drop-out behind blogging site Tumblr sells it to Marissa Mayer's Yahoo," *Daily Mail* (London), May 19, 2013, www .dailymail.co.uk/news/article-2326998/Yahoo-buys-Tumblr-1-1billion-Founder -David-Karp-tech-tycoon.html.

78. Sarah Perez, "@WalmartLabs buys adtech start-up Adchemy, its biggest talent deal yet," TechCrunch, May 5, 2014, http://techcrunch.com/2014/05/05/walmartlabs-buys-adtech-start-up-adchemy-its-biggest-talent-deal-yet.

79. www.sephora.com/about-us; Jason Del Rey, "In-store tech is so hot right now: Sephora acquires fragrance software start-up Scentsa," All Things D, August 7, 2013, http://allthingsd.com/20130807/in-store-tech-is-so-hot-right-now -sephora-acquires-fragrance-software-start-up-scentsa.

80. Colin Morrison, "How Axel Springer can be a digital media champion," Flashes and Flames, April 25, 2014, www.flashesandflames.com/2014/04/how -axel-springer-can-become-a-digital-media-champion.

81. Ibid.

82. David Meyer, "Axel Springer invests in privacy-friendly search start-up Qwant," Gigaom, June 19, 2014, http://gigaom.com/2014/06/19/axel-springer -invests-in-privacy-friendly-search-start-up-qwant.

Chapter 3. Getting Old Isn't What It Used to Be

1. Awesome-o, "Robovie R3 unveiled," Robotics Zeitgeist, April 22, 2010, http://robotzeitgeist.com/2010/04/robovie-r3-unveiled.html.

2. "Field listing: Median age," The World Factbook, US Central Intelligence Agency, www.cia.gov/library/publications/the-world-factbook/fields/2177.html; "Population ages 65 and above (% of total)," World Bank database, http://data .worldbank.org/indicator/SP.POP.65UP.TO.ZS.

3. "Fertility rate, total (births per woman)," World Bank database, http://data .worldbank.org/indicator/SP.DYN.TFRT.IN.

4. Daniel Gross, "Why Japan isn't rising," Slate, July 18, 2009, www.slate.com /articles/business/moneybox/2009/07/why_japan_isnt_rising.html.

5. "South Asia: Pakistan," The World Factbook, US Central Intelligence Agency, www.cia.gov/library/publications/the-world-factbook/geos/pk.html.

6. "Country comparison: Total fertility rate," The World Factbook, US Central Intelligence Agency, www.cia.gov/library/publications/the-world-factbook/rankorder/2127rank.html.

7. Elizabeth Kolbert, "Head count," *New Yorker*, October 21, 2013, www.newyorker.com/arts/critics/books/2013/10/21/131021crbo_books_kolbert?Currentpage=2.

8. "Country comparison," The World Factbook.

9. Ibid.

10. MGI analysis: Demographics and Employment, 2014.

11. Ibid.

12. Ibid.

13. Jay Winter and Michael Teitelbaum, *The Global Spread of Fertility Decline: Population, Fear, and Uncertainty* (New Haven, CT: Yale University Press, 2013).

14. "Fertility rate, total," World Bank database.

15. MGI analysis: Demographics and Employment, 2014.

16. "EU27 population is expected to peak by around 2040" (press release), Eurostat, European Commission, June 8, 2011, http://epp.eurostat.ec.europa.eu/cache/ITY_PUBLIC/3-08062011-BP/EN/3-08062011-BP-EN.PDF.

17. *The 2012 ageing report: Economic and budgetary projections for the 27 EU member states (2010–2060)*, European Commission, February 2012, http://ec.europa.eu/economy_finance/publications/european_economy/2012/pdf/ee-2012-2_en.pdf.

18. *The 2012 ageing report: Underlying assumptions and projection methodologies*, European Commission, April 2011, http://ec.europa.eu/economy_finance/publications/european_economy/2011/pdf/ee-2011-4_en.pdf.

19. Ibid.

20. MGI analysis: Demographics and Employment, 2014.

21. *World population prospects: The 2012 revision*, United Nations Department of Economic and Social Affairs, Population Division, June 2013, http://esa.un.org/wpp.

22. Ibid.

23. Sarah O'Connor, "World will have 13 'super-aged' nations by 2020," *Financial Times* (London), August 6, 2014, www.ft.com/cms/s/0/f356f8a0-1d8c-11e4-8f0c-00144feabdc0.html.

24. "Dean Xie Danyang blueprints Wuhan's future: An international city in 2040" (press release), EMBA Education Center of Wuhan University, April 16, 2014, http://emba.whu.edu.cn/en/News/News/2014-04-16/1287.php.

25. "Field listing: Median age," The World Factbook.

26. Richard Dobbs, Anu Madgavkar, Dominic Barton, Eric Labaye, James Minyika, Charles Roxburgh, Susan Lund, and Siddarth Madhav, "The world at work: Jobs, pay, and skills for 3.5 billion people," June 2012, McKinsey & Company.

27. Benjamin Shobert, "Bank on it," Slate, November 5, 2013, www.slate.com /articles/technology/future_tense/2013/11/feng_kexiong_s_volunteer_bank_ plan_to_care_for_china_s_elderly.html.

28. James Manyika, Michael Chui, Jacques Bughin, Richard Dobbs, Peter Bisson, and Alex Marrs, *Disruptive technologies: Advances that will transform life, business, and the global economy,* McKinsey Global Institute, May 2013.

29. Ibid.

30. Peter Baker, "Kagan is sworn in as the fourth woman, and 112th justice, on the Supreme Court," *New York Times,* August 7, 2010, www.nytimes.com /2010/08/08/us/08kagan.html?_r=0

31. Dobbs et al., "The world at work."

32. MGI analysis: Demographics and Employment, 2014.

33. Ibid.

34. Dobbs et al., "The world at work."

35. O'Connor, "World will have 13 'super-aged' nations by 2020."

36. Dobbs et al., "The world at work."

37. Suzanne Daley and Nicholas Kulish, "Germany fights population drop," *New York Times,* August 13, 2013.

38. "China reforms: One-child policy to be relaxed," BBC.com, November 15, 2013, www.bbc.com/news/world-asia-china-24957303; "Women at Work," *Finance & Development,* volume 50, number 2, International Monetary Fund, June 2013, www.imf.org/external/pubs/ft/fandd/2013/06/pdf/fd0613.pdf.

39. Dobbs et al., "The world at work."

40. Ibid.

41. Ibid.

42. Ibid.

43. *Global aging 2013: Rising to the challenge,* Standard & Poor's, March 20, 2013, www.mhfigi.com/societal-trends/global-aging-2013-rising-to-the -challenge.

44. Rafal Chomik and Edward R. Whitehouse, *Trends in pension eligibility ages and life expectancy, 1950–2050,* OECD Social, Employment and Migration working papers number 105, 2010.

45. Szu Ping Chan, "Pensions free-for-all 'risks leaving millions in poverty,'" *Telegraph* (London), March 29, 2014, www.telegraph.co.uk/finance/ personalfinance/pensions/10732126/Pensions-free-for-all-risks-leaving-millions -in-poverty.html.

46. Barbara A. Butrica, Howard M. Iams, Karen E. Smith, and Eric J. Toder, "The disappearing defined benefit pension and its potential impact on the retirement incomes of baby boomers," US Social Security Administration, *Social Security Bulletin* 69, no. 3, 2009, www.ssa.gov/policy/docs/ssb/v69n3/v69n3p1.html. More recent data from National Compensation Survey, US Bureau of Labor Statistics, March 2013.

47. "Defined benefit pensions: Plan freezes affect millions of participants and may pose retirement income challenges," US Government Accountability Office, 2008, www.gao.gov/new.items/d08817.pdf.

48. "Working longer: Older Americans' attitudes on work and retirement," Associated Press–NORC Center for Public Affairs Research, 2013, www.apnorc .org/projects/Pages/working-longer-older-americans-attitudes-on-work-and -retirement.aspx.

49. "Leading in the 21st century: An interview with HCA CEO Richard Bracken," McKinsey & Company, November 2013.

50. Rebecca L. Ray et al., *The state of human capital: False summit,* McKinsey & Company and The Conference Board, October 2012; *Sustainability report 2008,* Toyota Motor Corporation, July 2008, www.toyota-global.com/ sustainability/report/sr/08/pdf/sustainability_report08.pdf.

51. *French employment 2020: Five priorities for action,* McKinsey Global Institute, May 2012.

52. Ibid.; "Older employees driving value," News and views, Centrica, October 1, 2013, www.centrica.com/index.asp?Pageid=1042&blogid=695.

53. *Innovative Practices Executive Case Report No. 5,* Sloan Center on Aging and Work, 2012.

54. Georges Desvaux and Baudouin Regout, "Meeting the 2030 French consumer: How European-wide trends will shape the consumer landscape," *McKinsey Consumer and Shopper Insights,* May 2010.

55. Ibid.

56. Ibid.

57. Yuval Atsmon and Max Magni, "Meet the Chinese consumer of 2020," *McKinsey Quarterly,* March 2012.

58. www.eldertreks.com.

59. PT, "Thomas Cook launches 'Silver Breaks' for elderly travellers," *The Hindu* (Chennai), June 15, 2014, www.thehindubusinessline.com/companies/ thomas-cook-launches-silver-breaks-for-elderly-travellers/article6116909.ece.

60. http://info.singtel.com/personal/silverline.

61. www.youtube.com/watch?v=vilUhBhNnQc.

62. "Depend and the great American try on: Repositioning incontinence from the bathroom to the forefront of pop culture," PRWeek Awards 2013, http://awards .prweekus.com/depend-and-great-american-try-repositioning-incontinence -bathroom-forefront-pop-culture.

63. Olivia Goh, "Successful ageing—a review of Singapore's policy approaches," Civil Service College Singapore, *Ethos,* no. 1, October 2006, www .cscollege.gov.sg/Knowledge/Ethos/Issue%201%20Oct%202006/Pages/ Successful-Ageing-A-Review-of-Singapores-Policy-Approaches.aspx.

64. United Nations Department of Economic and Social Affairs, Population Division, "Magnitude and speed of population ageing," chapter 2 in *World*

Population Ageing 1950–2050 (NY: UN, 2002), www.un.org/esa/population/ publications/worldageing19502050/pdf/80chapterii.pdf.

65. Mansoor Dalal, "Senior living India . . . a need whose time has come!!!" Association of Senior Living India, www.asli.org.in/page-seniorlivingindia.html.

66. Japan retail market, Japan Retail News, www.japanretailnews.com/japans -retail-market.html.

67. Adam Westlake, "Aeon opens senior-focused shopping center," *Japan Daily Press,* April 25, 2012, http://japandailypress.com/aeon-opens-senior-focused -shopping-center-251330/; Louise Lucas, "Retailers target grey spending power," *Financial Times* (London), August 14, 2012, www.ft.com/cms/s/0/bb60a5b2 -e608-11e1-a430-00144feab49a.html#axzz3blwglwyg.

68. Christophe Nedopil, Youse and Bradley Schurman, "Age friendly banking: A global overview of best practices," AARP, June 27, 2014, www.aarpinternational.org /resource-library/resources/age-friendly-banking-a-global-overview-of-best-practices.

69. "Amazon launches 50+ Active and Healthy Living Store featuring hundreds of thousands of items in one single destination" (press release), Business Wire, April 15, 2013, www.businesswire.com/news/home/20130415005498/en/ Amazon-Launches-50-Active-Healthy-Living-Store#.U_s3ycwwkpc.

70. Roger Blitz, "Saga tests the water for stock market debut," *Financial Times* (London), February 16, 2014, www.ft.com/cms/s/0/55288bfc-970f-11e3-809f -00144feab7de.html; Saga market capitalisation, Hargreaves Lansdown, www.hl .co.uk/shares/shares-search-results/s/saga-plc-ordinary-1p.

71. www.cognifit.com.

72. "Raku-Raku phone series reaches 20 million unit sales in Japan" (press release), NTT Socomo, July 22, 2011, www.nttdocomo.co.jp/english/info/media _center/pr/2011/001534.html.

73. David Pierce, "Fujitsu's futuristic cane does so much more than help you walk," The Verge, February 27, 2013, www.theverge.com/2013/2/27/4036228/ fujitsus-futuristic-next-generation-cane-hands-on.

CHAPTER 4. TRADE, PEOPLE, FINANCE, AND DATA

1. Melody Ng, "Shanghai Pudong Airport to build world's biggest satellite concourse," The Moodie Report, February 10, 2014, www.moodiereport.com/ document.php?doc_id=38312.

2. "Ever wondered how everything you buy from China gets here? Welcome to the port of Shanghai—the size of 470 football pitches," *Daily Mail* (London), October 29, 2013, www.dailymail.co.uk/news/article-2478975/Shanghai-port -worlds-busiest-handles-736m-tonnes-year.html.

3. James Manyika, Jacques Bughin, Susan Lund, Olivia Nottebohm, David Poulter, Sebastian Jauch, and Sree Ramaswamy, *Global flows in a digital age: How trade, finance, people, and data connect the world economy,* McKinsey Global Institute, April 2014.

4. "Leading in the 21st century: An interview with Shell's Ann Pickard," McKinsey & Company, June 2014.

5. IMF e-library; Graeme Wearden, "IMF: World economy to shrink for first time in 60 years in 'Great Recession,'" *Guardian* (Manchester), March 10, 2009, www.theguardian.com/business/2009/mar/10/imf-great-recession.

6. Manyika et al., "Global flows in a digital age."

7. Ibid.

8. Ibid.

9. Ibid.

10. Ibid.

11. *South-South Trade Monitor*, no. 2, UNCTAD, July 2013; Manyika et al., *Global flows in a digital age.*

12. Dambisa Moyo, "China helps Africa to develop," *Huffington Post World Post*, March 31, 2014, www.huffingtonpost.com/dambisa-moyo/china-is-helping -emerging_b_5051623.html.

13. Manyika et al., "Global flows in a digital age."

14. Ibid.

15. Ibid.

16. Susan Lund, Toos Daruvala, Richard Dobbs, Philipp Härle, Ju-Hon Kwek, and Ricardo Falcón, *Financial globalization: Retreat or reset?* McKinsey Global Institute, March 2013.

17. Claire Gatinois, "Portugal indebted to Angola after economic reversal of fortune," *Guardian Weekly* (London), June 3, 2014, www.theguardian.com/world /2014/jun/03/portugal-economy-bailout-angola-invests.

18. Pankaj Mishra, "Infosys CEO SD Shibulal owns 700+ apartments in Seattle; now buying in Berlin, Frankfurt," *The Economic Times,* June 23, 2014, http://articles.economictimes.indiatimes.com/2014-06-23/news/50798685 _1_shruti-shibulal-infosys-ceo-sd-shibulal-tamara-coorg.

19. "Bright Food said to pay $960 million for Tnuva stake," *Bloomberg News,* May 22, 2014, www.bloomberg.com/news/2014-05-22/bright-food-said-to-pay -960-million-for-tnuva-stake.html.

20. Manyika et al., "Global flows in a digital age."

21. Charles Roxburgh, Susan Lund, Richard Dobbs, James Manyika, and Haihao Wu, *The emerging equity gap: Growth and stability in the new investor landscape,* McKinsey Global Institute, December 2011.

22. Lund et al., *Financial globalization.*

23. UN Department of Economic and Social Affairs, "Trends in total migrant stock: The 2005 tevision," February 2006, www.un.org/esa/population/ publications/migration/UN_Migrant_Stock_Documentation_2005.pdf; "Number of international migrants rises above 232 million, UN reports" (press release), United Nations News Centre, September 11, 2013, www.un.org/apps/ news/story.asp?Newsid=45819&Cr=migrants&Crl=#.U9_jcendvp0.

24. Mary Medeiros Kent, "More US scientists and engineers are foreign-born," Population Reference Bureau, January 2011, www.prb.org/Publications/Articles /2011/usforeignbornstem.aspx.

25. James Fontanella-Khan, "Romanians despair that wealthy Britain is taking all their doctors," *Financial Times* (London), January 14, 2014, www.ft.com/cms /s/0/f4c0b734-7c70-11e3-b514-00144feabdc0.html#axzz3bwxijwoo.

26. Maram Hussein, "Bangladeshi expats happy to work in Qatar, says envoy," Qatar Tribune, October 7, 2013, www.qatar-tribune.com/viewnews.aspx?N=DD 3FCF9D-5E03-47DC-B8AF-EFFDB77AF298&d=20131007; http://unbconnect .com/tofail-qatar/#&panel1-1.

27. Damien Cave, "Migrants' new paths reshaping Latin America," *New York Times,* January 5, 2012, www.nytimes.com/2012/01/06/world/americas/migrants -new-paths-reshaping-latin-america.html?Pagewanted=all&_r=0.

28. *UNWTO Tourism Highlights,* 2013 edition, United Nations World Tourism Organization; *Economic Impact of Travel & Tourism 2013 Annual Update,* World Travel & Tourism Council, 2013.

29. "US passports issued per fiscal year (2013–1996)," US Department of State, http://travel.state.gov/content/passports/english/passports/statistics.html; Andrew Bender, "Record number of Americans now hold passports," Forbes.com, January 30, 2012, www.forbes.com/sites/andrewbender/2012/01/30/record -number-of-americans-now-hold-passports.

30. *The Economist,* "Coming to a Beach Near You," April 2014. http://www .economist.com/news/international/21601028-how-growing-chinese-middle-class -changing-global-tourism-industry-coming.

31. *2012 Open Doors Report,* Institute of International Education, 2012.

32. Daniel Gross, "Myth of decline: US is stronger and faster than anywhere else," *Newsweek,* April 30, 2012, www.newsweek.com/myth-decline-us-stronger -and-faster-anywhere-else-64093.

33. Facebook website, http://newsroom.fb.com/company-info/; Kishore Mahbubani, "The global village has arrived," IMF, *Finance & Development* 49, no. 3, September 2012.

34. Manyika et al., "Global flows in a digital age."

35. Matthieu Pélissié du Rausas, James Manyika, Eric Hazan, Jacques Bughin, Michael Chui, and Rémi Said, *Internet matters: The Net's sweeping impact on growth, jobs, and prosperity,* McKinsey Global Institute, May 2011.

36. Olivia Nottebohm, James Manyika, Jacques Bughin, Michael Chui, and Abdur-Rahim Syed, *Online and upcoming: The Internet's impact on aspiring countries,* McKinsey & Company, January 2012.

37. *eTransform Africa: The transformational use of information and communication technologies in Africa,* World Bank and African Development Bank, December 2012; International Telecommunication Union statistics, 2012.

38. James Manyika, Armando Cabral, Lohini Moodley, Safroadu Yeboah-Amankwah, Suraj Moraje, Michael Chui, Jerry Anthonyrajah, and Ache Leke, *Lions go digital: The Internet's transformative potential in Africa,* McKinsey Global Institute, November 2013.

39. Damian Hattingh, Bill Russo, Ade Sun-Basorun, and Arend Van Wamelen, *The rise of the African consumer,* McKinsey & Company, October 2012.

40. Manyika et al., *Lions go digital.*

41. Michelle Atanga, "MTN ready to pour $400m into Africa and Middle East start-ups," VentureBurn, December 20, 2013, http://ventureburn.com/2013/12/mtn-ready-to-pour-in-400m-into-africa-middle-east-start-ups.

42. David Okwii, "Rocket Internet VC and start-up incubator takes on the Ugandan Internet space," Dignited, June 6, 2014, www.dignited.com/7977/rocket-internet-vc-start-up-incubator-takes-ugandan-internet-space.

43. Jonathan Cummings, James Manyika, Lenny Mendonca, Ezra Greenberg, Steven Aronowitz, Rohit Chopra, Katy Elkin, Sreenivas Ramaswamy, Jimmy Soni, and Allison Watson, *Growth and competitiveness in the United States: The role of its multinational companies,* McKinsey Global Institute, June 2010.

44. Manyika et al., "Global flows in a digital age."

45. Ibid.

46. Manyika et al., "Global flows in a digital age"; Pankaj Ghemawat and Steven A. Altman, "DHL Global Connectedness Index 2014," www.dhl.com/en/about_us/logistics_insights/studies_research/global_connectedness_index/global_connectedness_index.html#.VHnZWMkXn4Y.

47. "GE partners with the Millennium Challenge Corporation to provide $500 million in financing to Ghana 1000 project" (press release), August 5, 2014, http://allafrica.com/stories/201408061542.html; "GE to invest $2 billion in Africa by 2018" (press release), Business Wire, August 4, 2014, www.businesswire.com/news/home/20140803005030/en/GE-Invest-2-Billion-Africa-2018#.VDQoFvk7u-0.

48. Daniel Gross, "Coke applies supply-chain expertise to deliver AIDS drugs in Africa," The Daily Beast, September 25, 2012, www.thedailybeast.com/articles/2012/09/25/coke-applies-supply-chain-expertise-to-deliver-aids-drugs-in-africa.html.

49. Kenneth Rogoff, "Can Greece avoid the lion," *Project Syndicate,* February 3, 2010, www.project-syndicate.org/commentary/can-greece-avoid-the-lion-.

50. Stephen Hall, Dan Lovallo, and Reinier Musters, "How to put your money where your strategy is," *McKinsey Quarterly,* March 2012.

51. Katy George, Sree Ramaswamy, and Lou Rassey, "Next-shoring: A CEO's guide," *McKinsey Quarterly,* January 2014.

52. Mike Doheny, Venu Nagali, and Florian Weig, "Agile Manufacturing for volatile times," McKinsey & Company, 2012.

53. www.solarbrush.co.

54. www.shapeways.com.

55. "Portfolio: B & W Group," Sofina, www.sofina.be/EN/participation/bw
.php; Peter Marsh, "UK 'micro-multinationals' lead the way," *Financial Times*
(London), August 22, 2011, www.ft.com/cms/s/0/5c353610-c67f-11e0-bb50-001
44feabdc0.html#axzz39vspj1cz.

56. Marsh, "UK 'micro-multinationals' lead the way."

57. Nottebohm et al., *Online and upcoming*.

58. "Best new retail launch 2013—Jumia," World Retail Awards, September
30, 2014, www.worldretailawards.com/resources/best-new-retail-launch-2013
-%E2%80%93-jumia.

59. www.boeing.com/boeing/commercial/aviationservices/integrated-services
/digital-airline.page.

60. *Etsy Progress Report 2013,* http://extfiles.etsy.com/progress-report/2013
-Etsy-Progress-Report.pdf?Ref=progress_report_download.

61. http://openinnovation.astrazeneca.com.

62. www.unilever.com/innovation/collaborating-with-unilever/challenging
-and-wants.

63. www.bosch-pt.com/innovation/home.htm?Locale=en.

64. Manyika et al., "Global flows in a digital age."

65. *2014 Silicon Valley Index,* Joint Venture Silicon Valley and Silicon Valley
Community Foundation, www.siliconvalleycf.org/sites/default/files/publications
/2014-silicon-valley-index.pdf.

66. www.intelligentcommunity.org/index.php?Src=gendocs&ref=Smart21
_2012&link=Smart21_2012.

67. Richard Dobbs, Jaana Remes, Sven Smit, James Manyika, Jonathan Woetzel, and Yaw Agyenm-Boateng, "Urban world: The shifting global business
landscape," McKinsey Global Institute, October 2013.

68. Emily Glazer, "P&G unit bids goodbye to Cincinnati, hello to Asia," *Wall
Street Journal,* May 10, 2012, http://online.wsj.com/news/articles/SB1000142405
27023040703045773960536880815544.

69. Beth Brooks, "Unilever opens new global training centre in Asia for its
'future leaders,'" *The Grocer,* July 8, 2013, www.thegrocer.co.uk/people/unilever
-opens-global-training-centre-for-future-leaders/344935.article.

70. *Singapore Business News,* Singapore Economic Development Board, March
2013, www.edb.gov.sg/content/dam/edb/en/resources/pdfs/publications/Singapore
BusinessNews/march-2013/Singapore-Business-News-March-2013.pdf.

71. Rik Kirkland, "Leading in the 21st century: An interview with Ellen
Kullman," McKinsey & Company, September 2012.

72. Mike Doheny, Venu Nagali, and Florian Weig, "Agile Manufacturing for
volatile times," McKinsey & Company, 2012.

73. World Bank database; Isis Gaddis, Jacques Morisset, and Waly Wane, "A
well-kept secret: Tanzania's export performance," World Bank, March 4, 2013,

http://blogs.worldbank.org/africacan/a-well-kept-secret-tanzania-s-export
-performance.

CHAPTER 5. THE NEXT THREE BILLION

1. "Clarks ends shoemaking in Somerset," BBC.com, January 10, 2005, www
.bbc.co.uk/somerset/content/articles/2005/01/10/clarks_feature.shtml.

2. Mark Palmer, "A great British success: Why the world loves Clarks and its
shoes as it nears 200th anniversary," This is Money, April 19, 2013, www
.thisismoney.co.uk/money/markets/article-2311484/Clarks-A-family-firm-kept
-polish.html.

3. Patrick Barkham, "How the Chinese fell in love with Clarks shoes," *Guardian* (Manchester), March 8, 2011, www.theguardian.com/lifeandstyle/2011/mar
/09/chinese-love-clarks-shoes.

4. Ibid.

5. Olivia Goldhill, "Chinese tourists to spend £1bn in UK by 2017," *Telegraph*
(London), May 2, 2014, www.telegraph.co.uk/finance/china-business/10801908
/Chinese-tourists-to-spend-1bn-in-UK-by-2017.html; "Insight and research: UK
tourism dynamics," Barclays, www.barclayscorporate.com/insight-and-research/
research-and-reports/uk-tourism-dynamics.html.

6. "Chinese visitors surge to grab brands at Clarks Village outlet" (press release), Visit Somerset, January 15, 2014, www.visitsomerset.co.uk/blog/2014/1/15
/chinese-visitors-surge-to-grab-brands-at-clarks-village-outlet-a95.

7. Barkham, "How the Chinese fell in love with Clarks shoes."

8. Jo Tweedy, "Shoe travelled far? Clarks museum in Somerset proves unlikely
hit with Chinese tourists," *Daily Mail* (London), March 1, 2011, www.dailymail
.co.uk/travel/article-1361696/Chinese-tourists-flock-Clarks-shoe-museum
-Somerset.html#ixzz36nycck20.

9. "Poverty overview," World Bank, October 8, 2014, www.worldbank.org/en
/topic/poverty/overview; Richard Dobbs, Jaana Remes, James Manyika, Charles
Roxburgh, Sven Smit, and Fabian Schaer, *Urban world: Cities and the rise of the
consuming class,* McKinsey Global Institute, June 2012.

10. "Poverty: Not always with us," *The Economist,* May 30, 2013, www
.economist.com/news/briefing/21578643-world-has-astonishing-chance-take
-billion-people-out-extreme-poverty-2030-not; Dobbs et al., *Urban world.*

11. "Testimony on eradication of infectious diseases by Claire V. Broome, MD,
MPH, acting director, Centers for Disease Control and Prevention, US Department of Health and Human Services," May 20, 1998, www.hhs.gov/asl/testify/
t980520a.html; Annex Table 2, World Health Organization, *The World Health
Report 2004: Changing History* (Geneva: World Health Report, 2004); www.who
.int/whr/2004.

12. Dobbs et al., *Urban world.*

13. United Nations, "Introduction," in *The World at Six Billion* (NY: UN Department of Economic and Social Affairs, Population Division, October 12, 1999), www.un.org/esa/population/publications/sixbillion/sixbilpart1.pdf.

14. Sanjeev Sanyal, "Who are tomorrow's consumers?," Project Syndicate, August 9, 2012, www.project-syndicate.org/commentary/who-are-tomorrow -s-consumers-by-sanjeev-sanyal.

15. Yuval Atsmon, Ari Kertesz, and Ireena Vittal, "Is your emerging-market strategy local enough?," *McKinsey Quarterly*, April 2011.

16. Jonathan Ablett, Aadarsh Baijal, Eric Beinhocker, Anupam Bose, Diana Farrell, Ulrich Gersch, Ezra Greenberg, Shishir Gupta, and Sumit Gupta, *The "Bird of Gold": The rise of India's consumer market*, McKinsey Global Institute, May 2007.

17. Dominic Barton, "The rise of the middle class in China and its impact on the Chinese and world economies," chapter 7 in *US-China Economic Relations in the Next Ten Years: Towards Deeper Engagement and Mutual Benefit* (Hong Kong: China–United States Exchange Foundation, 2013), www.chinausfocus.com /2022/wp-content/uploads/Part+02-Chapter+07.pdf.

18. "China's next chapter," *McKinsey Quarterly*, no. 3, 2013.

19. Michael Yoshikami, "Why Tesla will win in China," CNBC.com, May 1, 2014, www.cnbc.com/id/101634065#.

20. Peter Bisson, Rik Kirkland, and Elizabeth Stephenson, "The great rebalancing," McKinsey & Company, June 2010,

21. Yuval Atsmon, Peter Child, and Udo Kopka, "The $30 trillion decathlon: How consumer companies can win in emerging markets," *McKinsey Perspectives on Retail and Consumer Goods,* spring 2013.

22. Dobbs et al., *Urban world*.

23. Kaylene Hong, "China's Internet population hit 618 million at the end of 2013, with 81% connecting via mobile," The Next Web, January 16, 2014, http://thenextweb.com/asia/2014/01/16/chinas-Internet-population-numbered -618m-end-2013-81-connecting-via-mobile.

24. Yuval Atsmon, Peter Child, Richard Dobbs, and Laxman Narasimhan, "Winning the $30 trillion decathlon," *McKinsey Quarterly*, August 2012.

25. Tushar Banerjee, "Five unusual ways in which Indians use mobile phones," BBC.com, February 11, 2014, www.bbc.com/news/world-asia-india-26028381.

26. Nilanjana Bhowmick, "37% of all the illiterate adults in the world are Indian," *Time*, January 29, 2014, http://world.time.com/2014/01/29/indian-adult -illiteracy.

27. Agustino Fontevecchia, "India's 243 million Internet users and the mobile e-commerce revolution," Forbes.com, July 7, 2014, www.forbes.com/sites/ afontevecchia/2014/07/07/indias-massive-e-commerce-opportunity-and-the -explosion-of-mobile.

28. www.techinasia.com/2013-china-surpasses-america-to-become-worlds-top-ecommerce-market/McKinsey Global Institute analysis.

29. Adrian Covert, "A decade of iTunes singles killed the music industry," CNN Money, April 25, 2013, http://money.cnn.com/2013/04/25/technology/itunes-music-decline.

30. Nathalie Remy, Jennifer Schmidt, Charlotte Werner, and Maggie Lu, *Unleashing fashion growth city by city*, McKinsey & Company, October 2013.

31. Dominic Barton, Yougang Chen, and Amy Jim, "Mapping China's middle class," *McKinsey Quarterly*, June 2013, www.mckinsey.com/insights/consumer_and_retail/mapping_chinas_middle_class.

32. Atsmon et al., "Winning the $30 trillion decathlon."

33. Sha Sha, Theodore Huang, and Erwin Gabardi, *Upward mobility: The future of China's premium car market*, McKinsey & Company, March 2013.

34. Remy et al., *Unleashing fashion growth city by city*.

35. MGI Cityscope database. For more detail, you can explore the evolving urban world though the free Android and Apple iOS app Urban World.

36. Acha Leke, Reinaldo Fiorini, Richard Dobbs, Fraser Thompson, Aliyu Suleiman, and David Wright, *Nigeria's renewal: Delivering inclusive growth in Africa's largest economy*, McKinsey Global Institute, July 2014.

37. Patti Waldmeir, "China's coffee industry is starting to stir," *Financial Times* (London), October 22, 2012, www.ft.com/cms/s/0/992ec1e6-1901-11e2-af88-00144feabdc0.html#axzz3f28g6jcq.

38. Atsmon et al., "Winning the $30 trillion decathlon."

39. "Master Kong is the most chosen brand in China," Kantar Worldpanel, May 20, 2014, www.kantarworldpanel.com/global/News/Master-Kong-is-the-Most-Chosen-Brand-in-China.

40. Kai Bi, "Tingyi will maintain its market leadership with a diversified product portfolio," analyst report, Morningstar, April 10, 2014, http://analysisreport.morningstar.com/stock/research?T=00322&region=hkg&culture=en-US&productcode=MLE.

41. Ishan Chatterjee, Jörn Küpper, Christian Mariager, Patrick Moore, and Steve Reis, "The decade ahead: Trends that will shape the consumer goods industry," McKinsey & Company, December 2010.

42. Bisson et al., "The great rebalancing."

43. Atsmon et al., "Winning the $30 trillion decathlon."

44. Chatterjee et al., "The decade ahead."

45. Tom Glaser, "2013 investor day," VF Corporation, June 11, 2013, www.vf17x17.com/pdf/2013%20VFC%20Investor%20Day-Glaser%20Transcript.pdf; Gary P. Pisano and Pamela Adams, *VF Brands: Global Supply Chain Strategy*, Harvard Business School case number 610–022, November 2009, www.hbs.edu/faculty/Pages/item.aspx?num=38127.

46. Atsmon et al., "Winning the $30 trillion decathlon."

47. Alejandro Diaz, Max Magni, and Felix Poh, "From oxcart to Wal-Mart: Four keys to reaching emerging-market consumers," *McKinsey Quarterly*, October 2012.

48. Atsmon et al., "Winning the $30 trillion decathlon."

49. Ibid.

50. Ibid.

51. Ibid.

52. Martin Dewhurst, Jonathan Harris, and Suzanne Heywood, "Understanding your 'globalization penalty,'" *McKinsey Quarterly*, July 2011.

53. Li Fangfang, "ABB sets sights on 'designed in China,'" *China Daily USA*, July 19, 2012, http://usa.chinadaily.com.cn/epaper/2012-07/19/content_15599833.htm.

54. Rick Newman, "Why US companies aren't so American anymore," *U.S. News & World Report*, June 30, 2011, http://money.usnews.com/money/blogs/flowchart/2011/06/30/why-us-companies-arent-so-american-anymore; William Lazonick, "A transformative jobs plan: What's good for IBM's top executives is not good for the US," Roosevelt Institute, May 2011, www.rooseveltinstitute.org/new-roosevelt/transformative-jobs-plan-what-s-good-ibm-s-top-executives-not-good-us; Martin Dewhurst, "An interview with Michael Cannon-Brookes, vice president, business development, China and India, IBM Corporation," in *Perspectives on global organizations*, McKinsey & Company, May 2012.

55. Rachel Layne, "GE moves 115-year-old X-ray unit's base to China to tap growth," *Bloomberg News*, July 25, 2011, www.bloomberg.com/news/2011-07-25/ge-healthcare-moves-x-ray-base-to-china-no-job-cuts-planned.html.

56. Hervé de Barbeyrac and Ruben Verhoeven, "Tilting the global balance: An interview with the CEO of Solvay," *McKinsey Quarterly*, October 2013.

57. Choe Soon-kyoo, "How LG surpassed Samsung in India," *Korea Times*, April 6, 2012, www.koreatimes.co.kr/www/news/bizfocus/2012/04/342_108490.html.

58. Atsmon et al., "Winning the $30 trillion decathlon."

59. Ibid.

CHAPTER 6. REVERSING THE CYCLE

1. Brian Whitaker, "How a man setting fire to himself sparked an uprising in Tunisia," *Guardian* (Manchester), December 28, 2010, www.theguardian.com/commentisfree/2010/dec/28/tunisia-ben-ali.

2. http://web.worldbank.org/WBSITE/EXTERNAL/COUNTRIES/MENAEXT/0,,contentmdk:20528258~pagepk:146736~pipk:226340~thesitepk:256299,00.html.

3. UN FAO Food Price Index, Food and Agriculture Organization of the United Nations, www.fao.org/worldfoodsituation/foodpriceindex/en/; United Nations, "The global food crises," chapter 4 in *The Global Social Crisis: Report on*

the World Social Situation 2011 (NY: United Nations, 2011), www.un.org/esa/socdev/rwss/docs/2011/chapter4.pdf.

4. UN FAO Food Price Index; Nafeez Ahmed, "Why food riots are likely to become the new normal," *Guardian* (Manchester), March 6, 2013, www.theguardian.com/environment/blog/2013/mar/06/food-riots-new-normal.

5. Marco Lagi, Karla Z. Bertrand, and Yaneer Bar-Yam, "The food crises and political instability in North Africa and the Middle East," New England Complex Systems Institute, September 28, 2011, necsi.edu/research/social/food_crises.pdf.

6. http://web.worldbank.org/WBSITE/EXTERNAL/NEWS/0,,contentmdk:22833439~pagepk:64257043~pipk:437376~thesitepk:4607,00.html.

7. Charlotte McDonald-Gibson, "Exclusive: Red Cross launches emergency food aid plan for UK's hungry," *Independent* (London), October 11, 2013, www.independent.co.uk/news/uk/home-news/exclusive-red-cross-launches-emergency-food-aid-plan-for-uks-hungry-8872496.html.

8. "Globally almost 870 million chronically undernourished—new hunger report," Food and Agriculture Organization of the United Nations, October 9, 2012, www.fao.org/news/story/en/item/161819/icode.

9. Jeff Cox, "Record 46 million Americans are on food stamps," CNBC.com, September 4, 2012, www.cnbc.com/id/48898378.

10. Richard Dobbs, Jeremy Oppenheim, Fraser Thompson, Sigurd Mareels, Scott Nyquist, and Sunil Sanghvi, *Resource revolution: Tracking global commodity markets*, McKinsey Global Institute, September 2013.

11. IMF staff, "Unparalleled growth, increased inequality: 20th century income trends," in *Globalization: Threat or opportunity?*, International Monetary Fund, April 12, 2000, www.imf.org/external/np/exr/ib/2000/041200to.htm#III.

12. Richard Dobbs, Jeremy Oppenheim, Adam Kendall, Fraser Thompson, Martin Bratt, and Fransje van der Marel, *Reverse the curse: Maximizing the potential of resource-driven economies,* McKinsey Global Institute, December 2013.

13. Dobbs, et. al. *Resource revolution: Tracking global commodity markets.*

14. Ibid.

15. Richard Dobbs, et. al. *Urban World.*

16. Dobbs et al., *Resource revolution: Tracking global commodity markets.*

17. Richard Dobbs, Jeremy Oppenheim, and Fraser Thompson, "A new era for commodities," *McKinsey Quarterly,* November 2011.

18. Dobbs et al., *Resource revolution: Tracking global commodity markets.*

19. World Steel Committee on Economic Studies, *Steel Statistical Yearbook* (Brussels: World Steel Association, 2001, 2013).

20. Richard Anderson, "Resource depletion: Opportunity or looming catastrophe?" BBC.com, June 11, 2012, www.bbc.com/news/business-16391040.

21. Dobbs et al., *Reverse the curse.*

22. Kenneth Rogoff, "Who's dependent now?," Project Syndicate, December 7, 2005, www.project-syndicate.org/commentary/who-s-dependent-now-.

23. David Cohen, "Earth audit," *New Scientist* 194, no. 2605, May 26, 2007; Lester R. Brown, *Plan B 2.0: Rescuing a Planet under Stress and a Civilization in Trouble* (New York: W. W. Norton, 2006).

24. Yoshihide Wada et al., "Global depletion of groundwater resources," *Geophysical Research Letters* 37, no. 20, October 2010.

25. Colin P. Fenton and Jonah Waxman, "Fundamentals or fads? Pipes, not punting, explain commodity prices and volatility," *Commodity Markets Outlook and Strategy,* J. P. Morgan Global Commodities Research, August 2011.

26. Javier Blas, "Costs rise for 'technological barrels' of oil," *Financial Times* (London), May 29, 2013.

27. Dobbs et al., *Resource revolution: Meeting the world's energy, materials, food, and water needs.*

28. Ibid.

29. Dobbs et al., *Resource revolution: Tracking global commodity markets*; Randy Schnepf, *Energy use in agriculture: Background and issues,* Congressional Research Service Reports, BiblioGov, 2013.

30. Dobbs et al., *Resource revolution: Tracking global commodity markets.*

31. Peter Bisson, Elizabeth Stephenson, and S. Patrick Viguerie, "Pricing the planet," McKinsey & Company, June 2010.

32. "Petroleum & other liquids: Data," US Energy Information Administration, www.eia.gov/dnav/pet/hist/leafhandler.ashx?N=PET&s=RWTC&f=D.

33. Sean Farrell, "Ukraine crisis sends wheat and corn prices soaring," *Guardian* (Manchester), March 3, 2014, www.theguardian.com/business/2014/mar/03/ukraine-crisis-crimea-hits-price-wheat-corn.

34. *Climate change 2013: The physical science basis,* Intergovernmental Panel on Climate Change, 2013, www.climatechange2013.org. The report uses four new scenarios for greenhouse-gas concentrations projecting that the global surface temperature is likely to have changed by more than 1.5 degrees Celsius by 2100 compared with the period from 1850 to 1900 in all but the lowest scenario, and by more than 2 degrees Celsius in its two high scenarios. The 2-degree threshold is widely thought of as the dividing line between acceptable warming and dangerous warming.

35. Edward Wong, "Cost of environmental damage in China growing rapidly amid industrialization," *New York Times*, March 29, 2013.

36. Amy Harder, "EPA sets draft rule to cut carbon emissions by 30% by 2030," *Wall Street Journal,* June 2, 2014, http://online.wsj.com/articles/epa-rule-to-cost-up-to-8-8-billion-annually-sources-say-1401710600.

37. Michael Greenstone and Adam Looney, *A strategy for America's energy future: Illuminating energy's full costs,* The Hamilton Project, Brookings Institution,

May 2011, www.brookings.edu/research/papers/2011/05/energy-greenstone-looney.

38. Dobbs et al., *Resource revolution: Tracking global commodity markets*.

39. *Evolution of the super cycle: What's changed and what may*, Goldman Sachs equity research, April 2013.

40. Dobbs et al., *Resource revolution: Meeting the world's energy, materials, food, and water needs*.

41. "How our cloud does more with less," Google Official Blog, September 8, 2011, http://googleblog.blogspot.com/2011/09/how-our-cloud-does-more-with-less.html.

42. www.enernoc.com.

43. "Waste prevention policy," Korean Ministry of Environment, http://eng.me.go.kr/eng/web/index.do?menuId=141&findDepth=1; Dobbs et al., *Resource revolution: Tracking global commodity markets*.

44. www.uplus.co.kr/cmg/engl/coif/pelu/retrievepelucsr04.hpi?Mid=5921.

45. Dobbs et al., *Resource revolution: Meeting the world's energy, materials, food, and water needs*.

46. Hanh Nguyen, Martin Stuchtey, and Markus Zils, "Remaking the industrial economy," *McKinsey Quarterly*, February 2014.

47. "The circular economy applied to the automotive industry," Ellen MacArthur Foundation, July 24, 2013.

48. "Ricoh grows services business expertise" (press release), Ricoh, July 26, 2013, www.ricoh-europe.com/about-ricoh/news/2013/Ricoh_grows_Services_Business_Expertise.aspx.

49. Nguyen et al., "Remaking the industrial economy."

50. Ibid.

51. Ibid.

52. *H&M Conscious Actions: Sustainability Report 2013*, http://sustainability.hm.com/content/dam/hm/about/documents/en/CSR/reports/Conscious%20Actions%20Sustainability%20Report%202013_en.pdf.

53. "Natural gas: Data," US Energy Information Administration, www.eia.gov/dnav/ng/hist/n9070us2m.htm.

54. *World Energy Outlook 2012 executive summary*, International Energy Agency, November 2012, www.iea.org/publications/freepublications/publication/English.pdf.

55. Dobbs et al., *Resource revolution: Tracking global commodity markets*.

56. Dobbs et al., *Resource revolution: Meeting the world's energy, materials, food, and water needs*.

57. European Photovoltaic Industry Association; Zachary Shahan, "World solar power capacity increased 35% in 2013 (charts)," CleanTechnica, April 13, 2014, http://cleantechnica.com/2014/04/13/world-solar-power-capacity-increased-35-2013-charts.

58. Global Wind Energy Council, *Global Wind Report, Annual Market Update 2013,*April 2014, www.gwec.net/wp-content/uploads/2014/04/GWEC-Global-Wind-Report_9-April-2014.pdf.

59. International Energy Agency, September 2014, www.iea.org/newsroomandevents/pressreleases/2014/september/how-solar-energy-could-be-the-largest-source-of-electricity-by-mid-century.html.

60. Thomas G. Kreutz and Joan M. Ogden, "Assessment of hydrogen-fueled proton exchange membrane fuel cells for distributed generation and cogeneration," *Proceedings of the 2000 US DOE Hydrogen Program Review,* US Department of Energy, October 2000.

Chapter 7. End of an Era

1. "Elevated rail corridor in Mumbai: Project information memorandum," Indian Railways, www.indianrailways.gov.in/railwayboard/uploads/directorate/infra/downloads/Project_Information_Memorandum.pdf.

2. AFP, "Death on wheels: Commuter anger rises over Mumbai's local trains," *Hindustan Times,* April 29, 2014, www.hindustantimes.com/india-news/mumbai/death-on-wheels-commuter-anger-rises-over-mumbai-s-local-trains/article1-1213404.aspx.

3. "How the Indian economy changed in 1991–2011," *Economic Times* (Mumbai), July 24, 2011, http://articles.economictimes.indiatimes.com/2011-07-24/news/29807511_1_market-economy-scooters-india-s-gdp; World Bank databases, including foreign direct investment and net inflows (BoP, current US$) at http://data.worldbank.org/indicator/BX.KLT.DINV.CD.WD and GDP Per capita (current US$) at http://data.worldbank.org/indicator/NY.GDP.PCAP.CD.

4. PTI, "India to become third largest economy by 2030: PwC," *The Hindu* (Chennai), July 5, 2014, www.thehindu.com/business/Economy/india-to-become-third-largest-economy-by-2030-pwc/article6180722.ece.

5. Shirish Sankhe, Ireena Vittal, Richard Dobbs, Ajit Mohan, Ankur Gulati, Jonathan Ablett, Shishir Gupta, Alex Kim, Sudipto Paul, Aditya Sanghvi, and Gurpreet Sethy, *India's urban awakening: Building inclusive cities, sustaining economic growth*, McKinsey Global Institute, April 2010.

6. Ibid.

7. Julien Bouissou, "Mumbai's rail commuters pay a high human price for public transport," *Guardian Weekly* (London), October 29, 2013, www.theguardian.com/world/2013/oct/29/india-mumbai-population-rail-accidents.

8. Sankhe et al., *India's urban awakening.*

9. Ibid.

10. Richard Dobbs, Susan Lund, Charles Roxburgh, James Manyika, Alex Kim, Andreas Schreiner, Riccardo Boin, Rohit Chopra, Sebastian Jauch, Hyun Kim, Megan McDonald, and John Piotrowski, *Farewell to cheap capital? The*

implications of long-term shifts in global investment and saving, McKinsey Global Institute, December 2010.

11. Richard Dobbs, Herbert Pohl, Diaan-Yi Lin, Jan Mischke, Nicklas Garemo, Jimmy Hexter, Stefan Matzinger, Robert Palter, and Rushad Nanavatty, *Infrastructure productivity: How to save $1 trillion a year,* McKinsey Global Institute, January 2013.

12. Lisa Smith, "The truth about real estate prices," Investopedia, www .investopedia.com/articles/mortages-real-estate/11/the-truth-about-the-real-estate -market.asp.

13. FIPE-ZAP index; Samantha Pearson, "Brazil housing bubble fears as economy teeters," *Financial Times* (London), February 14, 2014, www.ft.com/ cms/s/0/f5348f8c-9558-11e3-8371-00144feab7de.html#slide0.

14. "Halifax House Price Index," Lloyds Banking Group, www.lloydsbanking group.com/Media/economic-insight/halifax-house-price-index; http://monevator .monevator.netdna-cdn.com/wp-content/uploads/2011/12/house-prices.jpg.

15. "Location, location, location," *The Economist,* August 29, 2014, www .economist.com/blogs/dailychart/2011/11/global-house-prices.

16. Martin Feldstein, "When interest rates rise," Project Syndicate, March 30, 2103, www.project-syndicate.org/commentary/higher-interest-rates-and-financial -stability-by-martin-feldstein.

17. Economist Intelligence Unit; Global Insight; McKinsey Global Economic Growth Database; Oxford Economics; *World development indicators,* World Bank database, http:// data.worldbank.org/data-catalog/world-development-indicators; McKinsey Global Institute analysis.

18. Dobbs et al., *Urban world.*

19. Heinz-Peter Elstrodt, James Manyika, Jaana Remes, Patricia Ellen, and César Martins, *Connecting Brazil to the world: A path to inclusive growth,* McKinsey Global Institute, May 2014; "Countries of the world," Worldatlas.com, http://worldatlas.com/aatlas/populations/ctyareal.htm.

20. *The global competitiveness report 2013–2014,* World Economic Forum, www.weforum.org/reports/global-competitiveness-report-2013-2014.

21. Elstrodt et al., *Connecting Brazil to the world.*

22. Dobbs et al., *Farewell to cheap capital?*

23. World Bank database; Dobbs et al., *Farewell to cheap capital?* Since the 1970s, global investment as a share of GDP fell from 26.1 percent to a recent low of 20.8 percent in 2002. Total global investment from 1980 through 2008 averaged $700 billion per year less than it would have been had the investment rate of the 1970s persisted—a cumulative sum of $20 trillion.

24. *2013 report card for America's infrastructure,* American Society of Civil Engineers, www.infrastructurereportcard.org.

25. Dobbs et al., *Infrastructure productivity.*

26. Ibid.

27. Dobbs et al., *Farewell to cheap capital?*

28. Benedict Clements, Victoria Perry, and Juan Toro, *From stimulus to consolidation: Revenue and expenditure policies in advanced and emerging economies*, IMF, departmental paper no. 10/3, October 6, 2010, www.imf.org/external/pubs /ft/dp/2010/dp1003.pdf.

29. "Gross savings (% of GDP)," World Bank database, http://data.worldbank .org/indicator/NY.GNS.ICTR.ZS.

30. Guonan Ma and Wang Yi, *China's high saving rate: myth and reality,* Bank for International Settlements working papers number 312, June 2010, www.bis .org/publ/work312.htm.

31. "Gross savings (% of GDP)."

32. Dobbs et al., *Farewell to cheap capital?*

33. Ibid.

34. Ibid.

35. Richard Dobbs and Susan Lund, "Quantitative easing, not as we know it," *The Economist,* November 14, 2013, www.economist.com/blogs/freeexchange /2013/11/unconventional-monetary-policy.

36. EIU World Database; McKinsey Global Institute analysis.

37. *Historical tables,* Budget of the US government, Fiscal year 2015, Office of Management and Budget, www.whitehouse.gov/sites/default/files/omb/budget/ fy2015/assets/hist.pdf.

38. Dobbs and Lund, "Quantitative easing."

39. Ibid.

40. Ibid.

41. *Fiscal Monitor,* International Monetary Fund, April 2014, www.imf.org/ external/pubs/ft/fm/2014/01/pdf/fm1401.pdf.

42. Hiroko Tabuchi, "In Japan, a tenuous vow to cut," *New York Times,* September 1, 2011, www.nytimes.com/2011/09/02/business/global/japan-seeks -answers-to-debt-load-without-angering-voters.html?Pagewanted=all&_r=0.

43. Ben Chu, "European Central Bank imposes negative rates on banks in historic move," *Independent* (London), June 5, 2014, www.independent.co.uk/ news/business/news/european-central-bank-imposes-negative-rates-on-banks-in -historic-move-9494027.html.

44. Carmen M. Reinhart and Kenneth S. Rogoff, *Financial and sovereign debt crises: Some lessons learned and those forgotten,* IMF working paper no. 13/266, December 2013, www.imf.org/external/pubs/ft/wp/2013/wp13266.pdf.

45. *Global Benchmark of Cost and Schedule Performance for Mega Projects in Mining,* McKinsey & Company, 2013.

46. "Explosive growth," *The Economist,* November 19, 2009, www.economist .com/node/14931607.

47. Dobbs et al., *Infrastructure productivity.*

48. McKinsey Capital Productivity Practice case studies.

49. Katy George, Sree Ramaswamy, and Lou Rassey, "Next-shoring: A CEO's guide," McKinsey & Company, January 2014.

50. Andreas Behrendt, Malte Marwede, and Raymond Wittmann, "Building cars with less capital," *McKinsey Quarterly*, September 2014.

51. www.teslamotors.com/own.

52. US Securities and Exchange Commission Form 10-K, Tesla Motors, February 26, 2014, http://ir.teslamotors.com/secfiling.cfm?Filingid=1193125-14-69681& CIK=1318605.

53. US Securities and Exchange Commission Form 10-K, Amazon.com, January 31, 2014, http://phx.corporate-ir.net/phoenix.zhtml?c=97664&p=IROL -secToc&TOC=aHR0cDovL2FwaS50ZW5rd2l6YXJkLmNvbS9vdXRssa W5lLnhtbD9yZXBvPXRlbmsmaXBhZ2U9OTM1MTc0MSZzdWJzaWQ 9NTc%3d&ListAll=1&sXBRL=1.

54. Kelly Ungerman, "The secret of Amazon: Lessons for multichannel retailers," presentation at Chief Marketing and Sales Forum, McKinsey & Company, October 2012.

55. Abdullah Al-Hassan, Michael Papaioannou, Martin Skancke, and Cheng Chih Sung, *Sovereign wealth funds: Aspects of governance structures and investment management,* IMF working paper no. 13/231, November 2013, www.imf.org/ external/pubs/ft/wp/2013/wp13231.pdf.

56. "Global pension fund assets hit record high in 2013" (press release), Towers Watson, February 5, 2014, www.towerswatson.com/en-GB/Press/2014/02/Global -pension-fund-assets-hit-record-high-in-2013.

57. "Oil-fuelled caution," *The Economist,* May 22, 2014, www.economist.com /news/finance-and-economics/21602731-kingdom-does-not-splash-cash-other -gulf-states-oil-fuelled-caution.

58. Hugh Schofield, "PSG's dramatic rise to European giants," BBC.com, May 7, 2014, www.bbc.com/news/world-europe-27314338.

59. Sarfraz Thind, "Oil prices push sovereign wealth funds toward alternative investments," Institutional Investor, February 20, 2014, www.institutionalinvestor .com/Article/3311509/Investors-Sovereign-Wealth-Funds/Oil-Prices-Push -Sovereign-Wealth-Funds-Toward-Alternative-Investments.html#.vaoepcjdxpo.

60. Gus Delaporte, "Norway takes Manhattan," *Commercial Observer,* October 8, 2013; Gus Delaporte, "Norway's wealth fund to acquire stake in Times Square Tower for $684M," *Commercial Observer,* September 9, 2013.

61. Jeremy Grant, "Temasek's dealmaking reflects big bets on rise of the consumer," *Financial Times* (London), April 14, 2014, www.ft.com/cms/s/0 /79d9824e-bb9a-11e3-8d4a-00144feabdc0.html#axzz36evevz5a.

62. www.kiva.org/about.

63. "Stats," Kickstarter, www.kickstarter.com/help/stats?Ref=footer.

64. Rob Thomas, "The Veronica Mars movie project," Kickstarter, March 13, 2013, et seq., www.kickstarter.com/projects/559914737/the-veronica-mars-movie -project.

65. "Alibaba sells loan arm to Alipay parent in pre-IPO change," *Bloomberg News*, August 12, 2014, www.bloomberg.com/news/2014-08-12/alibaba-sells-loan-arm-to-alipay-parent-in-pre-ipo-change.html.

66. Jeff Glekin, "India's reliance on Chinese cash comes with risks," Reuters, January 17, 2012, http://in.reuters.com/article/2012/01/17/reliance-communications-on-chinese-cash-idindee80g0b420120117.

67. Dan Dunkley, "AMP sells stake to Japanese bank," Financial News, December 9, 2011, www.efinancialnews.com/story/2011-12-09/amp-australia-japanese-mitsubishi-bank-fundraising?Ea9c8a2de0ee111045601ab04d673622.

68. Elzio Barreto, "Brazil's BTG Pactual sells $1.8 billion stake," Reuters, December 6, 2010, www.reuters.com/article/2010/12/06/us-btgpactual-idustre6b553r20101206.

69. Emily Chasan, "Rising rates good news for corporate pensions," *Wall Street Journal*, July 24, 2013, http://blogs.wsj.com/cfo/2013/07/24/rising-rates-good-news-for-corporate-pensions.

70. Joe DePaola, "Pension gap—silent crisis in public-private pension funding—dodging the disaster: Reform critically needed or overstated," BizShifts-Trends, July 18, 2013, http://bizshifts-trends.com/2013/07/18/the-pension-gap-silent-crisis-in-public-private-pension-plan-funding-dodging-the-disaster-changes-desperately-needed.

71. Jonathan Moules, "Santander in peer-to-peer pact as alternative finance makes gains," *Financial Times* (London), June 17, 2014, www.ft.com/cms/s/0/b8890a26-f62a-11e3-a038-00144feabdc0.html.

72. Dominic Barton and Mark Wiseman, "Focusing capital on the long term," *Harvard Business Review,* January–February 2014, http://hbr.org/2014/01/focusing-capital-on-the-long-term/ar/1.

73. *Report on the management of the government's portfolio for the year 2012/13,* GIC Private Limited, 2013, www.gic.com.sg/images/pdf/GIC_Report_2013.pdf.

74. Barton and Wiseman, "Focusing capital on the long term."

CHAPTER 8. THE JOBS GAP

1. James Manyika, Susan Lund, Byron Auguste, Lenny Mendonca, Tim Welsh, and Sreenivas Ramaswamy, *An economy that works: Job creation and America's future*, McKinsey & Company, June 2011.

2. *Historical Income Tables: Households,* United States Census Bureau, US Department of Commerce, www.census.gov/hhes/www/income/data/historical/household/index.html.

3. *2014 global employment trends*, International Labor Organization, January 2014; "Specter of a jobless recovery in France," *New York Times,* February 26, 2005; *Heritage employment report: What the US can learn from Canada's recession and recovery,* November 2013, US Department of Labor website, www.dol.gov.

4. Richard Dobbs, Anu Madgavkar, Dominic Barton, Eric Labaye, James Minyika, Charles Roxburgh, Susan Lund, and Siddarth Madhav, "The world at work:

Jobs, pay, and skills for 3.5 billion people," June 2012, McKinsey & Company, www
.mckinsey.com/insights/employment_and_growth/the_world_at_work.

5. Danny Palmer, "Not enough data scientists, MIT expert tells Computing,"
Computing, September 4, 2013, www.computing.co.uk/ctg/news/2292485/not
-enough-data-scientists-mit-expert-tells-computing.

6. Thomas Wailgum, "Monday metric: 68% of companies struggle with big
data analytics," ASUG News, March 18, 2013, www.asugnews.com/article/
monday-metric-68-of-companies-struggle-with-big-data-analytics.

7. TJ McCue, "Manufacturing jobs changing but no severe job skills gap in
USA," Forbes.com, October 18, 2012, www.forbes.com/sites/tjmccue/2012/10/18
/manufacturing-jobs-changing-but-no-severe-job-skills-gap-in-usa.

8. Parija Bhatnagar, "Manufacturing boom: Trade school enrollment soars,"
CNN Money, July 31, 2012, http://money.cnn.com/2012/07/31/news/economy/
manufacturing-trade-schools/?Iid=EL.

9. Mona Mourshed, Diana Farrell, and Dominic Barton, *Education to employment: Designing a system that works*, McKinsey Center for Government, 2013.

10. Gordon G. Chang, "College grads are jobless in China's 'high-growth'
economy," Forbes.com, May 26, 2013.

11. Lilian Lin, "China's Graduates Face Glut," *Wall Street Journal*, August 22,
2012.

12. Voice of the Graduate, McKinsey & Company, May 2013; Bureau of
Labor Statistics, United States Department of Labor, www.bls.gov/news.release/
pdf/jolts.pdf.

13. Susan Lund, James Manyika, Scott Nyquist, Lenny Mendonca, and
Sreenivas Ramaswamy, *Game changers: Five opportunities for US growth and renewal*, McKinsey Global Institute, July 2013.

14. Steve Johnson, "H-1B visa cap reached after just five days as valley executives lobby to expand the program," *San Jose Mercury News*, April 7, 2014, www
.mercurynews.com/business/ci_25516535/h-1b-visa-cap-reached-after-just-five.

15. Sarah Mishkin, "Silicon Valley faces visa scramble for foreign workers,"
Financial Times (London), March 17, 2014, www.ft.com/intl/cms/s/0/7c14f76a
-aa0f-11e3-8497-00144feab7de.html#axzz3FYTuXcWB.

16. John Helyar, "Outsourcing: A passage out of India," *Bloomberg Businessweek*, March 15, 2012, www.businessweek.com/articles/2012-03-15/outsourcing
-a-passage-out-of-india.

17. *World development indicators*, World Bank database, http://data.worldbank
.org/data-catalog/world-development-indicators.

18. Richard Dobbs, Anu Madgavkar, Dominic Barton, Eric Labaye, James
Minyika, Charles Roxburgh, Susan Lund, and Siddarth Madhav, "The world at
work: Jobs, pay, and skills for 3.5 billion people," June 2012, McKinsey & Company, www.mckinsey.com/insights/employment_and_growth/the_world_at
_work.

19. Michael Chui, James Manyika, Jacques Bughin, Richard Dobbs, Charles Roxburgh, Hugo Sarrazin, Geoffrey Sands and Magdalena Westergren, *The social economy: Unlocking productivity and value through social technologies,* McKinsey Global Institute, July 2012.

20. "Nokia Mobile Mathematics empowers South African learners" (press release), Nokia.sa blog, October 24, 2013.

21. *Turning on mobile learning in Africa and the Middle East: Illustrative initiatives and policy implications,* UN Educational, Scientific and Cultural Organization, 2012, www.tostan.org/sites/default/files/resources/unesco_turning_on _mobile_learning_in_africa_and_the_middle_east.pdf.

22. Tahir Amin, "Mobilink announces to expand SMS-based literacy project," Business Recorder, March 26, 2010, www.brecorder.com/top-stories/single/595 /0/1035800.

23. Deborah Ball and Ilan Brat, "Spanish supermarket chain finds recipe," *Wall Street Journal,* October 23, 2012.

24. Mourshed et al., *Education to Employment.*

CHAPTER 9. FROM MINNOWS TO SHARKS

1. "California town on sale on eBay," BBC.com, April 4, 2006, http://news.bbc .co.uk/1/hi/world/americas/4875206.stm; Buck Wolf, "Hungry for miracles? Try Jesus on a fish stick," ABC News, November 30, 2004, http://abcnews.go.com/ Entertainment/WolfFiles/story?id=307227&page=1.

2. "eBay India marketplaces fast facts," eBay India, March 31, 2014, Fpages .ebay.in/community/aboutebay/news/infastfacts.html.

3. Pierre Omidyar and Meg Whitman, "A defining year for eBay," eBay: 2002 annual report, http://pages.ebay.com/2002annualreport/shareholderletter.html.

4. Justin Doebele, "Standing up to a giant," Forbes.com, April 25, 2005, www .forbes.com/global/2005/0425/030.html.

5. Kelvin Chan, "Alibaba expands beyond e-commerce," Business Week, May 9, 2014, www.businessweek.com/ap/2014-05-09/alibaba-expands-beyond-e-commerce.

6. William Barnett, Mi Feng, and Xiaoqu Luo, *Taobao vs. EBay China,* Stanford Graduate School of Business case no. IB88, 2010, www.gsb.stanford.edu/ faculty-research/case-studies/taobao-vs-ebay-china.

7. Elzio Barreto, "Alibaba IPO ranks as world's biggest after additional shares sold," Reuters, September 22, 2014, www.reuters.com/article/2014/09/22/us -alibaba-ipo-value-iduskcn0hh0a620140922.

8. US Securities and Exchange Commission Form F-1, Alibaba Group Holding Limited, May 6, 2014, www.sec.gov/Archives/edgar/data/1577552/0001193 12514184994/d709111df1.htm.

9. Bloomberg, November 28, 2014.

10. Dane Stangler and Sam Arbesman, *What does Fortune 500 turnover mean?* Ewing Marion Kauffman Foundation, June 2012, www.kauffman.org/~/media/

kauffman_org/research%20reports%20and%20covers/2012/06/fortune_500_turnover.pdf.

11. Richard Dobbs, Jaana Remes, Sven Smit, James Manyika, Jonathan Woetzel, and Yaw Agyenm-Boateng, *Urban world: The shifting global business landscape,* McKinsey Global Institute, October 2013.

12. Ibid.

13. "Creative destruction whips through corporate America," Innosight Executive Briefing, winter 2012, www.innosight.com/innovation-resources/strategy-innovation/upload/creative-destruction-whips-through-corporate-america_final2012.pdf.

14. *Microsoft's timeline from 1975–1990,* The History of Computing Project, www.thocp.net/companies/microsoft/microsoft_company.htm.

15. Christopher Steiner, "Meet the fastest growing company ever," Forbes.com, August 12, 2010, www.forbes.com/forbes/2010/0830/entrepreneurs-groupon-facebook-twitter-next-web-phenom.html.

16. *Annual Report 2012–2012,* Bharti Airtel Limited, 2013. *Annual Report 2012,* AT&T, 2013.

17. *Tata Fast Facts,* Tata, July 21, 2014, www.tata.com/htm/Group_fast_facts.htm; also see *Corporate sustainability in the UK: A selection of stories from Tata companies and employees,* Tata, 2013, www.uk.tata.com/pdf/uk_csr_booklet.pdf.

18. Yuval Atsmon, Michael Kloss, and Sven Smit, "Parsing the growth advantage of emerging-market companies," *McKinsey Quarterly,* May 2012.

19. Dobbs et al., *Urban world: The shifting global business landscape.*

20. Meisia Chandra, "Waze touches 50M users globally; Malaysia, Indonesia in top 10 list," e27, February 15, 2014, http://e27.co/waze-touches-50m-users-globally-malaysia-indonesia-in-top-10-list.

21. Steve O'Hear, "Amid reports Facebook is eyeing up financial services, TransferWire hits £1 billion in transfers," TechCrunch, April 14, 2014, http://techcrunch.com/2014/04/14/you-know-whats-cool.

22. Ibid.

23. www.expediainc.com/about.

24. TechCrunch.

25. Enders Analysis, onesource.

26. Rik Kirkland, "Leading in the 21st century: An interview with Carlos Ghosn," McKinsey & Company, September 2012.

27. *UK insurance aggregators 2012,* Datamonitor, www.datamonitor.com/store/product/uk_insurance_aggregators_2012?productid=CM00192-013.

28. Matt Scott, "Google is a 'real threat' to the insurance industry," Insurance Times, May 1, 2014, www.insurancetimes.co.uk/google-is-a-real-threat-to-the-insurance-industry/1408126.article.

29. Mark Sands, "Telematics: Taking the wheel?" Post Online, April 30, 2013, www.postonline.co.uk/post/analysis/2264472/telematics-taking-the-wheel.

30. Derek Thompson, "Is *House of Cards* really a hit?" *The Atlantic*, February 24, 2014, www.theatlantic.com/business/archive/2014/02/is-i-house-of-cards -i-really-a-hit/284035.

31. *Garages global tour*, GE Garages, www.gegarages.com/global-tour.

32. BMW website: www.bmwblog.com/2014/07/30/see-bmw-i3-parks-driver -aboard.

33. Daimler press release, September 2013, http://media.daimler.com/dcmedia /0-921-614307-1-1629819-1-0-0-0-0-0-11702-0-0-1-0-0-0-0-0.html.

34. AT&T press release, March 2014, http://about.att.com/story/audi_and_att _announce_pricing_for_first_ever_in_vehicle_4glte_connectivity.html.

35. Companies' 2013 annual reports and related press releases.

36. James Manyika, Armando Cabral, Lohini Moodley, Safroadu Yeboah-Amankwah, Suraj Moraje, Michael Chui, Jerry Anthonyrajah, and Ache Leke, *Lions go digital: The Internet's transformative potential in Africa*, McKinsey Global Institute, November 2013.

37. Pankaj Ghemawat, "Developing global leaders," *McKinsey Quarterly*, June 2012.

38. *Annual Report 2013*, Unilever, www.unilever.com/images/Unilever_AR13 _tcm13-383757.pdf.

39. Elga Reyes, "Unilever launches €50M leadership centre in Singapore," Eco-Business, July 1, 2013, www.eco-business.com/news/unilever-launches -leadership-centre-Singapore.

40. Stephen Hall, Dan Lovallo, and Reinier Musters, "How to put your money where your strategy is," *McKinsey Quarterly*, March 2012.

41. www.salesforce.com/customers/stories/burberry.

42. *Burberry's digital activism*, Enders Analysis, August 2012, www.enders analysis.com/content/publication/burberry%E2%80%99s-digital-activism.

43. Ella Alexander, "Burberry opens Regent Street flagship," *Vogue UK*, September 13, 2012, www.vogue.co.uk/news/2012/09/13/burberry-regent-street-flagship-opens.

44. Imran Amed, "CEO talk: Angela Ahrendts on Burberry's connected culture," The Business of Fashion, September 3, 2013, www.businessoffashion.com /2013/09/burberry-angela-ahrendts.html.

Chapter 10. Policy Matters

1. Christoph Bertram, *Germany: The Sick Man of Europe?* Project Syndicate, September 18, 1997, www.project-syndicate.org/commentary/germany--the-sick -man-of-europe-.

2. *World development indicators*, World Bank database, http:// data.worldbank .org/data-catalog/world-development-indicators.

3. Ibid.

4. "100,000 protest German reforms in Berlin," Deutsche Welle, November 2, 2003; www.dw.de/100000-protest-german-reforms-in-berlin/a-1019341.

5. Richard Dobbs, Anu Madgavkar, Dominic Barton, Eric Labaye, James Minyika, Charles Roxburgh, Susan Lund, and Siddarth Madhav, *The world at work: Jobs, pay, and skills for 3.5 billion people,* June 2012, McKinsey & Company.

6. *World development indicators.*

7. Dobbs et al., *The world at work.*

8. *Attitudes about aging: A global perspective,* Pew Research Global Attitudes Project, January 30, 2014, www.pewglobal.org/2014/01/30/attitudes-about-aging-a-global-perspective.

9. The Economist Intelligence Unit.

10. *2009 ageing report: Economic and budgetary projections for the EU-27 member states (2008–2060),* European Commission, February 2009, http://ec.europa.eu/economy_finance/publications/publication14992_en.pdf.

11. James Manyika, Jacques Bughin, Susan Lund, Olivia Nottebohm, David Poulter, Sebastian Jauch, and Sree Ramaswamy, *Global flows in a digital age: How trade, finance, people, and data connect the world economy,* McKinsey Global Institute, April 2014.

12. Julian Ku and John Yoo, "Globalization and Sovereignty," *Berkeley Journal of International Law* 31, no. 1, 2013, http://scholarship.law.berkeley.edu/bjil/vol31/iss1/6.

13. Chun Han Wong, "Singapore tightens hiring rules for foreign skilled labor," *Wall Street Journal,* September 23, 2013.

14. "Firms to consider Singaporeans fairly for jobs," Singapore Ministry of Manpower, September 23, 2013, www.mom.gov.sg/newsroom/Pages/PressReleases Detail.aspx?listid=523.

15. *Growing income inequality in OECD countries: What drives it and how can policy tackle it?* OECD, May 2011, www.oecd.org/social/soc/47723414.pdf.

16. World Inequality Database.

17. *A new multilateralism for the 21st century: The Richard Dimbleby lecture,* Christine Lagarde, International Monetary Fund, February 3, 2014, www.imf.org/external/np/speeches/2014/020314.htm.

18. James Manyika, David Hunt, Scott Nyquist, Jaana Remes, Vikram Malhotra, Lenny Mendonca, Byron Auguste, and Samantha Test, *Growth and Renewal in the United States: Retooling America's economic engine,* McKinsey Global Institute, February 2011.

19. James Manyika, Jonathan Woetzel, Richard Dobbs, Jaana Remes, Eric Labaye, Andrew Jordan, *Global growth: Can productivity save the day in an aging world?*, January 2015, McKinsey Global Institute.

20. OECD, *Government at a Glance 2013* (OECD Publishing, 2013), www.oecd.org/gov/govataglance.htm.

21. François Bouvard, Robert Carsouw, Eric Labaye, Alastair Levy, Lenny Mendonca, Jaana Remes, Charles Roxburgh, and Samantha Test, *Better for less: Improving public sector performance on a tight budget,* McKinsey & Company, July 2011.

22. Rajat Gupta, Shirish Sankhe, Richard Dobbs, Jonathan Woetzel, Anu Madgavkar, and Ashwin Hasyagar, *From poverty to empowerment: India's imperative for jobs, growth, and effective basic services,* McKinsey Global Institute, February 2014.

23. Justin Pritchard, "California pushes to finish driverless car rules," Associated Press, March 12, 2014, bigstory.ap.org/article/california-pushes-finish -driverless-car-rules.

24. "Striking back: Germany considers counterespionage against US," Spiegel Online International, February 18, 2014, www.spiegel.de/international/germany/ germany-considers-counterespionage-measures-against-united-states-a-953985.html.

25. "Merkel and Hollande to discuss European communication network avoiding US," Reuters, February 15, 2014, http://uk.reuters.com/article/2014/02/15/uk -germany-france-idUKBREA1E0IE20140215.

26. Richard Dobbs, Jeremy Oppenheim, Fraser Thompson, Sigurd Mareels, Scott Nyquist, and Sunil Sanghvi, *Resource revolution: Tracking global commodity markets*, McKinsey Global Institute, September 2013.

27. Richard Dobbs, Jeremy Oppenheim, Fraser Thompson, Marcel Brinkman, and Marc Zornes, *Resource revolution: Meeting the world's energy, materials, food, and water needs*, McKinsey Global Institute, November 2011.

28. Carmen M. Reinhart and Kenneth S. Rogoff, "From financial crash to debt crisis," *American Economic Review* 101, no. 5, August 2011, www.aeaweb.org /articles.php?doi=10.1257/aer.101.5.1676; also see David Beers and Jean-Sébastien Nadeau, *Introducing a new database of sovereign defaults,* Bank of Canada, technical report no. 101, February 2014.

29. *Delivery 2.0: The new challenge for governments,* McKinsey & Company, October 2012.

30. OECD, *Government at a Glance 2013.*

31. Ibid.

32. Ibid.

33. www.afi-global.org.

34. Ibid.

35. Ulf Rinne, Arne Uhlendorff, and Zhong Zhao, "Vouchers and caseworkers in public training programs: Evidence from the Hartz reform in Germany," IZA discussion paper no. 3910, December 2008, ftp.iza.org/dp3910.pdf.

36. www.trade.gov/nei.

37. Huiyao Wang, "China's return migration and its impact on home development," *UN Chronicle* L, no. 3, September 2013, http://unchronicle.un.org/article /chinas-return-migration-and-its-impact-home-development.

38. *World development indicators.*

39. *Starting strong II: Early childhood education and care,* OECD, September 2006, www.oecd.org/edu/school/startingstrongiiearlychildhoodeducationandcare .htm.

40. "Table 1368: Female labor force participation rates by country: 1980 to 2010," *Statistical Abstract of the United States 2012,* United States Census Bureau, US Department of Commerce, www.census.gov/compendia/statab/2012/tables /12s1368.pdf.

41. *Denmark in Figures 2013,* Statistics Denmark, February 2013, www.dst.dk /en/Statistik/Publikationer/VisPub.aspx?cid=17953.

42. Theresa Braine, "Reaching Mexico's poorest," *Bulletin of the World Health Organization* 84, no. 8, August 2006, www.who.int/bulletin/volumes/84/8/news 10806/en.

43. Christopher Harress, "Goodbye, oil: US Navy cracks new renewable energy technology to turn seawater into fuel, allowing ships to stay at sea longer," *International Business Times,* April 8, 2014, www.ibtimes.com/goodbye-oil-us -navy-cracks-new-renewable-energy-technology-turn-seawater-fuel-allowing -1568455.

44. David E. Bloom, David Canning, and Günther Fink, *Implications of population aging for economic growth,* NBER working paper no. 16705, January 2011, www.nber.org/papers/w16705.

45. *World development indicators*; Pensions at a glance 2013, OECD, 2013, www.oecd-ilibrary.org/finance-and-investment/pensions-at-a-glance-2013_ pension_glance-2013-en.

46. "Japan long-term care: Highlights from *Help Wanted? Providing and Paying for Long-Term Care,* OECD Publishing, 2011," May 18, 2011, www.oecd.org/els /health-systems/47891458.pdf, from Francesca Colombo, Ana Llena-Nozal, Jérôme Mercier, and Frits Tjadens, *Help Wanted? Providing and Paying for Long-Term Care* (OECD Health Policy Studies, OECD Publishing, 2011).

47. Chilean Ministry of Finance.

48. IMF, *World Economic Outlook: Transitions and tensions,* International Monetary Fund, 2013, www.imf.org/external/pubs/ft/weo/2013/02.

49. Sean Cockerham, "New York ruling on fracking bans might send tremors across US," *Miami Herald,* June 30, 2014, www.miamiherald.com/2014/06/30 /4211388/new-york-ruling-on-fracking-bans.html.

50. "Bulgaria bans shale gas drilling with 'fracking' method," BBC.com, January 19, 2012, www.bbc.co.uk/news/world-europe-16626580; Jan Hromadko and Harriet Torry, "Germany shelves shale-gas drilling for next seven years," *Wall Street Journal,* July 4, 2014, http://online.wsj.com/articles/germany-shelves-shale -gas-drilling-for-next-seven-years-1404481174.

51. Swedish Institute.

52. Germany Federal Environmental Agency.

53. Mona Mourshed, Diana Farrell, and Dominic Barton, *Education to employment: Designing a system that works,* McKinsey Center for Government, 2013.

54. Karim Tadjeddine, "'A duty to modernize': Reforming the French civil service," McKinsey & Company, April 2011.

55. James Manyika, Michael Chui, Diana Farrell, Steve Van Kuiken, Peter Groves, and Elizabeth Almasi Doshi, *Open data: Unlocking innovation and performance with liquid information*, McKinsey Global Institute, McKinsey Center for Government, and McKinsey Business Technology Office, October 2013.

56. Eric Braverman and Mary Kuntz, "Creating a 'coalition of the positive' in India: An interview with Nandan Nilekani" and Elana Berkowitz and Blaise Warren, "E-government in Estonia" in "Innovation in government: India and Estonia," McKinsey & Company, June 2012.

57. Marcos Cruz and Alexandre Lazarow, "Innovation in government: Brazil," McKinsey & Company, September 2012.

58. Smart Cities, Navigant Research, 2014, www.navigantresearch.com/research /smart-buildings/smart-cities.bus%20visi.

59. Vestas Annual Reports, 2005, 2009, and 2013.

60. *Draft Grundfos response to the European Commission's public consultation on resource efficiency*, Grundfos, February 24, 2012, http://ec.europa.eu/environment /resource_efficiency/pdf/Grundfos.pdf; *From solo enterprise to world leader*, Danfoss Trata, www.trata.danfoss.com/xxNewsx/2b005275-98ff-4165-a0a5-78efe1 46264a_CNP1.html.

CONCLUDING THOUGHTS

1. Rik Kirkland, "Leading in the 21st century: An interview with Daniel Vasella," McKinsey & Company, September 2012.

2. "Leading in the 21st century: An interview with Ford's Alan Mulally," McKinsey & Company, November 2013.

3. William Samuelson and Richard Zeckhauser, "Status quo bias in decision making," *Journal of Risk and Uncertainty* 1, no. 1, March 1988, www.hks.harvard .edu/fs/rzeckhau/SQBDM.pdf.

4. See Stephen Hall, Dan Lovallo, and Reinier Musters, "How to put your money where your strategy is," *McKinsey Quarterly*, March 2012; and Mladen Fruk, Stephen Hall, and Devesh Mittal, "Never let a good crisis go to waste," *McKinsey Quarterly*, October 2013.

5. Nate Boaz and Erica Ariel Fox, "Change leader, change thyself," *McKinsey Quarterly*, March 2014.

6. Suzanne Heywood, Aaron De Smet, and Allen Webb, "Tom Peters on leading the 21st-century organization," *McKinsey Quarterly*, September 2014.

7. Bill Javetski, "Leading in the 21st century: An interview with Larry Fink," McKinsey & Company, September 2012.

8. Boaz and Fox, "Change leader, change thyself."

SELECTED BIBLIOGRAPHY
AND FURTHER READING

Atsmon, Yuval, Peter Child, Richard Dobbs, and Laxman Narasimhan, "Winning the $30 trillion decathlon: Going for gold in emerging markets," *McKinsey Quarterly*, August 2012.

Atsmon, Yuval, and Max Magni, "Meet the Chinese consumer of 2020," *McKinsey Quarterly*, March 2012.

Banfi, Francesco, Paul-Louis Caylar, Ewan Duncan, and Ken Kajii, "E-journey: Digital marketing and the 'path to purchase,'" McKinsey & Company, January 2013.

Barton, Dominic, Andrew Grant, and Michelle Horn, "Leading in the 21st century," *McKinsey Quarterly*, June 2012.

Barton, Dominic, and Mark Wiseman, "Focusing capital on the long term," *Harvard Business Review*, January–February 2014.

Bouton, Shannon, David Cis, Lenny Mendonca, Herbert Pohl, Jaana Remes, Henry Ritchie, and Jonathan Woetzel, *How to make a city great*, McKinsey & Company, September 2013.

Bouvard, François, Robert Carsouw, Eric Labaye, Alastair Levy, Lenny Mendonca, Jaana Remes, Charles Roxburgh, and Samantha Test, *Better for less: Improving public sector performance on a tight budget*, McKinsey & Company, July 2011.

Brynjolffson, Eric, and Andrew McAfee, *The Second Machine Age: Work, Progress, and Prosperity in a Time of Brillliant Technologies* (New York: W. W. Norton, 2014).

Bughin, Jacques, Michael Chui, and James Manyika, "Ten IT-enabled business trends for the decade ahead," *McKinsey on Business Technology* 33, spring 2014.

Bughin, Jacques, and James Manyika, "Measuring the full impact of digital capital," *McKinsey Quarterly*, July 2013.

Chatterjee, Ishan, Jöm Küpper, Christian Mariager, Patrick Moore, and Steve Reis, "The decade ahead: Trends that will shape the consumer goods industry," McKinsey & Company, December 2010.

Chomik, Rafal, and Edward R. Whitehouse, *Trends in pension eligibility ages and life expectancy, 1950–2050,* OECD Social, Employment and Migration working papers no. 105, 2010.

Chui, Michael, James Manyika, Jacques Bughin, Richard Dobbs, Charles Roxburgh, Hugo Sarrazin, Geoffrey Sands, and Magdalena Westergren, *The social economy: Unlocking productivity and value through social technologies,* McKinsey Global Institute, July 2012.

Clements, Benedict, Victoria Perry, and Juan Toro, *From stimulus to consolidation: Revenue and expenditure policies in advanced and emerging economies,* IMF, departmental paper no. 10/3, October 6, 2010, www.imf.org/external/pubs/ft /dp/2010/dp1003.pdf.

Cummings, Jonathan, James Manyika, Lenny Mendonca, Ezra Greenberg, Steven Aronowitz, Rohit Chopra, Katy Elkin, Sreenivas Ramaswamy, Jimmy Soni, and Allison Watson, *Growth and competitiveness in the United States: The role of its multinational companies,* McKinsey Global Institute, June 2010.

Dobbs, Richard, Susan Lund, Charles Roxburgh, James Manyika, Alex Kim, Andreas Schreiner, Riccardo Boin, Rohit Chopra, Sebastian Jauch, Hyun Kim, Megan McDonald, and John Piotrowski, *Farewell to cheap capital? The implications of long-term shifts in global investment and saving,* McKinsey Global Institute, December 2010.

Dobbs, Richard, Anu Madgavakar, Dominic Barton, Eric Labaye, James Manyika, Charles Roxburgh, Susan Lund, and Siddarth Madhav, *The world at work: Jobs, pay, and skills for 3.5 billion people,* McKinsey Global Institute, June 2012.

Dobbs, Richard, Jeremy Oppenheim, Adam Kendall, Fraser Thompson, Martin Bratt, and Fransje van der Marel, *Reverse the curse: Maximizing the potential of resource-driven economies,* McKinsey Global Institute, December 2013.

Dobbs, Richard, Jeremy Oppenheim, Fraser Thompson, Marcel Brinkman, and Marc Zornes, *Resource revolution: Meeting the world's energy, materials, food, and water needs,* McKinsey Global Institute, November 2011.

Dobbs, Richard, Herbert Pohl, Diaan-Yi Lin, Jan Mischke, Nicklas Garemo, Jimmy Hexter, Stefan Matzinger, Robert Palter, and Rushad Nanavatty, *Infrastructure productivity: How to save $1 trillion a year,* McKinsey Global Institute, January 2013.

Dobbs, Richard, Jaana Remes, James Manyika, Charles Roxburgh, Sven Smit, and Fabian Schaer, *Urban world: Cities and the rise of the consuming class,* McKinsey Global Institute, June 2012.

Dobbs, Richard, Jaana Remes, Sven Smit, James Manyika, Jonathan Woetzel, and Yaw Agyenm-Boateng, *Urban world: The shifting global business landscape,* McKinsey Global Institute, October 2013.

Dobbs, Richard, and Shirish Sankhe, "Comparing urbanization in China and India," McKinsey & Company, July 2010.

Dobbs, Richard, Sven Smit, Jaana Remes, James Manyika, Charles Roxburgh, and Alejandra Restrepo, *Urban world: Mapping the economic power of cities,* McKinsey Global Institute, March 2011.

Doheny, Mike, Venu Nagali, and Florian Weig, "Agile Manufacturing for a volatile world case studies," McKinsey & Company, 2012.

Elstrodt, Heinz-Peter, James Manyika, Jaana Remes, Patricia Ellen, and César Martins, *Connecting Brazil to the world: A path to inclusive growth,* McKinsey Global Institute, May 2014.

European Commission, *The 2012 ageing report: Economic and budgetary projections for the 27 EU member states (2010–2060),* European Commission, February 2012.

Garemo, Nicklas, Jan Mischke, and Jonathan Woetzel, "A dose of innovation to ease infrastructure strains?" *McKinsey Quarterly,* September 2014.

George, Katy, Sree Ramaswamy, and Lou Rassey, "Next-shoring: A CEO's guide," McKinsey & Company, January 2014.

Greenstone, Michael, and Adam Looney, *A strategy for America's energy future: Illuminating energy's full costs,* The Hamilton Project, Brookings Institution, May 2011.

Gupta, Rajat, Shirish Sankhe, Richard Dobbs, Jonathan Woetzel, Anu Madgavkar, and Ashwin Hasyagar, *From poverty to empowerment: India's imperative for jobs, growth, and effective basic services,* McKinsey Global Institute, February 2014.

Hattingh, Damian, Bill Russo, Ade Sun-Basorun, and Arend Van Wamelen, *The rise of the African consumer,* McKinsey & Company, October 2012.

Heck, Stefan, and Matt Rogers, *Resource Revolution: How to Capture the Biggest Business Opportunity in a Century* (New York: New Harvest, 2014).

Hirt, Martin, and Paul Willmott, "Strategic principles for competing in the digital age," *McKinsey Quarterly,* May 2014.

Li, Guangyu, and Jonathan Woetzel, "What China's five-year plan means for business," *McKinsey Quarterly,* July 2011.

Lund, Susan, Toos Daruvala, Richard Dobbs, Philipp Härle, Ju-Hon Kwek, and Ricardo Falcón, *Financial globalization: Retreat or reset?,* McKinsey Global Institute, March 2013.

Ma, Guonan, and Wang Yi, *China's high saving rate: Myth and reality,* Bank for International Settlements working papers no. 312, June 2010.

Manyika, James, Jacques Bughin, Susan Lund, Olivia Nottebohm, David Poulter, Sebastian Jauch, and Sree Ramaswamy, *Global flows in a digital age: How trade, finance, people, and data connect the world economy,* McKinsey Global Institute, April 2014.

Manyika, James, Armando Cabral, Lohini Moodley, Safroadu Yeboah-Amankwah, Suraj Moraje, Michael Chui, Jerry Anthonyrajah, and Ache Leke, *Lions go digital: The Internet's transformative potential in Africa*, McKinsey Global Institute, November 2013.

Manyika, James, Michael Chui, Brad Brown, Jacques Bughin, Richard Dobbs, Charles Roxburgh, and Angela Hung Byers, *Big data: The next frontier for innovation, competition, and productivity*, McKinsey Global Institute, May 2011.

Manyika, James, Michael Chui, Jacques Bughin, Richard Dobbs, Peter Bisson, and Alex Marrs, *Disruptive technologies: Advances that will transform life, business, and the global economy*, McKinsey Global Institute, May 2013.

Manyika, James, Michael Chui, Diana Farrell, Steve Van Kuiken, Peter Groves, and Elizabeth Almasi Doshi, *Open data: Unlocking innovation and performance with liquid information*, McKinsey Global Institute, McKinsey Center for Government, and McKinsey Business Technology Office, October 2013.

Manyika, James, David Hunt, Scott Nyquist, Jaana Remes, Vikram Malhotra, Lenny Mendonca, Byron Auguste, and Samantha Test, *Growth and renewal in the United States: Retooling America's economic engine*, McKinsey Global Institute, February 2011.

Manyika, James, Jaana Remes, Jonathan Woetzel. "A productivity perspective on the future of growth," *McKinsey Quarterly*, September 2014.

Manyika, James, Jeff Sinclair, Richard Dobbs, Gernot Strube, Louis Rassey, Jan Mischke, Jaana Remes, Charles Roxburgh, Katy George, David O'Halloran, and Sreenivas Ramaswamy, *Manufacturing the future: The next era of global growth and innovation*, McKinsey Global Institute, November 2012.

Nguyen, Hanh, Martin Stuchtey, and Markus Zils, "Remaking the industrial economy," *McKinsey Quarterly*, February 2014.

Pélissié du Rausas, Matthieu, James Manyika, Eric Hazan, Jacques Bughin, Michael Chui, and Rémi Said, *Internet matters: The Net's sweeping impact on growth, jobs, and prosperity*, McKinsey Global Institute, May 2011.

Reinhart, Carmen M., and Kenneth S. Rogoff, *Financial and sovereign debt crises: Some lessons learned and those forgotten*, IMF working paper no. 13/266, December 2013.

———, *This Time Is Different: Eight Centuries of Financial Folly* (Princeton, NJ: Princeton University Press, 2011).

Sankhe, Shirish, Ireena Vittal, Richard Dobbs, Ajit Mohan, Ankur Gulati, Jonathan Ablett, Shishir Gupta, Alex Kim, Sudipto Paul, Aditya Sanghvi, and Gurpreet Sethy, *India's urban awakening: Building inclusive cities, sustaining economic growth*, McKinsey Global Institute, April 2010.

Spence, Michael, *The Next Convergence: The Future of Economic Growth in a Multispeed World* (New York: Farrar, Straus & Giroux, 2011).

Stock, James H., and Mark W. Watson, "Has the business cycle changed and why?," National Bureau of Economic Research working paper no. 9127, August 2002, www.nber.org/papers/w9127.

Towson, Jeffrey, and Jonathan Woetzel, "All you need to know about business in China," *McKinsey Quarterly,* April 2014.

United Nations, *World population prospects: The 2012 revision,* UN Department of Economic and Social Affairs, Population Division, June 2013, http://esa.un.org/wpp.

Winter, Jay, and Michael Teitelbaum, *The Global Spread of Fertility Decline: Population, Fear, and Uncertainty* (New Haven, CT: Yale University Press, 2013).

Woetzel, Jonathan, Gordon Orr, Alan Lau, Yougang Chen, Elsie Chang, Jeongmin Seong, Michael Chui, Autumn Qiu, *China's digital transformation: The Internet's impact on productivity and growth,* McKinsey Global Institute, July 2014.

World Bank and African Development Bank. *eTransform Africa: The transformational use of information and communication technologies in Africa,* World Bank and African Development Bank, December 2012.

INDEX

McKinsey Global Institute (MGI), the business and economics research arm of McKinsey & Company, was established in 1990 to develop a deeper understanding of the evolving global economy and provide leaders in the commercial, public, and social sectors with facts and insights on which to base management and policy decisions. MGI research combines the analytical tools of economics with the insights of business leaders and examines microeconomic industry trends to better understand the broad macroeconomic forces affecting business strategy and public policy. MGI's in-depth reports have covered more than twenty countries and thirty industries. The partners of McKinsey & Company fund MGI's research in its entirety. For further information about MGI and to download reports for free, please visit www.mckinsey.com/mgi.

Richard Dobbs, James Manyika, and **Jonathan Woetzel** have been with McKinsey for a collective total of around seventy-five years and are based in London, San Francisco, and Shanghai respectively. They are the directors of McKinsey and of the McKinsey Global Institute. For 25 years the McKinsey Global Institute has provided leaders in the commercial, public, and social sectors with the facts and insights on which to base management and policy decisions.

Richard Dobbs is a graduate of Oxford and, as a Fulbright scholar, Stanford. He has worked with clients in a range of industries, from high technology to petroleum, banking, and utilities. He has been based in London for fifteen years, Seoul for six, and in India for two, and was coleader of McKinsey's Corporate Finance Practice. At MGI, he has led research on global economic trends, including urbanization, resources, capital markets, lifestyle diseases, productivity, and growth. Richard has taught at Oxford, Seoul National, and Tsinghua Universities and is the author of *Value: The Four Cornerstones of Corporate Finance.*

James Manyika received a doctorate in electrical engineering and robotics from Oxford where he was a Rhodes Scholar. Based in Silicon Valley since 1994, James has advised the leaders of many of the world's leading technology companies. At MGI he leads work on the global economy, growth and productivity, competitiveness, and on technology and the digital economy. He was appointed by President Obama as vice chair of the President's Global Development Council. He has served on the US Department of Commerce Innovation Advisory Board and is a board member of the Aspen Institute, the Oxford Internet Institute, and Harvard's Hutchins Center. He is a Senior Fellow at the Brookings Institution.

Jonathan Woetzel, based in China since 1985, cofounded McKinsey's practice there. He leads McKinsey's Cities Special Initiative and cochairs the nonprofit think tank Urban China Initiative. At MGI he has led research on urbanization, sustainability, resources, economic development, and technology and has worked with governments and businesses globally on these issues. He lectures at the Guanghua School of Business, has authored four books on China, and holds a doctorate in political science from the University of Southern California.

PublicAffairs is a publishing house founded in 1997. It is a tribute to the standards, values, and flair of three persons who have served as mentors to countless reporters, writers, editors, and book people of all kinds, including me.

I. F. STONE, proprietor of *I. F. Stone's Weekly*, combined a commitment to the First Amendment with entrepreneurial zeal and reporting skill and became one of the great independent journalists in American history. At the age of eighty, Izzy published *The Trial of Socrates*, which was a national bestseller. He wrote the book after he taught himself ancient Greek.

BENJAMIN C. BRADLEE was for nearly thirty years the charismatic editorial leader of *The Washington Post*. It was Ben who gave the *Post* the range and courage to pursue such historic issues as Watergate. He supported his reporters with a tenacity that made them fearless and it is no accident that so many became authors of influential, best-selling books.

ROBERT L. BERNSTEIN, the chief executive of Random House for more than a quarter century, guided one of the nation's premier publishing houses. Bob was personally responsible for many books of political dissent and argument that challenged tyranny around the globe. He is also the founder and longtime chair of Human Rights Watch, one of the most respected human rights organizations in the world.

·   ·   ·

For fifty years, the banner of Public Affairs Press was carried by its owner Morris B. Schnapper, who published Gandhi, Nasser, Toynbee, Truman, and about 1,500 other authors. In 1983, Schnapper was described by *The Washington Post* as "a redoubtable gadfly." His legacy will endure in the books to come.

Peter Osnos, *Founder and Editor-at-Large*